FLY FISHING
THE
SIERRA NEVADA

To Jay —

Thanks for Monache Meadows;
Thanks for Golden Trout;
Thanks for cooking;
Thanks for the friendship.
See you on the water.

Bill

8/10/99

Jay —
You 'da Monache Man!
Thanks for a great Golden
experience with more to
come I'm sure.
Your Pal,   8/10
Rich —

FLY FISHING
THE
SIERRA NEVADA

BY BILL SUNDERLAND

Aguabonita
Books

FOR INFORMATION WRITE:
Aguabonita Books
PO Box 40429
San Francisco, CA 94140

Text Copyright © 1999 by Bill Sunderland
Maps Copyright © 1999 Aguabonita Books

PHOTOGRAPHY CREDITS:
Front cover, front flap, back cover all except upper right column image
Copyright © 1999 by Paolo Marchesi. Back cover upper right column
image and back flap Copyright © 1999 by Bill Sunderland.
Pages 2, 8, 9, 16, 20, 54, 58, 64, 67, 70, 81, 82, 90, 94, 99, 104-105, 108, 112,
115 Copyright © 1999 by Paolo Marchesi. Pages 11, 14, 38, 40, Copyright
© 1999 by Kenneth Susman. Pages 12, 24, 48, 52, 72, 86, Copyright ©
1999 by Bill Sunderland. Pages 19, 28, 34, 43, 46, 51, 60-61, 100, Copyright © 1999 by Rick E. Martin. Page 44, Copyright © 1999 by Ken
Morrish. Page 78, Copyright © 1999 by Rick Bean.

Maps by Litton Design, San Francisco

Library of Congress Catalog Card Number: 99-73087.
ISBN: 0-9652566-0-X

Printed in Hong Kong

First Edition
M 10 9 8 7 6 5 4 3 2 1

This edition produced for Aguabonita Books by:
Barich Books
870 Market Street, Suite 690
San Francisco, CA 94102

To My Grandchildren
Chelsea
Zachary
Sammy

May there always be wild trout for them to catch.

TABLE OF CONTENTS

INTRODUCTION

Fly-Fishing Prejudices; Here are Mine

Paolo Marchesi

THE objective of this book is to provide fly fishers accurate information on where to ply their talents in the Sierra. That said, there are a lot of "ifs," "ands," "whys," and "buts."

Like anybody else who has spent a lifetime wielding a fly rod, I have my own prejudices and preferences. You should know them when you read this book because although I've tried to be fair in describing areas and waters, what I like could creep into my reporting.

First, I prefer moving water—I'd rather fish a stream flowing into or out of a lake than the lake itself. This is relative, of course, since I'll fish the lake if the best angling is in that body of water. There also are major exceptions, like the Hex hatch on Lake Almanor, the late-season weed beds on Lake Crowley, Lahontan cutthroat in Heenan Lake, and the big brookies in Kirman Lake. These all are stillwater experiences not to be missed, as is made clear on the following pages.

I'm also a wild-trout person. Stockers from the hatchery pens of the California Department of Fish and Game in most cases don't really interest me. Unfortunately (to my mind), that eliminates a majority of state waters because the main thrust of the DFG for many years was to maintain put-and-take fisheries where folks could drive up, toss in a worm,

Some Sierra rivers, such as the East Walker (above), give anglers a chance at catching large hook-jawed brown trout (left).

and go home with a limit of cookie-cutter rainbows that had never eaten anything but pellets.

Give me those waters where the trout population sustains itself, or where the stocking is such that the hatchery-bred fish survive over the winter, long enough to become wild themselves. I like catching big fish as well as the next angler, but I also thrill to the sparkle of a little brookie or a twelve-inch brown that can be enticed to the surface in a stream that should hold only ten-inchers. Note that I use the term "wild trout." Native fish are something else, and there are only a few of them around, such as the Lahontan cutthroat and the famous High Sierra golden. In fact, most of the Lahontans and some of the goldens of today are bred and planted by the DFG, so although they are native, they might not qualify as wild. There's no such thing here as a native brown or brook trout, either—browns were imported from Germany and Scotland, and the brookies came from eastern U.S. waters. But now they offer some of the best wild-trout fishing available.

The wild-trout movement in California started in the late 1960s at Hat Creek (which is not in the Sierra Nevada) and gained impetus in 1972 with the beginning of the DFG's Wild Trout Program. It was bolstered in 1979 by a state law mandating that 25 miles of stream and one lake annually be added to catch-and-release waters. Fly-fishers, played a key role in both these movements.

9

Today, the Wild Trout and Catch-and-Release Programs are well established within the DFG and, for the most part, accepted by anglers. For fly fishers, who by the nature of their craft tend to release most of their catch, the programs have been a success. Even though most Wild Trout waters also allow lure fishing, the fact is that fly-line anglers are those who make the most use of this resource.

Perhaps the major negative is that California is running out of the type of water, particularly lakes, that are logical additions to the Wild Trout and/or Catch-and-Release programs. As John M. Deinstadt, the now-retired head of the DFG's Wild Trout Program says, "We've identified most of the Hot Creeks and Fall Rivers in California, and I'd be very surprised if something pops up that we didn't know about. Now we are down to working with waters that are more and more difficult." That's a disheartening statement because only about 3.5 percent of California streams or rivers and fewer than 1 percent of its lakes are in the programs.

There are exceptions to this emphasis on wild trout in what follows, of course, and where stocked waters offer something out of the ordinary, they are included. If you know of or find an accessible creek, river, or lake that isn't in the book, it probably carries stocked fish or doesn't qualify as first-rate angling. Hey, fish it anyway—it is a lot of fun to catch smaller trout, and working your own piece of water is a rewarding experience. Besides, you might stumble onto some first-rate fishing that I don't know about.

The high backcountry is honeycombed with little streams and dotted with hundreds of lakes, many of them with fish. Some can be reached by hiking for a few hours; some may take a day or more of slogging to get there. (Personally, I prefer going in on horseback with pack horses to carry the load.) If you are an avid backpacker, you'll have your own favorite spots, many of them little lakes that can't sustain the pressure of regular fishing. This is a case where I'm going to offer only occasional suggestions, most of them day hikes, so if this is your bag, haul out the U.S. Forest Service and topographical maps and do your own exploring. I wish I still had the legs to keep up with you.

The eastern slope of the Sierra drops sharply toward the Nevada border, but since little of the range is in Nevada, we've stayed with California waters. On the western side, there are myriad foothill lakes and reservoirs, along with rivers dropping into the Sacramento and San Joaquin Valleys. Some of them, particularly reservoirs, have good fishing but aren't really prime fly fishing water. So for the most part, I've neglected the lower western-slope areas. except for a few spots where fishing is better than normal. I'll take you down the whole Sierra chain, from north to south, and then to some of the east-slope hot spots, but there are some preliminaries we should go over first.

The first three chapters give a profile of the Sierra and their fishing and deal with being prepared to go fishing there, including information on insect hatches and the flies that imitate them. The main thing you need in order to be prepared for fly fishing the Sierra, however, is gear, and if you're already a fly-line angler, you're probably ready to go. Pretty much any trout rod that will throw a line will do because it depends on how well you can use it. But for novices, here are some guidelines.

RODS

On many of the smaller streams, a lightweight rod with a 3-weight or even 2-weight line works great. I like them fairly long, 8 or 9 feet, because sometimes I need to dap by shoving the rod through the brush and letting the fly fall where fish are holding. There's another viewpoint on this, that shorter rods in lengths of 6 or 7 feet make it a lot easier to cast in tight quarters. Lighter rods also are more fun because they give a better feel for smaller fish.

On larger rivers, I use a 5-weight, or even a 6-weight, particularly where there is wind. An example is the upper Owens River, which is perfect for a rod as light as a 3-weight, but which has a hellish and almost constant wind that makes casting with a light rod impossible.

LINES

Most of the time I use a floating line. If I hit areas where I need to fish a nymph deep, I generally just make the leader long enough to get it down. On some lakes, a sink-tip line is necessary, but not much Sierra water calls for a full-sinking line.

LEADERS

My theory is that longer and lighter leaders catch bigger trout. In some waters (Hot Creek, the East Walker, the upper Owens River, for example) using them is a must. Tossing a 12-foot leader with a 7X tippet is necessary because resident trout have been fished for so frequently that they are extremely spooky, and if you can make it 15 feet and 8X, so much the better. But get on a little mountain stream with ten-inch brookies and a 9-foot leader and 5X or 6X tippet works great. When nymphing, you can make your leaders even shorter.

FLIES

Here's where things can get out of hand, since it seems every fly fisher and every store that sells fly-fishing gear in the Sierra Nevada has a favorite selection. So let's stick to generalities. Caddisflies are the most plentiful aquatic insect, followed by mayflies, midges, and stoneflies. And let's not forget damselflies, leeches, scuds, and even snails, not to mention terrestrials such as grasshoppers and ants. For extensive fishing, an angler needs imitations for all of them. A few across-the-board suggestions, though, hold up well throughout the Sierra and should be part of an angler's fly box. If you want

Kenneth Susman

A typical fly box for fishing the Sierra has to include a variety of dries and nymphs ranging in size from #12 to #18, or even smaller, along with a few Woolly Buggers and hopper imitations.

a more detailed discussion of the aquatic insects and fly patterns of the Sierra, see Chapter 3.

NYMPHS

Gold-Ribbed Hare's Ears, Pheasant Tails, Bird's Nests, Princes, and Zug Bugs, size 12 to 18, with or without bead heads. You'll also need a damselfly imitation, size 10 to 14, and mosquito and midge imitations in size 18, 20, or even smaller. On the other end, don't forget stonefly imitations as large as size 6.

DRIES

A selection of caddis imitations, including the Elk Hair Caddis in various shades from black to light tan. The Adams, particularly in the parachute version, is the favored mayfly, but there are myriad other upwing imitations that work. Be sure to have Pale Morning Duns, Pale Evening Duns, Blue-Winged Olives, and Little Yellow Stones. That's a lot of flies, particularly when you need them from size 10 to size 18 and even size 20. You'll need specialty flies such as a big yellow imitation for the Lake Almanor Hex hatch or big orange imitations for those rivers that have a spring Salmon Fly hatch.

For attractors, Red or Yellow Humpies are the general favorite, but I like to fish a Royal Wulff because I can see it better.

TERRESTRIALS

Black and cinnamon ants are extremely effective, as are hoppers later in the summer. Cricket patterns occasionally work, too.

MISCELLANEOUS

Woolly Buggers and Woolly Worms, size 6 to 12, in black, brown, purple, and even yellow should be part of the angler's arsenal, along with streamers such as Zonkers and Matukas in various colors and sizes. Scuds work well on some lakes, and I've been successful with emergers (including LaFontaine's and the cul-de-canard) that can be fished in the surface film. Don't forget to have a cripple or two, particularly the Quiggly Cripple.

Of course, we could always suggest you use a Power Bait pattern in the stocked waters in the Sierra Nevada. But it doesn't give a fly-line angler much guidance to list a couple of dozen streams in a region and describe them by saying they are typical Sierra creeks with stocked rainbows. Although some of them may offer good fishing, this book emphasizes wild-trout areas. That's where most of the best fly fishing is. I'll admit that I've left out a few places that have excellent fishing but that would not be able to survive heavy fishing pressure. If you find them, go to it!

CHAPTER I: THE SIERRA NEVADA

Where is It? What is It?

Bill Sunderland

THERE'S no firm delineation or boundary for the Sierra Nevada. Geologists say one thing, botanists another. But for practical purposes, it starts in the north at Lake Almanor in Plumas County and runs southeast to the headwaters of the Kern River, where the mountain range swings south and ends at Tehatchapi Pass. The peaks and passes of California's 430-mile-long backbone become higher as it stretches south, climaxing with Mount Whitney, at 14,496 feet the tallest mountain in the contiguous forty-eight states. There are some 500 peaks that are higher than 12,000 feet, including 10 that are over 14,000 feet.

Geologically, the range is a huge granite slab between 60 and 80 miles wide that slopes gradually upward to the east and then drops sharply off, forming the precipitous eastern slope. As a result, the crest of the range is near the eastern border, and at the higher, southern end, sharp drop-offs can result in a 7,000-foot plunge in elevation in the space of a few miles.

There are a limited number of east-west passes over the Sierra, becoming progressively higher to the south. They are Beckwourth Pass on Highway 70, 5,221 feet above sea level; Yuba Pass on Highway 49, 6,701 feet; Donner Pass on Inter-

The eastern escarpment of the Sierra presents a dramatic background for fly fishing.

state 80, 7,135 feet; Echo Summit on Highway 50, 7,380 feet; Carson Pass on Highway 88, 8,573 feet; Ebbetts Pass on Highway 4, 8,730 feet; Sonora Pass on Highway 108, 9,642 feet, and Tioga Pass on Highway 120, 9,941 feet. At the southern end, on Highway 178 from Bakersfield, there is Walker Pass, 5,250 feet above sea level. Except for Highways 70, 80, and 50, which are kept open by Caltrans, the east-west passes are closed by snow in the winter. When they are opened in the spring depends on how deep the snowpack is and how fast the snow melts.

According to geologists, the "High Sierra" means that region above 8,000 feet that extends from just north of Yosemite National Park some 150 miles south to Cottonwood Pass and includes relatively flat and open highlands between peaks. I'm in the habit of referring to the high Sierra (note the lowercase "h" in "high") as the upper region of whatever section of the Sierra Nevada that I'm writing about, so please forgive me this geological trespass.

There are approximately 2,000 lakes in the Sierra Nevada and probably just as many streams. But there are only 15 major river systems, most of them flowing to the west. On the eastern slope flowing east there are the Truckee, Carson, Walker, and Owens Rivers. Ten major rivers flow west—the Feather, Yuba, American, Mokelumne, Stanislaus, Tuolumne, Merced, San Joaquin, Kings, and Kaweah. The Kern River flows south out of the southern end of the range before turning west. Smaller systems that flow to the west include the Consumnes, Calaveras, and Tule Rivers.

Ice Age glaciers were a predominant force in shaping the Sierra Nevada of today, scooping out valleys, leaving moraines, and scouring granite rock surfaces. Although the last Ice Age ended about 10,000 years ago, there are probably sixty small glaciers left in the Sierra, most of them less than half a mile long. These glacierets, as they are called, can be differentiated from seasonal snowfields by the flow of milky water that issues from under them. The milkiness is caused by finely ground rock generated by the slow movement of the glacier.

The recorded history of the Sierra Nevada began on April 2, 1772, when a Catholic missionary, Pedro Font, saw the mountains at a distance from the western edge of the San Joaquin Valley. He described them in his diary as "una grand sierra nevada," which translates from the Spanish as "a great snowy range." "Sierra Nevada" became the accepted name for these mountains—the Snowy Range.

Although many of the rivers were named in following years, it wasn't until October 1827, that non-native Americans—Jedediah Smith and two companions—crossed the mountains, probably somewhere near Ebbetts Pass. Four years later, Joseph Walker and a party of fifty climbed the eastern slope and made their way across to the Central Valley. He also was the first person to see the Yosemite Valley.

An expedition led by John C. Fremont and guided by Kit Carson saw Lake Tahoe on February 14, 1844. Beginning with the Gold Rush five years later, the entire area was explored and settled. And with that began the changes that have led to the present-day degradation of the Sierra Nevada's ecosystems.

Their status is detailed in *The Status of the Sierra Nevada* by the Sierra Nevada Ecosystem Project (SNEP), published in 1996 after two years of research by eighteen team members and nineteen special consultants. This massive, multivolume report details what has happened to the Sierra and projects what might befall it in the future, along with suggestions on what can be done. Here are some of the major points that affect anglers.

POPULATION

During the Gold Rush, from 150,000 to 175,000 people inhabited the Sierra Nevada. In 1970, the population was about 300,000, and in 1990 over 650,000 Californians lived in the Sierra, many in the western foothills near major highways. About 40 percent of the growth was in Nevada, Placer, and El Dorado Counties. Projections are that between 1.5 million and 2.4 million people will call the Sierra Nevada home by 2040. The report noted that "new residents are increasingly drawn by the amenity values of Sierra Nevada resources as they seek a high-quality living environment" and that despite the burst in population, there has been almost no growth in agriculture, timber harvesting, and mining. Recreation and tourism now provide as much income as those traditional, commodity-based industries.

FISH

The introduction of non-native fish, mostly brown and brook trout, along with the planting of trout in previously barren lakes, has "greatly altered aquatic ecosystems through impacts on native fish, amphibians and invertebrate assemblages." The report said that "historically, only about 20 high-elevation lakes contained fish, whereas there are now more than 2,000 lakes containing fish. This human-mediated ecological transformation has had severe detrimental impacts on native aquatic invertebrates and amphibians, causing drastic reductions in distribution and population sizes. Merely through cessation of stocking, as many as one-third of the lakes could revert to fishless condition."

The report also noted that "chinook salmon and steelhead once ran in most of the major Sierran streams but now have been nearly eliminated from the range due to dams and impoundments, which profoundly alter stream-flow patterns and water temperatures. Decline in other native fish species is also evident, especially at lower elevations."

ANIMALS

About 400 species of mammals, birds, reptiles and amphibians are in the Sierra Nevada. Three modern species have become extinct: the grizzly bear, the California condor, and Bell's vireo, a type of bird. At the same time, about 15 species have moved into the Sierra, some of which are having detrimental effects on native species. The report singles out the brown-headed cowbird, noting that "the spread of this nest-parasitizing bird has mirrored the spread of farmland, grazing, clear-cut logging and suburban development. Cowbirds are implicated or directly charged with the decline of several songbirds in the Sierra Nevada."

FORESTS

Despite 150 years of "Euro-American timber harvest," the report said that "clear-cut blocks larger than 5-10 acres are at present uncommon in the conifer forests of the Sierra Nevada and tree cover is relatively continuous....Early large clear-cuts have reforested and more recent clear-cuts in the Sierra have been small in area and limited in scope."

GRAZING

"Historic unregulated grazing, which ended in the early 1900s, created widespread, profound and, in some places, irreversible ecological impacts." The report said that "grazing has been a pervasive activity throughout the Sierra Nevada for more than 130 years," and although current practices

Kenneth Susman

reduce grazing, it still has a significant impact on biodiversity and ecological processes of many rangelands in the middle to high elevations. Restoration of stream channels and biodiversity can take decades.

THE FUTURE

The report not only outlines the problems, but opens the way for a new process: "The people must examine the ideas and test them against their own sense of validity and the need for change." What it leaves unresolved, however, "is the question of whether our society has the will and the capability to correct such problems. Implementation of new approaches or possible solutions is the responsibility of the public and its institutions. The beginning is to acknowledge that problems exist: willing minds and able hands can find solutions."

THE PRESENT

In some cases, they already have. Some Sierra streams are in better condition than they were ten or fifteen years ago. Despite the effects that continued land development, mining, logging, and grazing have had on the environment and especially on the fishing in the Sierra, and despite uncertainties about the future, there is plenty to excite the fly angler in what the region has to offer. Here are a few examples.

The Hex hatch on Lake Almanor isn't to be missed. (See the Feather River Country chapter.) It is pure excitement and fun, and whether you catch anything or not, you'll come away with the adrenaline flowing. If you do catch fish, it's a given that they'll be big ones. While you are in the area, be sure to fish nearby Yellow Creek. It doesn't qualify as blue-ribbon water, but the area is so beautiful that it's worth the trip.

Dropping to the other end of the Sierra, a visit to one of the golden-trout streams is an unforgettable experience. (See the Golden Trout Country chapter.) You'll never forget that first golden, and no matter how many you hook after that, each one is a thing of awe, so beautiful it makes you hurt. Although several streams are good, I like the South Fork of the Kern at Monache Meadows, despite the 4x4 banging it takes to get in. Just kick the cattle out of the way and go do it, or hike upstream above the meadow. No matter where, you'll catch fish.

I love the eastern slope and believe it has most of the best big-trout fishing in the mountain range. There's the upper Owens River, particularly in the spring or fall, when the browns or rainbows are moving upriver to spawn. (See the Owens River Area chapter.) Even during the summer, there are plenty of fish and very few people around Long Ears or Benton's Crossing, and you can have a stretch of stream to yourself, accompanied only by swarms of mosquitoes. In the late summer and fall, the Lake Crowley weed beds are great

for float tubing, although you'll see more fly fishers than mosquitoes in this case.

Hot Creek? Too many folks with new gear who don't have a clue what they're doing. Still, it can be fun early in the day or late in the evening, when fewer people are about.

Moving north, Green Creek, not far from Bridgeport, is one of my favorite trout waters. (See the Bridgeport Area chapter.) It is tough fishing, and I've had to work for every trout I've caught there. That's satisfying, knowing you've done the right things and they have paid off. I've also done the right things on Green Creek and they haven't paid off, but that's fishing.

One of many creeks in the Markleeville area that is fun small-stream fishing is Wolf Creek, (See the Carson River chapter.) Wolf Creek is nice because anglers can walk upstream fairly easily and find wild trout. Not big fish, but lots of fun.

The North Fork of the Stanislaus is a favorite because it is the closest thing I have to home water—my parents used to have a home not far from Arnold. I opened many a season on Beaver Creek all by myself, catching small trout by the dozens and enjoying every minute of it. (See the Highway 4 chapter.)

This overview just hits some of the high spots. Of course, there's good fishing to be had all around and between these destinations, as well. You'll soon have your own favorites. Before you go, however, there a few things you should know about the mountains and the flies you need to fish them.

◆ ◆ ◆ ◆ ◆

To purchase the *Status of the Sierra Nevada*, write The Centers for Water and Wildland Resources, University of California, 1 Shields Avenue, Davis, CA 95616-8750, or call them at (916) 752-8070. Access to a computer-based catalogue of all public databases, maps, and other digitally stored information used in the project is via the internet at http://alexandria.sdc.ucsb.edu/.

West slope streams, such as Deer Creek, have a different sort of beauty than waters of the arid east slope.

CHAPTER 2: DANGER—LOOK OUT!
It's Wild Out There.

Paolo Marchesi

THE old expression "It's a jungle out there" can be taken at face value when it comes to life outdoors in the Sierra. Even if you step out of your car at a campground parking place and walk twenty feet to a river or creek, there can be danger. Bushwhackers who clamber down steep hillsides and force their way through the underbrush are adding yet other elements of peril. The Sierra Nevada is mountainous country with large, predatory animals, snakes, slippery hillsides, crumbling, unstable rock, and all the other things that make wild country wild—and attract us to it. We also wade on slippery rocks in rushing rivers and float around in inner tubes that can burst or turn over in the middle of a lake.

One thing underlies all the advice people give about journeys in the Sierra. There is nothing like common sense to keep you safe, but if something does go wrong, the more you know about what to do in such a situation, the better your chances of coming out of it without permanent damage. You don't need to be scared—just be alert, always, and cautious when the need arises.

This isn't the definitive work on mountain dangers and how to deal with them, but a reminder of what can happen to a fly fisher intent on angling. You just need to keep your wits about you. The best suggestions I can offer on dealing with

Take time to study the water before you begin wading. If you slip and go for a swim, rapids, falls or fast water downstream can compound the danger.

backcountry dangers, apart from using common sense, are: buy a small pocket guide on wilderness medicine, then read it beforehand and keep it in your fishing vest; always carry a first-aid kit; and take the first-aid classes generally available to the public through hospitals and clinics.

Also, whenever possible, fish with another person. If you go alone, leave word with your spouse or a responsible friend exactly where you are going and when you'll be back. Then be responsible yourself and go to that place and tell your friend when you have safely returned so he or she won't start a search party while you're at the local bistro.

Finally, know what you can do physically. An hour's hike deep into a steep canyon can mean a two-hour climb coming out. And you'll need plenty of drinking water on hot summer days.

Here are some of the everyday perils you may face and what to do about them.

GIARDIA LAMBLIA

This one-celled protozoan carried by both domestic and wild animals exists in water throughout the Sierra Nevada (and just about every other "pristine" wilderness in the western United States). It is a nasty little bug that at best causes diarrhea and at worst can make you very, very sick. It is the reason not to drink the clear, cold, inviting water in the streams you fish. It takes a week to ten days to gestate in your intestines (nine days is the norm), so it might not ruin a fishing trip, but can make you miserable afterward. If you get sick, go to a doctor—*Giardia* can be cured with drugs. If you don't take medical action, *Giardia* cysts can perpetuate the disease and you probably will get worse.

I've had it once. I made the mistake of holding the leader in my mouth while changing a fly, and apparently there still was a drop of *Giardia*-bearing water on the leader. Violent cramps, diarrhea, and flatulence were the unwelcome result.

If you must drink water from a river or creek, disinfect it. That means boiling it thoroughly, adding chlorine or iodine, or using a filter that can screen *Giardia* out. Stores that cater to backpackers sell these filters, as well as disinfecting tablets that can be carried in your fishing vest.

POISON OAK

The way to deal with this is to know what it looks like in all its forms and seasons and stay away from it. Since it is a fairly distinctive plant, it is easy to identify, although it is surprising how many folks don't seem willing to spend a few minutes on the subject to avoid what can be a painful situation.

An excellent pamphlet is put out by the State Compensation Insurance Fund (525 Golden Gate Avenue, San Francisco, CA 94102, Safety Pamphlet No. 10015) that shows color pictures of poison oak in all four of its seasons and offers advice in both English and Spanish.

Poison oak is recognizable by its three-leaf pattern, bright green with heavy veins in the spring, yellow-green, pink, or reddish, with small white or tan berries in the summer, and deep red or russet brown in the fall. In the winter, the plant can be recognized by its bare, whiplike stems or in some cases its climbing vines. The plant can come in the form of a vine, bush, or spindly plant and is very common up to about 5,000 feet.

It is the sap from poison oak that irritates the skin and causes humans to break out. You can get the oil by direct contact, by having it transmitted (by a dog, for example), and even from the smoke caused by burning poison oak.

If you know you've touched it, wash the area thoroughly with soap and water at the first opportunity. If it's too late for that, there are medications and other remedies, such as calamine lotion. There also are protective creams that can be spread on exposed areas of your skin if you know you will be in poison oak country.

Some people are more susceptible to poison oak than others, but that is a situation that can change—it won't bother you, perhaps for years, then, without warning, your body will become susceptible to being irritated by the plant.

RATTLESNAKES

They can be anyplace. There are two types of people—those who are terrified of snakes and those who aren't. Nobody seems ambivalent on the subject. It is the type, like myself, who aren't scared of snakes, who sometimes become negli-

gent in watching out for them. Be careful where you put your hands and feet, particularly your hands if you are climbing over a rocky hillside in the scramble to get to a canyon stream. A snake can be quietly sunning itself on a rock and isn't going to be happy if you accidentally grab it when all you are expecting is a granite handhold.

Rattlesnake bites aren't as dangerous as popular mythology makes them. In an estimated 20 percent of bites, the snake does not inject venom, and in another 10 percent, only a small amount of venom is injected. These bites can become infected, like any cut, but aren't life-threatening.

For the record, there aren't any "timber rattlers" in the Sierra Nevada. What we have are varieties of the Western rattlesnake, mostly the Pacific Coast brand. They come in a number of different sizes and colors depending on the terrain they inhabit, but they are all the same species. There are a few other types of rattlers in the desert country at the southeastern tip of the Sierra Nevada, but that isn't the area we are fishing.

It isn't difficult to identify rattlesnakes—the loud buzz they make with the rattles on their tails is distinctive and very, very alarming. If you have never heard a rattlesnake, don't worry. There are other things that may sound like a rattlesnake, but if and when you hear one, there will be absolutely no doubt in your mind what it is.

If you hear it, don't jump, because you might jump into the rattlesnake. Freeze long enough to determine where the rattlesnake is, and then get away from it. It can strike only about half the length of its body, although if it is coiled and in the strike position, it can be hard to tell exactly how long it is.

Rattlesnakes buzz when disturbed or frightened. It's when they are snoozing in the sun and you step on them or put your hand on them that the most danger exists. A remedy is to follow well-trodden paths and make enough noise to give fair warning to any snake in front of you. They don't want to have anything to do with you any more than you want to have anything to do with them.

About 3,000 people are bitten by rattlesnakes every year, and only a few of them die. And many of the people who were bitten were inviting disaster by handling the snakes.

If bitten, determine if venom was injected. The symptoms are burning pain near the wound, rapid swelling of the affected area, tingling, and a metallic taste in the victim's mouth. The muscles may twitch and the victim become weak.

Anyone who is bitten should stay as calm as possible, remain stationary, and remove any jewelry (for example, rings, if the bite is in the hand or arm) in case the limb swells. If close to transportation, a fifteen or twenty-minute walk at the most, head for the hospital. But in an isolated area, a companion should go immediately for help—the victim shouldn't try to hike out.

What you don't do is cut the bite and attempt to suck out

the blood or poison. Doctors found years ago that this was more dangerous than the bite itself. However, there is a little tool that can be carried while hiking—a Sawyer Extractor Pump designed to suck out poison. They don't cost much and can be bought at most outdoor stores. Make it part of your first-aid kit.

BEARS

These smart animals have learned to equate campers with food, which is why most encounters with them are in campgrounds while they are trying to get into somebody's larder. Avoid inviting them in by putting food in the bear-proof boxes provided at many campsites, hanging food from a tree if hiking, or putting it in the trunk of your car where (most of the time) they can't get at it. Whatever you do, don't leave it lying around the camp or, worse yet, take it into your tent, or chances are high you'll have a very unwelcome and potentially dangerous visitor. If worse comes to worst, let the bear have the food—it is an extremely strong animal, and you don't want to mix with it. Don't forget that things like toothpaste and even some types of soap smell like food to a bear, so tuck them away with the food items, not in your tent.

If you fish isolated Sierra Nevada streams and rivers regularly, you've almost certainly been surprised by—and probably surprised—a bear. They'll normally take off, and you'll be left with just a pounding heart and a story for your friends. Just be extra careful of mama bears with cubs, since that's a recipe for trouble. Quickly back off (don't run) so she can collect her cubs and disappear. If you run into a cub by itself, get out of there, because mother bear is nearby.

When was the last time somebody in California was killed by a bear? I don't even remember. Have I run into bears? Regularly. Have I ever been threatened? Never. Have I been scared? Hell yes.

MOUNTAIN LIONS

This is a beautiful animal, and you're lucky if you ever see one. They are all over the place, particularly where deer are abundant, and in recent years, humans have been killed by lions that apparently mistook them for prey. The strategy for dealing with a mountain lion is: don't run, make yourself as large and formidable as possible by raising your arms over your head, and, if you can, even throw rocks. If attacked, fight back with anything at hand. What it boils down to is making it clear to the lion that you aren't dinner. Get that across and it will buzz off.

WASPS, BEES, AND YELLOW JACKETS

These are generally just a nuisance, but in some cases they are a danger. If you have an allergic reaction to stings, called anaphylactic shock, then you should always carry a bee-sting kit that contains Adrenaline and an antihistamine as part of your first-aid gear—and you probably do, since you real-

ize the danger you are in. You probably should carry one anyway as a precaution. The kits don't cost much and don't take up much room, but you need a doctor's prescription to get them from a pharmacy.

The other danger is running into a wasps' or bees' nest and triggering a situation where you may suffer from multiple stings. Bees build their hives in such places as tree hollows and in rock crevasses, and these generally are easy to see because of the activity. Wasps build their football-shaped papier-mâché nests in trees. yellow jackets often build their nests underground or in tree stumps.

If stung, ease the stinger out by scraping it with a knife or a needle, or even a credit card. Trying to pinch it out will empty the venom sac into the sting.

P.S. Don't swat at these insects—it just irritates them.

BUBONIC PLAGUE

Yeah, this is the same "Black Death" that wiped out millions of Europeans during the Dark Ages. And it is still very much around, although easily treatable with antibiotics. Still, it's much easier to avoid it than to treat it.

Plague is a bacterium transmitted by fleas that get it from host rodents such as mice, squirrels, cute little chipmunks, and cuddly rabbits. Generally, it is quickly identified by forest personnel and the area where it is prevalent is closed to the public. The infected animals usually die, so do not handle any dead rodents or other animals, since larger mammals, particularly those that eat rodents, can have it, too. And don't be tempted to set up your camp anywhere near one of those infected campgrounds because plague-bearing fleas are out looking for a new meal. The incubation period for plague is two to six days after being bitten and is accompanied by fever, enlarged lymph nodes, and occasionally pneumonia.

WADING

I used to be what's called an "aggressive wader," which means I did whatever I could to get into position to cast to fish. It brought so many dunkings that everything in my fishing vest, including the camera, was waterproof. As my legs (and a few other parts of my body) have aged, I've become much more cautious (some would say less stupid) about wading.

Not that there's anything the matter with aggressive wading, but help yourself by carrying a wading staff and go slowly, using the staff as a third leg. If you're with a friend, it is very effective to hold hands as you ford a difficult area of fast or deep water. Another trick, if one of you is a much stronger or taller wader, is for the strong wader to stay just upstream, which helps break the current for the weaker or smaller person.

Another rule: wear a tight chest belt to keep your waders from taking on water if you fall. With skin-tight neoprenes

Rick E. Martin

There's nothing like being on a High Sierra lake with a float tube. Great fishing is all but guaranteed — and so is cold water, so be prepared.

it isn't so bad, but with loose waders, all that water inside can keep you from regaining your feet.

Above all, don't be stupid and get into water you can't deal with. No fish is worth it.

FLOAT TUBES

I have a friend who is an expert fly fisher and who has logged about as much time in a float tube as a commercial airline pilot in a plane. But on an aggressive, long cast a couple of years ago he turned over a U-shaped tube and the lap buckle jammed. He came extremely close to drowning before another tuber realized what was happening and paddled to his aid.

Such accidents may not happen often, but if they can happen to somebody as experienced as my friend, they can happen to anybody who uses a float tube. (By the way, the incident was serious enough that the manufacturer changed the buckle-release design on the float tube.)

If you're a new float tuber, or have a new tube, try it out in a swimming pool with a buddy to help out. That way you can get the feel of just how hard it is to turn it over. It also helps to capsize deliberately and practice getting out. You might also try it while wearing waders—don't forget a wading belt.

Remember, if a circular tube is turned over, it is impossible to get right-side up again. Get out of the tube by swimming straight down to clear yourself from the seat—the hardest part is getting your fins through the leg holes—and then come

up outside the tube. Tubes have a quick-release catch for the seat that can help, but remembering to snap it loose with your upper body under water takes a certain amount of calmness under pressure.

Most float tubes now have a backup bladder that is used as a back rest and that will keep you from sinking if there is a major leak or blowout. I used an old tube for years that didn't have such a backup, but I always wore a pair of suspenders that could be inflated with CO_2 cartridges and used as a life jacket.

WEATHER

Living in some areas of California makes it easy to forget there really is such a thing as weather. But in the Sierra Nevada, you better believe it exists and that it can change within minutes. What starts as a sunny midsummer day in the high country can end with freezing cold, rain, lightning, or even snow. So be prepared.

The two major dangers are hypothermia and lightning. Obviously, hypothermia can be avoided by bringing clothing that will keep you dry and warm. Even having a plastic garbage bag in your fishing vest that can be used as emergency rain gear helps. Don't forget matches in a waterproof container. A thermal reflector blanket that weighs only a few ounces and folds almost to handkerchief size could be a lifesaver in an emergency, too.

If a lightning storm hits, and they can develop in the mountains with amazing rapidity, don't be stupid and continue fishing. Waving a lightning rod (a.k.a. a graphite fishing rod) in the middle of a creek or river during a storm is not very bright. Lightning takes the quickest way to the ground, and that involves hitting the tallest thing around. That could be you and your fishing rod, if you're in the middle of a open piece of water. So stash the rod someplace and take cover—not under the tallest tree around or under the only tree in the middle of a meadow, but in a stand of low trees surrounded by higher trees.

If you are caught in the middle of an open area with no protection, crouch down or roll into a ball. You may not feel dignified doing this, but survival can mean doing whatever is necessary. Sitting in your car during a storm is fine if the car is a hardtop. Convertibles offer no protection from lightening.

The short form of all these recommendations is this: be alert when things are going well, know how they can go wrong, and be prepared to deal with what happens when they do. Compared with, say, the northern Rockies or the Olympics, the Sierra Nevada is a pretty benign place, as major mountain chains go, but it's still a major mountain chain. Be prepared.

CHAPTER 3: SIERRA INSECTS
Matching the Bugs Trout Eat

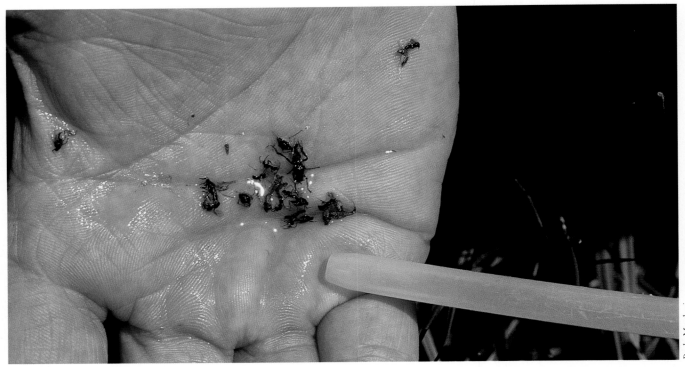

Paolo Marchesi

IS that insect flitting above the water a "light-colored bug," a "Speckled Dun," an "Adams," or a *"Callibaetis"*? They may all be one and the same, but to each angler the answer depends on how deeply he or she is involved in the entomology of the insects on which trout feed and the patterns used to imitate them.

Fly fishers need to know something about the insects their flies are imitating, not only to determine what trout are eating, but to understand how imitations should be fished in order to make them realistic. There's no doubt that the more you know, the better your imitation and presentation can be, but there's also the question of how much is too much.

For some anglers, there's no such thing as too much, and for such aficionados, I've included a list of several excellent fly-fishing entomology books at the end of this chapter. Buy them and you can memorize Latin names to your heart's content. For the rest of us, a generalized knowledge of common insects and their imitations should more than suffice.

Unlike some other regions, particularly Eastern fly-fishing waters, the Sierra Nevada does not have the scientific documentation that comes from years of stream-by-stream studies that tell exactly what insects inhabit an area and

You'll increase your chances for hookups if your flies imitate the insects the trout are eating.

when they hatch. It would be logical to expect such studies from the California Department of Fish and Game, but the state agency instead has focused its work on using aquatic insects as a pollution indicator. Because of this, DFG biologists mostly have studied streams that have problems —not the best trout-fishing waters.

Lack of scientific documentation probably doesn't make that much difference to the fly-line angler because most Sierra Nevada waters contain more or less the same mayflies, caddisflies, stoneflies, and midges. There just aren't that many fisheries that have unusual or specific hatches greatly different from the rest of the streams and lakes in the Sierra.

This allows for a great deal of generalization, particularly on the western slope, where for the most part, trout are more opportunistic feeders than on the eastern slope, where hatches are more prolific, and fish tend to zero in on a specific bug. If you're not really that interested in the bugs themselves, the Introduction's list of what a fly box for general fishing in the Sierra Nevada should contain may be all you need. You can get by with less, or you can cram your vest with much, much more. For anglers who want more information on what these patterns imitate, along with when the major hatches take place, here is a list of the top dozen aquatic insects in the Sierra Nevada.

SIERRA HATCHES

MAYFLIES

Mayflies belong to the order Ephemeroptera. There are over 600 species of them in the United States, about 200 of them in California. They are in almost every freshwater habitat. Females lay eggs in the water, where they hatch and become nymphs that feed on aquatic plants. The nymphs grow steadily and molt a number of times before their emergence as a dun, technically called a "subimago." This is the point at which they make their way to the surface, shed their skin, and take to the air. It is the stage most imitated by dry-fly fishers.

Duns have dull colors and generally fly to vegetation near the water, where they undergo one more molt to become a spinner, or "imago." This final stage is the sexually mature insect that mates, lays its eggs (if it is a female), and then dies. Adult mayflies are easily identifiable by their upright wings, slender bodies, and long tails. They hover, but do not fly forward very well.

Some of the more prolific mayflies found in the Sierra Nevada, along with the flies that imitate them, include the following.

BAETIS (BLUE-WINGED OLIVES)

The major *Baetis* hatches occur from March through June and again in September into November. The duns are a dull olive-gray or brown, generally hatching in the afternoon in large numbers, particularly on overcast days. *Baetis* nymphs are active swimmers. Duns can drift atop the surface for some distance, giving trout ample opportunity to get to them. The nymphs live in a wide range of moving water, everywhere from eddies to riffles. Mayflies are small and can be overlooked by anglers, but are an important food for trout, even during multiple hatches when larger insects also are available.

NYMPHS: Pheasant Tail, Hare's Ear and Bird's Nest, both conventional and beadhead, size 14 to 20.
DUNS: Blue-Winged Olive, size 14 to 22.
SPINNERS: Rusty Spinner, size 16 to 22.

CALLIBAETIS (SPECKLED DUN)

There are hatches of *Callibaetis* throughout the trout season, from April into October. Like the *Baetis*, the duns are a dull olive-gray, but with mottled wings. Hatches tend to occur in the afternoon in large numbers, particularly on overcast days. *Callibaetis* live in still or slow-moving water. There are up to three major hatches during the summer, with each of the later hatches producing smaller bugs than the one before. Anglers should inspect the insects and try to match the size. Generally speaking, the spring hatch is about size 12, the summer size 14, and the fall size 16.

NYMPHS: Pheasant Tail, Hare's Ear and Bird's Nest, both conventional and bead head, size 12 to 18.
DUNS: Adams, Gray Quill, and Light Cahill, size 12 to 18.
SPINNERS: Rusty Spinner, size 16 to 20.

EPHEMERELLA INFREQUENS AND INERMIS (PALE MORNING DUN)

These hatch from May to September in the morning or evening and even during midday when weather is overcast or cold. Infrequens and inermis look the same, with pale green to yellowish bodies and pale gray wings. Infrequens, the larger of the two, hatches first, followed by inermis.

NYMPHS: Pheasant Tail, Bird's Nest and Hare's Ear, both conventional and beadhead, size 14 to 20.
DUNS: PMD Sparkle Dun, PMD Comparadun, or Light Cahill, size 16 to 20.
SPINNERS: Pale olive-yellow spinner, size 16 to 20.

TRICORYTHODES (TRICOS)

Tricos hatch from June to October. These tiny mayflies are tough to fish, but trout love them. Olive-bodied, gray-winged duns hatch early in the day and quickly molt to become spinners, which are olive or black, with long tails. The spinners are the most important part of the hatch for anglers. Tricos live in moving water, usually in the slow sections, and hatch in the morning.

NYMPHS: These are so small they generally aren't fished, but if you want to try it, tie a brown nymph on a size 20 to 24 size hook.
DUNS: Sparkle Duns in both olive and black, size 18 to 24.
SPINNERS: Trico Spinner, size 18 to 24, and Parachute Trico, size 18 to 24.

CADDISFLIES

Mayflies seem to get the publicity, but caddisflies (order Trichoptera), or sedges, as they are called in England, are the most important insect for anglers fishing the Sierra Nevada. Caddisflies are common, numerous, and live in all sorts of water.

Females lay eggs in clusters, either on top of the water or by crawling under the surface to deposit them. The eggs hatch into larvae, many of which construct cases for themselves of sand, small pebbles, or sticks. They metamorphose into pupae with external wing pads before cutting their way free of the shell and making their way to the surface, where they unfold their wings and fly away. This breaking from the pupal case can take only a few seconds, and trout take caddis emergers aggressively, rather than leisurely sipping them from the surface. Caddisflies mate on foliage near the water, and then the females return to the water to lay their eggs.

All caddisflies have distinctive, tent-shaped wings when at rest and flutter when they are flying. The most common caddis in the Sierra Nevada, along with the flies that imitate them, include the following.

RHYACOPHILA (LITTLE GREEN ROCK WORM)

Caddisflies of the genus Rhyacophila hatch from May through September, and the several species are widespread, particularly in freestone streams such as those found in the Sierra. They are not case builders, so the larval stage is a popular food for trout and therefore important to anglers. Colors range from tan to green, and weighted flies work best because usually the larvae are on or near the bottom.

LARVAE: Green Rock Worm, Zug Bug, Latex Caddis Larva,
*   size 8 to 16.*
EMERGING PUPAE: Wet-hackle flies such as the Partridge and Green
*   and the LaFontaine Deep Sparkle Pupa and Emergent Sparkle Pupa*
*   in brown and bright green, size 10 to 16, are good imitations.*
ADULTS: Dark Bucktail Caddis, size 10 to 14.

HYDROPSYCHE (SPOTTED SEDGE)

Caddisflies of the genus Hydropsyche hatch from April through September. This widespread caddis is plentiful in all the running waters of the Sierra, from small streams to the larger rivers at lower elevations. It builds shelters from sand or other matter and spins nets in the current to strain food, leaving its shelter only to graze on what is trapped in the net.

LARVAE: These are similar to Rhyacophila larvae and can be imitated
*   by the same Green Rock Worm, Zug Bug, and Latex Caddis Larva*
*   patterns, sizes 10 to 16. Hare's Ear Nymphs also work.*
EMERGING PUPAE: Wet-hackle flies in light and dark brown and
*   the LaFontaine Deep Sparkle Pupa and Emergent Sparkle Pupa*
*   in brown and yellow, size 10 to 16, are good imitations.*
ADULTS: Elk Hair Caddis or Ginger Bucktail Caddis, size 10 to 16.

LEPIDOSTOMA (GRANNOM)

Hatches of this case-making caddis genus occur from April through September. They mostly inhabit running water and can be found in both riffles and pools, but sometimes also live in lakes. The larvae are slow-moving and can only crawl, not swim. All make various types of cases.

LARVAE: The best cased-caddis imitation is a Herl Nymph,
*   size 10 to 16.*
EMERGING PUPAE: Wet-hackle flies in light and dark brown and
*   the LaFontaine Deep Sparkle Pupa*
*   and Emergent Sparkle Pupa in brown, size 10 to 16.*
ADULTS: Imitations depend on the species, which can be light tan to
*   almost black and come in a variety of sizes.*

LIMNEPHILIDAE (OCTOBER CADDIS, FALL CADDIS, CINNAMON SEDGE, DARK SEDGE)

This is a large family that contains 100 or more species in the West, many of them in the Sierra Nevada. They live in all types of water, but all of them are case makers. The Discmoecus, often known as the October Caddis or Fall Caddis, is the most famous species for fly fishers. These big, orange caddisflies come off in the early fall and can provide a bonanza both for trout and anglers.

LARVAE: Cased-caddis imitations, as large as size 6 for the October
*   Caddis.*
EMERGING PUPAE: Wet-hackle flies in light and dark brown and
*   the LaFontaine Deep Sparkle Pupa and Emergent Sparkle Pupa in a*
*   variety of colors for this diverse family, size 10 to 16. Orange wet*
*   hackles and the LaFontaine Deep Sparkle Pupa and Emergent Sparkle*
*   Pupa in orange and brown, up to size 6 for the October Caddis.*
ADULTS: October Caddis imitations, size 6 or size 8 with orange
*   bodies and tan wings. A Stimulator is my favorite.*

STONEFLIES

Stoneflies (order Plecoptera) live in moving water and require a high concentration of oxygen, which means they are plentiful in most Sierra streams. Like mayflies, they lay their eggs in the water. These hatch into larvae and emerge as adults, with no pupal stage. Unlike mayflies, however, they are sexually mature as adults and do not have a spinner stage.

Stoneflies at rest can be identified because they fold their wings flat over their body. The best-known of the stoneflies are the Golden Stones and Salmon Flies, both large insects that can trigger a feeding frenzy among trout and other fish.

ISOPERLA AND ISOGENUS (LITTLE YELLOW STONES)

Hatches are from April to August, but are heaviest in May and June. At higher elevations, hatches also may be heavy in July. Little Yellow Stones are found in almost all running waters of the Sierra Nevada and can be important to anglers when hatches are under way.

LARVAE: Little Yellow Stone, light yellow to dark brown,
*   size 10 to 14.*
ADULTS: Little Yellow Stone, yellow-bodied Bucktail Caddis or
*   Elk Hair Caddis, size 10 to 14.*

ACRONEURIA CALIFORNICA (GOLDEN STONE)

This large stonefly hatches from mid-May through June, with temperatures determining timing. They live mostly in the riffles of larger rivers. As larvae, Golden Stones are predators and crawl along the bottom, searching for prey. When ready to emerge as adults, they crawl to the bank and onto streamside rocks and vegetation. Trout feed on them heavily during their underwater migration to the bank, as well as when adults deposit their eggs in the water.

LARVAE: Yellow Stone Nymph or Golden Stone Nymph,
*   size 4 to 8.*

*ADULTS: Stimulator, Golden Stone, or yellow-bodied
   Bucktail Caddis, size 4 to 8.*

PTERONARCYS CALIFORNICA (SALMON FLY)

Larger than the Golden Stone, Salmon Flies hatch a bit earlier, beginning in mid-April. For the most part, they inhabit bigger rivers, but some are found in smaller mountain streams, although not in as large numbers. Although they are not as voracious feeders as Golden Stones, these orange-colored flies have similar habits.

NYMPHS: Montana Stone, size 4 to 6.
*ADULTS: Stimulator, Bird's Stone Fly, Sofa Pillows,
   or an orange-bodied Bucktail Caddis, size 4 to 6.*

MIDGES

Midges *(family Chironomidae)* are only part of the group that make up the order of True Flies *(Diptera)*, but they are the most important members for the angler. They hatch all year long, and trout will feed on them just about any time. When there is no hatch of other insects, a smart angler often will try a midge pattern. Although they also live in moving water, they are most important for the fly-line angler in still water.

As the name indicates, midges tend to be small, some so tiny they are hard for the human eye to see, which puts off many anglers. For nymph imitations, the Griffith's Gnat in size 18 to 22 (as small as size 28, if you are brave) is the easiest to tie, but there are other varieties, such as Dave Whitlock's Midge Larva and Emerging Pupa that are effective.

Adults are imitated by any midge patterns, in colors ranging from cream to black, size 16 to 22 and smaller.

◆ ◆ ◆ ◆ ◆

ADDITIONAL INFORMATION

There are a number of excellent books for fly fishers who want to hone their entomological skills, but the basic text for every angler in California still has to be *The Complete Book of Western Hatches,* by Rick Hafele and Dave Hughes, published by Frank Amato Publications, P.O. Box 82112, Portland, OR 97202, (503) 653-8108.

Other books include the following.

Caddisflies, by Gary LaFontaine, published by Lyons and Burford, 31 West 21st Street, New York, NY 10010.

Sierra Trout Guide, by Ralph Cutter, published by Frank Amato Publications, P.O. Box 82112, Portland, OR, 97202, (503) 653-8108.

Caddis Super Hatches, by Carl Richards and Bob Braendle, published by Frank Amato Publications, P.O. Box 82112, Portland, OR, 97202, (503) 653-8108.

Selective Trout, by Doug Swisher and Carl Richards, published by New Century Publishers, 220 Old New Brunswick Road, Piscataway, NJ 08854.

CHAPTER 4: THE FEATHER RIVER COUNTRY
Big Beautiful, and Lots of Fly Fishing

Bill Sunderland

THE FEATHER RIVER country, the northernmost section of the Sierra Nevada, covers a large area offering a wide variety of fly fishing—prolific lakes, both big and small, good-sized rivers with easy access or difficult hiking, and small streams that range from freestone to spring creek.

Mostly within Plumas County and dominated by the Plumas National Forest, this is an area geared for tourism. Public and private camping abounds, along with lodging, restaurants, and every type of shop that can eke a living out of the visitor. Fishing of all sorts is popular, but so are the numerous golf courses and country-club-style amenities that are available.

Let's get the one slightly negative element out of the way first. There is lots and lots of good fly fishing, but little excellent fishing, such as can be found on some Sierra Nevada eastern-slope streams like the Owens River, Hot Creek, and the East Walker River. That said, there are so many positive things about the area and its fishing that this becomes a minor point

Trout fishing, after all, is for most fly-line anglers the overall experience. The clear water of a mountain stream, the wildlife, the silence of a forest, the majesty of the surrounding mountains, or the golden sweep of a meadow are

Yellow Creek and Humbug Valley rank among the prettiest places of the Sierra Nevada. The split-rail fence keeps cattle out.

as much a part of the sport of angling for a trout with flies as catching them. At least that's so for me, and I don't think I'm that much different from the rest of you who take rod in hand to do battle with rainbows, browns, and brookies.

And that's why the Feather River country is so nice. It's hard to beat the beauty of a meadow like Humbug Valley, surrounded by a ring of timbered mountains and bisected by the rambling, spring-fed waters of Yellow Creek, or of Lower Sardine Lake, with snow-covered crags in the background. So who cares if you catch fish.

Whoa, wait a minute. Let's not get carried away. Fishing is part of the game, too, and tricking a few dozen rainbows or browns or brookies to come to the hook isn't to be sneered at, even if some of them aren't that big.

The Spanish explorer Luis Arguello gave the Feather River its name in 1820, calling it Rio de las Plumas (that's "Feather River" in Spanish) because he saw what looked like bird feathers floating on the water. Thirty years later, mining took over when the area became part of the great California Gold Rush. There now are about 22,000 residents within the county's 2,618 square miles—along with one stoplight (in Quincy). Three-quarters of its land is national forest, with the largest, Plumas National Forest, in the middle, Lassen National Forest at the northern end, and Tahoe National Forest to the south and east.

You can get here by way of Highway 36 from Red Bluff, Highway 70 from Sacramento and Oroville, Highway 89 by following it north from Interstate 80 at Truckee, or via Highway 70 from Highway 395, just north of Reno. Highways 70 and 89 bisect the area, along with stretches of Highway 36 to the north and Highway 49 to the southeast.

Plumas County boasts more than 100 lakes and 1,000 miles of rivers and creeks. To deal with so much water, we'll take it area by area, from northern Plumas County (including the North Fork and Hamilton Branch of the Feather River, Lake Almanor, Butt Valley Reservoir, and Yellow Creek), through the central and eastern area (Spanish Creek, the Middle Fork of the Feather River, Nelson Creek, Lake Davis, and Frenchman Lake, among others), to the south (the South Fork of the Feather River and the Lakes Basin area).

THE NORTH FORK AND HAMILTON BRANCH OF THE FEATHER RIVER

There are two sections of the North Fork, one northwest of and flowing into Lake Almanor and the other flowing south, out of the lake. Also feeding Lake Almanor from the east is the Hamilton Branch of the Feather, a 4-mile stretch of water that flows out of Mountain Meadows Reservoir.

The upper North Fork and all the other tributaries flowing into the lake don't open to fishing until the Saturday before Memorial Day, a regulation that protects rainbow trout entering streams in the spring to spawn. Otherwise, the area is subject to general fishing regulations

The upper North Fork originates among the myriad streams that have their origin on the slopes of Mount Lassen and flows into Lake Almanor just north of the town of Chester. Near Chester, the river is stocked, but to the northeast, where numerous tributaries flow into the North Fork, there is a crisscross of dirt roads that make exploring fun. Creeks such as **Rice Creek, Lost Creek,** and **Willow Creek,** just to name a few, have excellent wild, small-trout populations. It isn't big-fish country, but even the novice fly fisher can do well here.

From Chester, go north on Feather River Drive, which becomes Warner Valley Road and parallels the North Fork, with access via a number of dirt roads. Another way to get to the area is to take the Wilson Lake Road north from Highway 36 about 13 miles west of Chester. This dirt road winds past Wilson Lake then crosses the North Fork of the Feather and Rice Creek. There are numerous side roads that provide access to other area creeks—so many that a U.S. Forest Service map is a must.

The Hamilton Branch is stocked, although there are also a number of native trout in the harder-to-reach sections. This is a favorite fishing area for all sorts of angling. What can't be accessed by road can be reached via the trails that parallel the river.

To get to the Hamilton Branch, take Highway 36 east from Chester and County Road A13 south to where it crosses the river near Lake Almanor. You can follow Highway 147 north along the river for about 2 miles until it intersects Clear Creek. Both the river and the trout are smaller upstream from that intersection.

The North Fork after it flows out of the southern end of Lake Almanor is not particularly accessible, but does have good fishing. To get to this stretch of the river, follow Seneca Road south from Highway 89 at the southern end of Lake Almanor, then park at the bridge over the river about 5.5 miles along the road and hike either upstream or downstream. Seneca Road doesn't rejoin the river until near the town of Caribou, where access is from the powerhouse road and a trail leads upstream.

From Caribou downstream, Seneca Road is paved until it meets Highway 70 at Gansner Bar. This 7-mile stretch is very popular, with three campgrounds and heavy stocking. Still, some of the pools hold big brown trout, and there always are holdover planted rainbows that have reached a respectable size.

The North Fork and the East Branch of the North Fork join at Gansner Bar and flow south into Lake Oroville. The East Branch flows out of Indian Valley near Greenville, on Highway 89, and is paralleled by Highway 70 all the way to Lake Oroville. With easy access, it is stocked by the DFG, so while there are plenty of fish to be caught, it isn't prime water for the wild-trout angler.

In the lower sections there are smallmouth and largemouth bass, which replace trout as the water becomes warmer. While there certainly are big trout in this section, they generally are there only in the spring, when high water makes fly fishing difficult, returning to Lake Oroville as the river temperature rises.

LAKE ALMANOR

Let me breathe two little words into your shell-like ear: "Hex hatch!" Although Lake Almanor offers good fishing, with rainbows, browns, salmon, smallmouth bass, and catfish, most of the time it is more easily probed by bait and lure anglers than by fly fishers. But in the summer, beginning in late June and continuing well into July, there are magnificent hatches of the big *Hexagenia limbata* mayflies when big fish in the lake gorge themselves with wild abandon and fly-line anglers are in their glory.

The trick, of course, is to be on the lake during the Hex hatch, which varies both in time and numbers, but generally peaks about the Fourth of July. Hexagenia live as nymphs in the mud or sand bottom of lakes or slow-moving streams, then, like most mayflies, wiggle to the surface, break open their shucks, and take to the air. They undergo one more metamorphosis on land, changing into sexually mature males and females, mate as a swarm, and then the females lay their eggs by dipping into the water until they tire and die. These spinners fall dead and dying on the surface of the water, where trout take them at their leisure. The most exciting fishing, however, is when the nymphs are making their way to the sur-

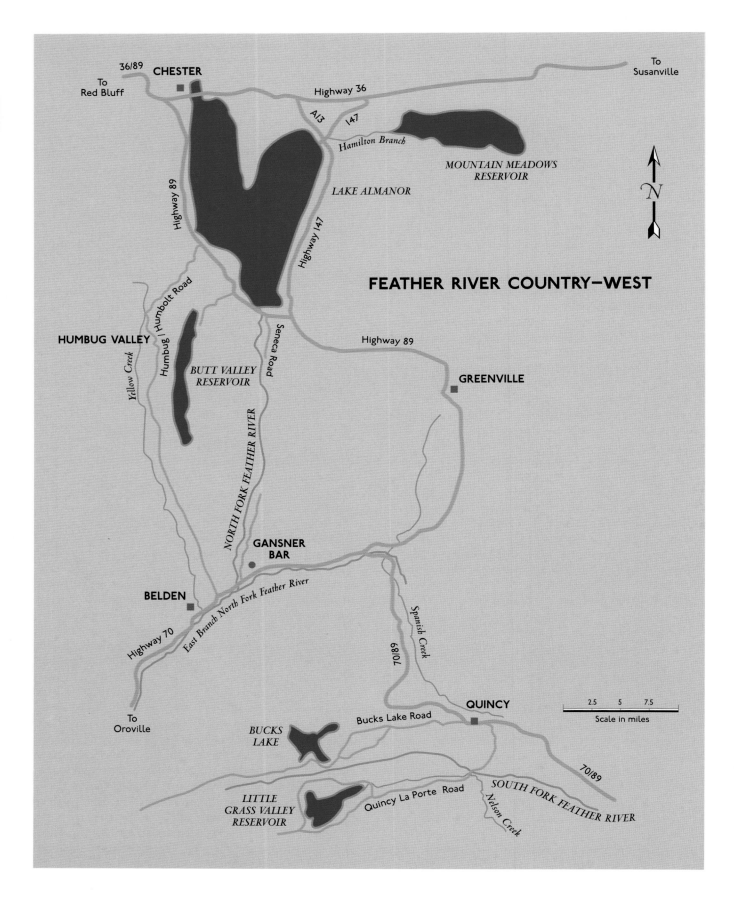

face as emergers and the newly hatched mayflies are floating on the surface, waiting for their wings to dry so they can fly away.

The Lake Almanor Hex hatch is late in the day, the last few minutes before dark, and even into dark. These flies are so big that just about everything that feeds on bugs has a banquet, including trout, bass, ducks, and even bats.

Harry Reeves, an avid fly-line angler who lives in Quincy, captures the Hex hatch excitement in this description: "They're so big that when they pop out of their shuck you can hear them. They come out just at dark, and when there is a big hatch, ducks are scooping them up, bass are coming up, trout are slurping them up. You break off a fly and can't see what you're doing and they're all around you!"

Fish key first on the emerging nymphs, which are not strong swimmers as they make their way to the surface. The best imitation is a light-colored orange or yellow nymph tied on a size 6 or size 8 hook. Get the nymph deep into the water and then do a slow retrieve.

For dries, also tied on a size 6 or size 8 hook, use a bright yellow body, yellow hackle, and a long, upturned abdomen and tail. Try to pinpoint a feeding fish, figure out which way it is moving, and cast a few feet in front of it. It sounds simple, but....With dries, let the fly sit on the water for a few seconds and then strip it a few inches—this imitates the action of mayflies that are trying to take off, but can't quite make it.

Don't go light on the tippet—we're talking fish of two to six pounds and six-pound or seven-pound tippet material.

Much of the Hex hatch takes place in coves and near the shore, particularly on both sides of the south end of the lake. Another favored place is the so-called A-Frame on the eastern side of the Lake Almanor Peninsula, which pokes into the middle of the east side of the lake. Wading is possible, but small boats or float tubes offer more mobility. Good entry points for float tubers are at the boat ramp at the south end of the lake above the dam or at the East Shore Picnic Ground, just across the lake.

If you're unlucky enough to miss the Hex hatch, there still is fly fishing at Lake Almanor, which is about 16 miles long and 6 miles wide and sits at 4,510 feet. The better areas are the north arm near the Highway 36 causeway early or late in the season, the mouth of the Hamilton Branch of the Feather River, and in several of the coves on the southeast or southwest side of the lake. If you can spot a hatch, it might mean some dry-fly fishing for trout, but generally, float tubing with black or olive Woolly Buggers or with standard nymphs such as Pheasant Tails or Bird's Nests, size 12 to 14, is the best bet. And don't forget the bass that inhabit the lake—they can be fun on a fly rod, too.

On the subject of lakes in this area, a word about **Butt Valley Reservoir,** just southeast of Lake Almanor: this for years was a good fly-fishing lake and had its own Hex hatch, but engineers feared the dam would collapse in an earthquake and drained it in 1996 for repairs. It was filled during the winter, but again drained in 1997. The repairs were finished in late 1997, the reservoir was refilled during the 1997–98 winter, and fish were restocked. Indications are that it once again offers good fishing and even its own *Hexagenia limbata* hatch.

YELLOW CREEK

You can't visit the Feather River country without a pilgrimage to Yellow Creek. This spring-fed stream meanders through Humbug Valley about 8 miles from the western shore of Lake Almanor, a monument to what can be done when fishing and commercial organizations combine their efforts to save a bit of water from the ravages of civilization.

First, a bit of history. The grass-lush valley cut by Yellow Creek was long a favored Maidu Indian spot, then was settled by whites just prior to the Gold Rush. In 1849, Thomas Stoddard claimed he discovered gold while prospecting the area and went for help, bringing back several miners he had hired to tap the vein. But he couldn't find his strike again, and the disgruntled miners named it Humbug Valley.

A resort hotel was built in 1909 and prospered for some years before it burned. It never was replaced. Cattle became the main industry of the valley, fattening quickly on the land's abundant grass.

This was great for the cattle and their owners, but tough on Yellow Creek. The herds all but wiped out the meadow trout fishing, trampling the banks, muddying the water, and driving the big brown and rainbow trout into the lower reaches of the stream.

In 1971, the nonprofit fishing organization California Trout (CalTrout) took Yellow Creek under its wing as part of a movement to restore wild trout and wild-trout habitat in California. It was one of the streams originally nominated for the Department of Fish and Game's Wild Trout Program, but the wrong portion of the creek was included, so CalTrout led the drive to get volunteers to restore what it felt was the best section of the stream. CalTrout was joined in the project by the DFG, the Pacific Gas & Electric Company, which owned most of the land, the Dye Creek Cattle Company, the Plumas County Fish and Game Commission, and the U.S. Forest Service.

To keep cattle away from the stream, volunteers erected split-cedar fencing that blended with the countryside along a half-mile meadow stretch of Yellow Creek. Within five years, the trout population in this area had jumped by 600 percent. More money was raised, more volunteers were solicited, and the fencing was extended along most of the creek in the meadow.

Today, the fish are there, most of them brown trout and some of them large. They aren't present in the tremendous numbers that can be found in some other California angling Meccas, but there are enough to make fishing fun.

The meadow section is a special-regulation stream—no bait, barbless flies or lures, and only two trout ten inches or smaller can be kept. The creek is born from the waters at Big

Rick E. Martin

A live Hexagenia limbata *mayfly from Lake Almanor and an imitation—both about two inches long.*

Springs, at the upper end of Humbug Valley. It is a typical spring creek as it meanders through the valley, with clear water, deep runs, and undercut banks that shelter wary fish. There is little bankside vegetation to shield the angler, so caution and long, pinpoint casts are necessary. Anglers generally do much better casting to specific fish than just covering likely spots.

Hatches are prolific in the nutrient-rich water—mayflies, caddisflies, and stoneflies, including the big orange Salmon Flies that offer trout a spring feast. There are so many hatches that often it is difficult to determine just what the trout are eating. Sometimes it is not the most obvious bug, so don't hesitate to try larger or smaller flies when you can't get a take.

Many of the anglers who fish Yellow Creek wait for an evening hatch, but in reality, the fishing is just about as good at noon as it is when shadows fall. Try mayfly and caddis imitations, sizes 12 to 16 for dries, and the usual Sierra nymphs—Pheasant Tails, Bird's Nests, and Zug Bugs, size 12 or 14. And don't forget black or olive Woolly Buggers, size 6 or 8, particularly in the spring. Strip them in along the undercut banks, where the big ones lurk. Ant imitations are always good, and as the summer wears on, grasshopper imitations can draw out big browns. Locals favor the Corkendall, a

black-bodied fly with a jungle-cock tail and a buff-colored hackle, that can be fished dry or in the surface film. Try the Quincy fly shops (listed below) for a few of them.

An alternative to the meadow's spring-creek fishing is downstream from Yellow Creek Campground, where the stream drops into a canyon and becomes a more typical mountain pocket-water creek. In fact, those in the know say this is where the really big fish are and, if it matters, there are no special regulations. The end of the special-regulation part of Yellow Creek is clearly marked by a large wooden sign.

Yellow Creek Campground, owned and run by PG&E, has only ten campsites and is a popular place to stay for anglers and nonanglers alike. Apart from the fishing, it offers a great view of the meadow wildlife, everything from birds to bears.

To get to Yellow Creek from Highway 89 on the southwest side of Lake Almanor, take Humbug / Humboldt Road 8 miles to Humbug Valley. This dirt road, used heavily for logging, is suitable for all but the largest RVs. About half a mile after leaving Highway 89 there is an unmarked fork in the road—stay left. The right branch also goes to Humbug Valley, but it is twice as far that way, although the right branch is a slightly better road.

There are numerous cross and side roads and no signs, so drivers sometimes have to guess which is the main road. As the road enters Humbug Valley, there are two white houses to the right, with the unmarked turnoff to Yellow Creek

Campground on the left, across Humbug Creek. The campground is 1.3 miles from the turnoff.

On the road to the campground there is a spring, protected by a PG&E-built gazebo, that gushes pure, cold soda water. Early in this century, visitors at the nearby hotel (the one that burned down) traditionally used the water to make lemonade, so take along some fresh lemons and give it a try.

Just before the campground, the road forks, with the campground to the right. The left-hand branch offers a mile or so of easy access to Yellow Creek where it enters the canyon, then moves up the hillside and many twisty miles later finally runs into Caribou Road near Gansner Bar Campground. The campground is 2 miles from Highway 70 and 25 miles west of Quincy. This is not a good road, and access to Yellow Creek is by bushwhacking down the hillside.

The mouth of Yellow Creek where it feeds the North Fork of the Feather River at Belden, 27 miles west of Quincy on Highway 70, is accessible by parking at the rest stop next to the power station and then following the marked trail upstream. The trail, which has a number of washouts and is not in very good shape, goes about 2 miles into the canyon, and fishing the tumbling pocket water can be good. From there, upstream anglers can clamber through the canyon to get to likely spots.

SPANISH CREEK

Fished heavily by locals, Spanish Creek flows through the town of Quincy and empties into the east branch of the North Fork. Although it is heavily stocked, there are wild trout and holdover rainbows.

A spot in Quincy that offers access is at Gansner Park, where the Highway 70 bridge crosses Spanish Creek on the west side of town. From Gansner Park, fish downstream to the sewage treatment plant, where private property begins. You can pick the creek up again on Chandler Road, which goes all the way around the town of Quincy. Another access at Quincy is above or below the private Oakland Camp, just northeast of town. The road paralleling the creek goes right through Oakland Camp, but it is a public road. It becomes impassable after a couple of miles, but anglers can fish the creek all the way to Keddie.

Spanish Creek also is accessible at Keddie, a little town 7 miles from Quincy, north on Highway 70/89. There is a residential street called Old Highway that leads to Spanish Creek, and from there an easy trail—once a wagon road—follows the water.

BUCKS LAKE

A popular and well-developed vacation area, 5,155-foot-high Bucks Lake is a lovely 17-mile drive from Quincy via Bucks Lake Road. In addition to rainbows, browns, and brookies, there also are Mackinaw trout and kokanee in both Bucks and Lower Bucks, which is located just below the main lake.

Because the shoreline drops off rapidly, fly fishing from the bank can be productive at Bucks in the spring or fall. Look for rising fish and cast to them. Float tubing also works well on the lake, particularly in the inlets where Mill Creek, Bucks Creek, Haskins Creek, and Right Hand Creek come in. It is in these areas in the fall that the browns try to move into the creeks to spawn, and the rainbows—and Mackinaws—follow them right into the shallows. Also in the fall there is a dark caddis hatch, during which black-bodied flies can be extremely effective. At **Lower Bucks Lake,** the best fishing area is the inlet from Bucks Lake when the water is flowing. There are numerous campgrounds around Bucks Lake, along with motels, restaurants, private campgrounds, boat ramps, and all the other amenities of a vacation lake.

THE MIDDLE FORK OF THE FEATHER RIVER

This is the centerpiece of fly fishing in the Feather River country, cutting southwest through the middle of Plumas County on its 85-mile journey to Lake Oroville. Officially designated a Wild and Scenic River, It presents a dual personality—easily accessible fishing, or canyon areas that can be reached only via a tangle of rugged mountain roads and major bushwhacking. Feeder streams, some with pull-up areas, others that can be reached only by hiking, abound as well. All of them have fish.

The upper reaches of the Middle Fork, from near Beckwourth and Portola to the Highway 89 bridge at Graeagle, don't offer the best fly fishing on the river, but there certainly are fish, and they certainly can be caught with flies. If you do want to fish the upper stretch, there is good access at Rocky Point Road just east of Portola. It swings along the river for a couple of miles before rejoining Highway 70.

The most accessible fishing is from the Highway 89 Bridge at Graeagle to the town of Sloat. For most of this distance, railway tracks run along the river, and a number of roads from Highway 70/89 go to the Middle Fork, including Two Rivers Road (closed off, but it's an easy walk to the river), Layman's Camp Road, Cromberg Cemetery Road, and Sloat Road. The little town of Sloat, about a mile off Highway 70/89, is a favorite fishing area, and anglers can walk upstream or downstream along the river.

In fact, by using any of these roads to get to the Middle Fork, fly fishers can work their way upstream and downstream to cover as much water as they like. There isn't any particular area that is better than any other, although getting away from the access points increases the chance of hooking wild trout, since this section of the Middle Fork has hatchery fish.

This is almost entirely freestone water with pools and is fished like just about any other Sierra Nevada freestone stream or river. Recommended nymphs are Bird's Nests, Pheasant Tails, Hare's Ears, and Zug Bugs, size 12 and 14, along with larger stonefly nymphs in May and June, when the Golden Stones are hatching. Caddisflies are plentiful, so be sure to have Green Rock Worm and LaFontaine's Sparkle Pupa or Emerger patterns to imitate them.

For the most part, attractors such as Yellow Humpies and Royal Wulffs suffice, but using an Adams, Elk Hair Caddis, or Little Yellow Sally, along with a Stimulator to match the big stoneflies, probably will catch a few more fish. Mostly the size is either 14 or 16. As usual, olive or black Woolly Buggers, along with ant and grasshopper imitations, should be part of the angler's arsenal.

From Sloat downstream, which is to the southwest, the Middle Fork flows into a rugged canyon where there is almost no easy access, but which offers perhaps the best wild-trout fishing in the Feather River country. Be warned: this is not for the faint-hearted or couch potato. It involves exploring mountain logging roads, some of which require four-wheel drive and then peter out, and hiking or bushwhacking from high ridges down to the river. The going is rough and steep, and camping on the river overnight is a must for an angler who wants to do any serious fishing.

Buy the latest Plumas National Forest map and begin probing likely roads to find one that goes within hiking distance of the river. Take plenty of equipment, and don't go alone. For fishing, any of the flies that work on the more accessible section of the Middle Fork will work in this water. Fishing this area can be a fantastic experience, but you aren't going to be able to do it in a hurry, and you aren't going to be able to do it without some work.

There is a drive-up access to the canyon section of the Middle Fork via La Porte Road, which turns south from Highway 70/89 just east of Quincy. This two-lane blacktop winds through Thompson Valley and into the mountains, crossing the Middle Fork after 8.3 miles. There are campgrounds on either side of the bridge, and the angler can use this as a starting point to go either up or down the river

Another 2.5 miles along La Porte Road leads to **Nelson Creek,** a typical Sierra freestone stream that offers fine fly fishing. From the bridge over the creek, a short, rough trail on the left, near side of the bridge drops down to Nelson Creek. An angler's survey box marks the head of the trail.

Fishing upstream means clambering over rocks and wading, but it is worth it. Working downstream is just as good, and after about a mile, Nelson Creek flows into the Middle Fork of the Feather. There are a lot of large rainbows in Nelson Creek, and they rise readily to dries, including attractors. Bring the same selection of flies that you would use anywhere in the region and be prepared for a fine day of fly fishing.

Just about any feeder stream that flows into the Middle Fork has trout in it, so don't hesitate to toss a fly on the water. One particularly worth mentioning is **Jamison Creek,** which originates in the Lakes Basin, then flows through Plumas Eureka State Park near Graeagle and into the Middle Fork at Two Rivers. Jamison Creek is accessible at several points inside the park, including at the Upper Jamison Campground. It also can be fished upstream from where it flows into the Middle Fork.

LAKE DAVIS

Off Highway 70, 6 miles north of Portola, Lake Davis is a fly-fishing hot spot that can provide some of the best action in the Feather River country. Although open to fishing all year (which means ice fishing in the winter, since it freezes over), once ice-out begins in April, the lake turns on.

Anglers can make their way to one of the coves at the southwest end of the lake—which ones depends on how much snow there is—and cast out from shore. The hatch is blood midges, imitated with a blood-midge pattern or a Brassie, size 12 or 14, and the rainbows are there because they want to go up any available tributary to spawn. Retrieve using a very slow strip, or fish the midge pattern under an indicator. Either way can give you a multifish day, most of them big because it is the adult spawners who are in the area. (In reality, they are all holdover planted fish, since spawning is minimal in the lake.)

There are boat ramps at Mallard Cove and Honker Cove on the eastern side, and if they are open, a small boat is a good way to fish, although those willing to brave the icy temperatures also can use float tubes. It isn't really necessary to be on the water—wading and casting from the shore can be just as effective.

In May and June, the damselfly hatch peaks, another prime time for fly fishers. It is a "gentleman's hatch" that begins about 9 A.M., so you don't need to rush breakfast and be on the water before dawn. An effective way to fish the hatch is with a damselfly nymph imitation and a long leader greased with floatant to within a few inches of the nymph, which allows you to control the sink depth. Straighten your line and then let it be—the trout are cruising and slurping up any damselflies they can find, and they probably will find yours. Even better: if you can spot a moving fish, put your nymph in front of it. Sizes 12 and size 14 are about right, and the color depends on the time, since it changes throughout the hatch. Usually, the hatch starts with dark nymphs and progresses until they are off-brown or even gold. Stay with a 3X or heavier tippet, since the moving fish provide a hard take.

The last major fly-fishing time on the lake is in late September and October, when the fish come into the shallows to feed heavily before ice arrives for the winter. Big flies such as size 2 to 6 Woolly Buggers in cinnamon, olive, and black are effective. Cast and strip with a sink-tip line when in deep water, or switch to a floating line and do the same in the shallows. This is an excellent period for float-tube aficionados, although small boats such as prams and canoes work just as well.

During this period, the fish are eating snails. If you don't believe it, catch a lunker and pick it up with your hand under its belly—you can feel and hear the snail shells that cram its stomach. It is amazing how many snails or blood midges or damselfly nymphs the belly of one big trout can hold.

Although those are the high points, there are numerous other hatches, particularly mayflies, throughout the summer. Float tubing from any of the many coves on the western side of the lake—where the weed growth is the heaviest—can be productive, particularly in the evening.

There are plenty of camping facilities, along with boat ramps and a store, at the lake.

The trout in Davis are planters, including a rainbow-kokanee strain and Eagle Lake trout. The lake is so nutrient-rich that they grow extremely fast, developing the small-head, big-body football shape that mark such trout.

Lake Davis was the scene of a much-publicized legal battle in 1997. Northern pike were introduced illegally into Davis in 1994 and thrived. The DFG announced plans in 1997 to poison the entire lake to rid it of that voracious species, which feeds on smaller fish, including trout. The proposal touched off a firestorm of local opposition, with one of the main objections focusing on the fact that Portola takes its drinking water from the lake.

With legal challenges out of the way and provisions made to protect Portola's water supply, the DFG in October 1997, poisoned all the fish in Lake Davis. The poison was supposed to dissipate quickly, but instead, traces remained in the lake until the summer of 1998, forcing the DFG to keep Davis closed to fishing well into the season and touching off a new round of legal battles.

Once the poison was out of the lake, it was stocked heavily with trout of all sizes. If the experience at nearby Frenchman Lake (see below) is any indication, it could take a year or two after the restocking before fishing in Lake Davis regains its former glory.

FRENCHMAN LAKE

Located at the eastern edge of Plumas County, eight miles off Highway 70, Frenchman Lake has long been known as a haven for bait and lure anglers and for families from Reno, 30 miles away. But it is coming on as a fly-fishing lake, particularly late in the season.

Unlike Davis, which is fairly shallow, Frenchman Lake is mostly deep, with only a few shallow areas. It is in those areas, located on the northern and northwestern ends of the lake, where fly fishing is best. The shallow areas, particularly Lunker Bay and Snaligaster Bay, have the same hatches and characteristics as Lake Davis. In the spring, there is a prolific damselfly hatch, and in the late fall, big fish move into shallow areas to feed heavily in preparation for winter. Snails make up a good portion of the trout food, so black or brown Woolly Buggers can be effective.

Early in the year, **Last Chance Creek,** which flows out of Frenchman Lake and is accessible at several areas along the road to the lake, offers good fishing. On opening day, many anglers gather just below the spillway where Last Chance Creek flows from the lake and where big trout hold that have come upstream to spawn. Fly fishers have to take their chances with elbow-to-elbow bait and lure anglers, so it can be tough going. Later in the season, the flow slows and the fishing drops off.

Both campgrounds and boat ramps are available at Frenchman.

The lake was poisoned by the state in the late 1980s to get rid of northern pike that had been illegally introduced. According to Dick Wiggin, who for thirty years has owned Wiggin's Trading Post at the intersection of Highway 70 and the road to Frenchman Lake, it took several years for fishing in the lake to return to normal. Frenchman is planted regularly with hatchery trout, and in 1998 received an extra 1,100,000 trout that were to have been planted in Davis, but had to be put elsewhere because of the residue of poison in Davis.

THE SOUTH FORK OF THE FEATHER RIVER

The South Fork of the Feather starts just above Little Grass Valley Reservoir, near La Porte, flows into and out of the reservoir, and then makes its way through a majestic canyon to Lake Oroville. Access is via La Porte Road off Highway 70, just east of Quincy.

Little Grass Valley Reservoir is a popular area, with camping and boat ramps. The South Fork is accessible both above and below the reservoir from a series of roads, but compared with the Middle Fork and some of the other Feather River country lakes, this provides mediocre fishing, even though it does offer great scenery.

THE LAKES BASIN

There are more than thirty mountain lakes 5,000 to 6,000 feet high in this beautiful recreation area near Graeagle, most of them with trout and many of them suitable for fly fishers.

This is a matter of how hard you want to work—there are drive-up lakes with stocked fish, there are fine hike-in lakes that can be reached in an hour's walk, or there are any number of lakes that are reached only by some serious hiking.

The Lakes Basin Recreation Area can be reached either by way of Gold Lake Forest Highway, which goes south off Highway 89 in Graeagle or, at the other end, from Highway 49 at Bassetts, on the North Fork of the Yuba River. (See the Yuba River chapter.)

Gold Lake, the largest of the lakes, is the centerpiece of the area, with camping, a boat ramp, a resort, and plenty of fish. It also can be extremely windy and as far as the fly fisher is concerned isn't the best bet in this area, even though it has big rainbows, browns, and Mackinaws. If you are going to fish it, try the coves, where there are evening hatches.

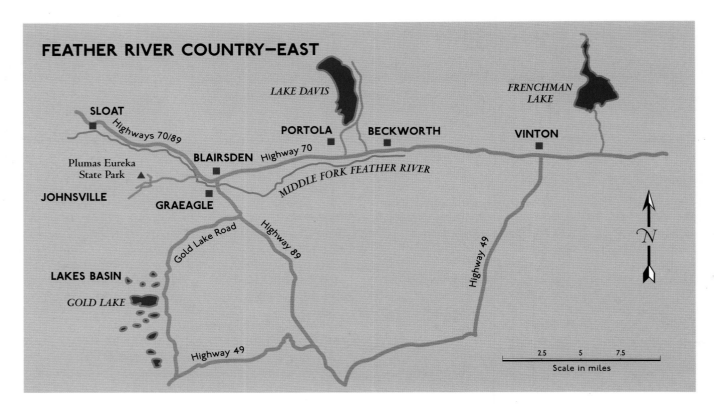

Gold Lake got its name during the Gold Rush, when Thomas Stoddard (the same guy who claimed he found gold in Humbug Valley) showed a pocketful of gold nuggets and said he had picked them up along the shore of a "lake of gold." This led to a long and fruitless search by many prospectors and to the naming of this—and any number of other waters—"Gold Lake."

The other easy-access lakes in this area are **Lower Sardine, Packer,** and **Upper Salmon Lakes,** all of which have resorts, camping, and both stocked and wild fish. Lower Sardine Lake in particular offers a spectacular setting, with the Sierra Buttes climbing to 8,587 feet directly behind it—a great place for photographs. Float tubes are effective, as are small boats (there's a ramp and a 5-mile-per-hour speed limit).

From Lower Sardine Lake, a four-wheel-drive road climbs a few hundred yards up to Upper Sardine Lake, which can be fished from shore. It's a rough road, so unless you want to give your 4x4 a workout, do it on foot.

Here are recommendations on some of the lakes.

Grass Lake, Rock Lake, Jamison Lake, and **Wades Lake** all are reached via trails from Plumas Eureka State Park, starting at the Upper Jamison Campground or the Jamison Mine at the southern end of the park. Grass Lake, about a 1.75-mile walk, offers good fly fishing for brown and rainbow trout, even though access is pretty much contained to one side of the lake. If you can, carry a float tube up so you can fish the whole lake.

It's another 2 miles to Jamison and Rock Lakes, which are only a couple of hundred yards apart. Wades Lake is about

the same distance, but on a separate trail that splits off after passing Grass Lake.

Jamison Lake is probably the best of these lakes for fly fishing, with plenty of access from the bank. Dark nymphs, Rio Grande Kings, and bee imitations such as the McGinty are favored here. Damselfly nymphs also work. Most of the trout in Jamison, as well as the other upper lakes, are brookies.

Another series of lakes good for fly fishers includes **Big Bear, Little Bear,** and **Cub,** all of which are reached by Round Lake Trail, which has its trailhead on Gold Lake Forest Highway about a mile north of the Gold Lake turnoff. It is about a half-mile walk to Big Bear, with Little Bear and Cub nearby.

SUMMING UP

For big-stream fishing, the **Middle Fork of the Feather River** is the most popular, with easy access via Highways 70 and 89 from Graeagle to Sloat. This section of the Feather, which is a Wild and Scenic River along its entire length to Lake Oroville, is planted, but has plenty of holdovers and wild trout to go along with hatchery rainbows.

Adventurous anglers with good legs can get into some great wild-trout fishing on the Middle Fork downstream from Sloat, where the river drops into a deep canyon. You have to probe the series of logging roads, some of them strictly for four-wheel-drive vehicles, until you find someplace to hike down to the river. This isn't easy going, but the fishing can be worth it.

While in the Feather River country, be sure to spend

some time at **Yellow Creek,** where a project sponsored by California Trout put this spring creek back on the fishing map. Fishing is good, but not great. Still, it is a beautiful setting, and the fishing for browns is productive enough to warrant the trip.

Lake Almanor is big water, but with enough shallow coves so that fly fishers can use float tubes or small boats to get to good fishing. What makes it exceptional, however, is the *Hexagenia limbata* hatch that begins in late June and peaks around the Fourth of July. This is a major mayfly hatch and seems to draw just about every fish in the lake—along with ducks and bats—to feed on these huge bugs. It's a fisherman's delight, so try to work it into your schedule.

Lake Davis, near Portola, at the eastern end of Feather River country, offers good fly fishing most of the season, with heavy action just after ice-out in April, as well as in the spring, when damselflies hatch, and in the fall, when trout come into the shallows to feed voraciously before ice once again covers the lake for the winter.

There are so many feeder creeks flowing into the forks of the Feather that offer good fishing that it's hard to pick the best. So anytime you see a likely spot, toss in a fly, and you'll almost certainly find fish.

◆ ◆ ◆ ◆ ◆

ADDITIONAL INFORMATION

FLY SHOPS
Sportsmen's Den, 1580 East Main Street, Quincy; (530) 283-2733. A full-service fly shop.

Sierra Mountain Sports, 501 Main Street (across from the courthouse), Quincy; (530) 283-2323. A sporting-goods store with a large fly-fishing section.

Ayoob's Sports, 201 Main Street, Chester; (530) 258-2611. Some fly-fishing gear is available.

Grizzly Country Store, Lake Davis, (530) 832-0270. This store was closed during the period after the poisoning of Lake Davis, but was sold and was scheduled to reopen.

Wiggin's Trading Post, located at the intersection of Highway 70 and the road to Frenchman Lake, (530) 993-4583. Some fly-fishing terminal tackle and flies.

HOSPITALS
Quincy: Plumas District Hospital, 1065 Buck's Lake Road, Quincy; (530) 283-2121.

Chester: Seneca District Hospital, 130 Brentwood Drive, Chester; (530) 258-2151.

Greenville: Indian Valley Hospital, 184 Hot Springs Road, Greenville; (530) 284-7191.

Portola: Eastern Plumas Hospital, 500 First Avenue, Portola; (530) 832-4277.

PUBLIC CAMPING
There are many public and private campgrounds throughout the area. For a list of campgrounds call, write, or e-mail the Plumas County Visitors Bureau, 550 Crescent Street, Quincy, CA 95970; (800) 326-2247 or (530) 283-6345. Fax: (530) 283-5465. E-mail: plumasco@psln.com.

All campgrounds tend to fill up quickly during summer holidays such as Memorial Day, the Fourth of July, and Labor Day, so either get there early or reserve a spot.

For information on U.S. Forest Service campgrounds only, call or write the Plumas National Forest Headquarters, 159 Lawrence Street, Quincy, CA 95971; (530) 283-2050. Most campgrounds are on a first-come, first-served basis, but some can be reserved. For reservations, call (800) 280-CAMP.

There also are a number of campgrounds owned and run by PG&E, of which all but group campgrounds are first-come, first-served. For information only, call (800) 743-5000. To reserve a group campground, call (530) 386-5164.

MORE SOURCES
The Plumas County Visitors Bureau, 550 Crescent Street, Quincy, CA 95970; (800) 326-2247 or (530) 283-6345. Fax: (530) 283-5465. E-mail: plumasco@psln.com.

The Chester–Lake Almanor Chamber of Commerce, 529 Main Street, Chester, CA 96020; (800) 350-4838 or (530) 258-2426. Fax: (530) 258-2760.

The Eastern Plumas Chamber of Commerce, 73136 Highway 70, Portola, CA 96122; (800) 995-6057 or (530) 832-5444. Fax: (530) 832-1938.

The Indian Valley Chamber of Commerce, 410 Main Street, Greenville, CA 95947; (530) 284-6633. Fax: (530) 284-6907. E-mail: ivchmbr@psln.com.

Plumas National Forest Headquarters, 159 Lawrence Street, Quincy, CA 95971: (530) 283-2050.

CHAPTER 5: THE YUBA RIVER

More Than Meets the Eye

Rick E. Martin

THE North, Middle, and South Forks of the Yuba River tumble down the western slope of the Sierra Nevada northwest of the Lake Tahoe area, beautiful mountain streams that start as trickles and end as full-fledged rivers pouring into man-made reservoirs in the foothills. Although all three hold trout, access limits fishing to only a few spots on the Middle and South forks. But the North Fork parallels Highway 49 for almost 40 miles and is favored trout water for many foothill dwellers and Sacramento-area anglers.

The Yuba is a typical snowmelt river: it is high and off-color during the spring runoff, hard to fish for fly-line types, and then slows to more manageable water as the summer heats up and the snow disappears. Mostly it is pocket water, a combination of tumbling falls and pools, with a few slicks and occasional riffles.

Fishing is good, a combination of hatchery and wild rainbows and wild browns, along with some brookies. Although trout in the eight-to-fourteen-inch range are normal, there are bigger fish, including large German browns. Every year a few browns weighing in at five or six pounds are caught. Major feeder streams are plentiful and offer just as good fishing as the Yuba itself.

Michael Fisher works the pool below Pauley Creek Falls on Pauley Creek near Downieville.

An added bonus is the rugged beauty of the countryside, along with the tourist charm of the Gold Rush towns of Downieville and Sierra City. This is the heart of the California gold country, and almost every foot of its rivers and creeks was prospected, with streambeds dug and panned and sluiced in the search for what the forty-niners called "color."

Prospecting continues, much of it at the family level of panning likely spots over the weekend or during a holiday. There still are mining claims to be found, however, so make it a point to treat any you find as private property. Some miners are friendly, some aren't, and all of them have dogs.

Highway 49, known as the Gold Country Highway, is the key to the Yuba. It crosses Interstate 80 at Auburn and heads north through Grass Valley and Nevada City, picking up the North Fork of the Yuba at the Highway 49 bridge above Bullard's Bar Reservoir. From this bridge to the headwaters at Yuba Pass is about 40 miles, and the highway parallels the river all the way, with easy access and numerous campgrounds for the angler.

There are other ways to get to the North Fork of the Yuba. From the town of Truckee near Lake Tahoe, follow Highway 89 northwest until it crosses Highway 49, then take 49 west to Yuba Pass. Farther north on Highway 89, at Graeagle, Gold Lake Road winds south through the Lakes

Basin Recreation Area (see the chapter on the Feather River country) to Bassetts, a resort on Highway 49 about 7 miles below Yuba Pass.

THE NORTH FORK OF THE YUBA RIVER

The best way to fly fish the North Fork is to drive along the river until you see an area you'd like to fish—then find a place to park and fish it. This isn't a river with "hot spots," but it has a respectable number of trout scattered along its entire length. The secret, according to those who fish it heavily, is to keep moving—if you don't get fish right away, don't pound the water, just move along.

Michael Fisher, who owns the Nevada City Anglers fly shop in Nevada City and who grew up in Downieville, says, "I drive along the water until I see some place I want to fish and then go fish it. I stay away from campground areas because of fishing pressure and immediately upstream or downstream of any bridge because you get a lot of stocked fish that will hold there." He also offers these words of wisdom: "The tailouts tend not to hold large fish. Try the center sections or toward the tailouts for larger fish, but not in the tailouts themselves."

From its inception at Yuba Pass at 6,701 feet, the river begins as little more than a trickle, a stream of water anglers can step across as it tumbles sharply down the rocky mountainside. About a mile below the pass, there is a semiflat meadow area where beaver ponds once offered difficult, but productive fishing for small brookies. However, some of the ponds were taken out by a home owner in the area, and the heavy winter rains in early 1997 washed out the rest of them. Beavers being what they are—persistent—the ponds could be rebuilt at any time, and if so will produce interesting fishing.

The boggy ground of beaver ponds makes for tough walking, and each step sends a tremor that can be transmitted to the fish throughout a large surrounding area, scaring them into hiding. Go as light-footedly as possible, and then wait for a while before casting to give fish time to get over any nervousness.

As it moves downstream, the Yuba is fed by numerous creeks, and by the time Salmon Creek runs into it half a mile below Bassetts Resort, it is becoming a full-fledged river. This upper area is the type of small river or creek typical of the Sierra—a freestone stream with small falls, rapids, and pocket water, and with brush crowding in from both sides. Fishing the pocket water is the angler's best bet, since the trout hold where there is the easiest lie, and the rushing water brings a steady supply of food. Access is simple. Just park at any turnout and clamber down to the river.

The only special-regulation section on the river is from Sierra City downstream to Ladies Canyon Creek, a distance of 4.7 miles. It is restricted to artificial lures and flies with barbless hooks, and the take limit is two trout of ten inches or more. There is plenty of access to this Wild Trout section, and indeed it holds a fair number of fish—about the same as in the rest of the river. The positive point about the area is that none of them are hatchery fish because there is no planting here.

Haypress Creek enters the Yuba at Sierra City about 13 miles below the summit, while at Downieville, 26 miles from the summit, the Downie River, Lavezzola Creek, and Pauley Creek feed the Yuba. They all offer good fly fishing. All are dealt with below. Downieville in particular is a great little town, so plan to spend some sightseeing time there. It's the kind of place that makes the gold country fascinating and gives your nonangling spouse something to do while you are pounding the water.

At the little town of Goodyear's Bar, you can cross a bridge over the Yuba to Old Toll Bridge Road, which parallels the river for almost 2 miles. Three feeder streams flow into the Yuba at Goodyear's Bar just below the bridge—**Goodyear's Creek** from the north, and **Brush** and **Rock Creeks** from the south.

From Downieville south to where the Highway 49 bridge offers the last drive-up access to the Yuba is about 13 miles, and there are pullouts and campgrounds just about everywhere. At the Rocky Rest Campground in Indian Valley there is a footbridge across the river, which makes access easier. However, this is a popular area, with numerous campgrounds and planted fish, so it wouldn't be my first choice as a spot to stop.

At the Highway 49 bridge, there is walk-in access to several miles of the North Fork from Shenanigan Flat Road, which parallels the river along a steep gorge. The road is gated and closed to vehicular traffic, but there are no restrictions against sidestepping the gate and walking along the river. The road goes for about 2 miles, and then there is a trail that follows the Yuba to Bullard's Bar Reservoir, another 6 or 7 miles. At one time there was a U.S. Forest Service campground at Shenanigan Flat, but it has long been closed.

Shenanigan Flat also is the trailhead to **Canyon Creek,** which Michael Fisher describes as "a pretty-good-sized creek" that offers good fishing. He suggests mountain biking to the trailhead and then walking from there.

For fly fishers who like to get away from easy-access areas to bite off a piece of a stream for themselves, there are a number of excellent tributaries that run cold and clear most of the summer and fall. With limited access points, they involve hiking and rock scrambling, but the reward can be multifish days. The fish may be smaller than in the North Fork of the Yuba, but this is not a hard and fast rule. There always seems to be that huge brown lurking in a small pool if you're good enough, or lucky enough, to catch it.

Here are some of the prime fishing tributaries to the North Fork following Highway 49 downstream from Yuba Pass.

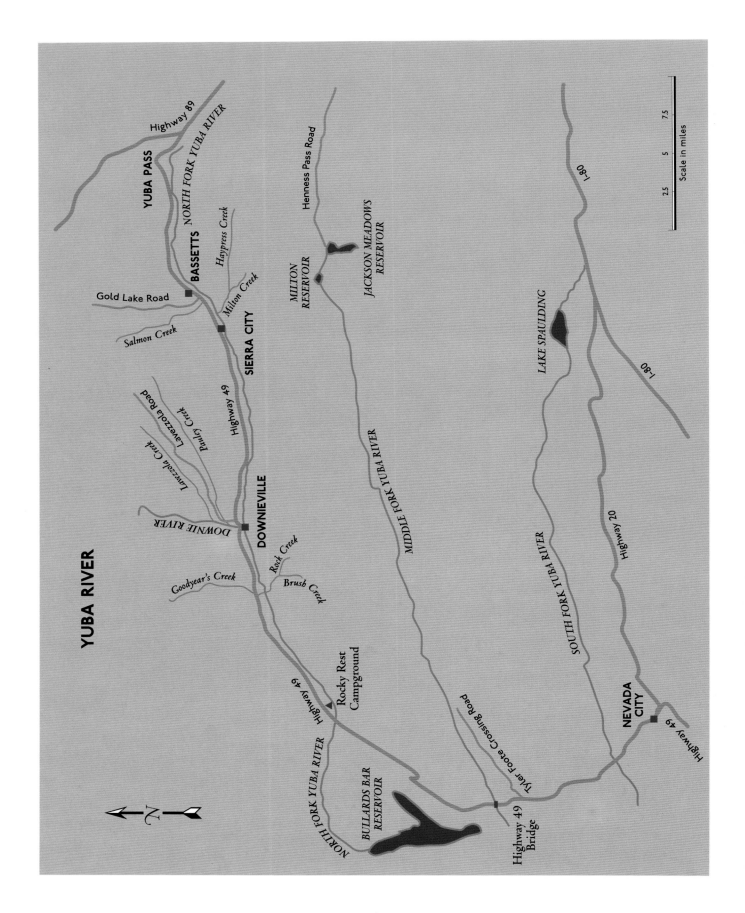

HAYPRESS CREEK

Haypress enters the Yuba at Sierra City and is accessed via Wild Plum Road, which leads to Wild Plum Campground. From the campground, a trail parallels the creek about 4 miles upstream and crosses the Pacific Crest Trail. One spot to try on Haypress is the pool just below the power station just upstream of Wild Plum Campground. **Milton Creek** also flows into Haypress Creek upstream of the campground and is accessible by hiking south on the Pacific Crest Trail.

SALMON CREEK

This creek is a major tributary to the Yuba and flows into the river half a mile downstream from Bassetts. The upper section is in the Lakes Basin Recreation Area, but it also can be fished from its confluence with the Yuba. Since it drops steeply to the Yuba, it is a series of falls and pools. There are fish, but it is tough going.

THE DOWNIE RIVER

The Downie River enters the North Fork of the Yuba right at Downieville. The lower section of the river that goes through the town is planted and heavily fished. The best in-town access to the Downie River is from the PG&E substation and adjoining water treatment plant at the northern end of Main Street near Hospital Bridge. Park and walk around the chain-link fence and follow the trail, which also is an access to Pauley Creek's lower stretches.

For fly-line anglers, the upper section of the Downie River is better and can be reached by following Downieville's Main Street and then taking Gold Bluff Road, which branches left from Main Street just before it crosses the Downie River at Hospital Bridge. Make a left turn on Sailor Ravine Road and follow the road about 6 miles. A four-wheel-drive vehicle is recommended. Note that Downieville's Main Street is not Highway 49, which runs through town, but is a narrow road branching north from Highway 49 in the middle of town.

Sailor Ravine Road goes high on the hillside and then drops down close enough to allow river access. It ends after several miles, but a trail continues along the Downie River so you can fish as much water as your legs allow. This upper section offers small-stream fishing, with plenty of wild rainbows and a few browns.

If you choose to follow Gold Bluff Road, it ends at a locked gate where you can park and walk down to the river. Hike upstream a short distance to where Lavezzola Creek enters the Downie. From there, it is possible to work upstream on the Downie or to fish Lavezzola Creek upstream.

LAVEZZOLA CREEK

Lavezzola Creek can be accessed either where it enters the Downie River (see above) or via Lavezzola Ranch Road, which is reached by following Main Street across Hospital Bridge and then going right when the road forks. This narrow dirt road, which has its share of traffic in both logging trucks and conventional vehicles, rises high on the hillside before dropping down to cross Lavezzola Creek about 3 miles into the drive.

There is an earlier access point at the so-called First Divide. Each of the "divides" is a summit of the road. There is no sign here, but look for a chain-link fence to the left. Park in a cleared area, go around the fence, and follow the switchback trail down to Lavezzola Creek. At the bridge, there are undeveloped camping areas on both sides of the stream. You can fish upstream or downstream as long as you are willing to scramble and indulge in typical Sierra pocket-water angling.

Continuing along Lavezzola Ranch Road takes you to the Third Divide, where Third Divide Trail drops to Lavezzola Creek, and a footbridge allows access to the far side. This is perhaps the best fishing on the creek, and as a result is popular. But hiking upstream or downstream isn't that tough here, so there is plenty of water for everybody.

Lavezzola Ranch Road ends at the locked gate of the Lavezzola Ranch about 5 miles from Downieville. Access to the creek from here involves parking alongside the road and walking about a mile along the road to the stream.

PAULEY CREEK

Pauley Creek merges with the Downie River at Hospital Bridge on Downieville's Main Street. Access here is by way of the PG&E plant. A little ways upstream is Pauley Creek Falls, and fish can be had from the pool below the falls. Otherwise, fish upstream and hit the pools, all of which should hold fish.

The upper stretches of Pauley Creek can be reached via Lavezzola Ranch Road (see above). Pauley Creek flows in a canyon to the east of the road, while Lavezzola Creek is in the adjoining canyon to the west. At First Divide, on the right-hand side, opposite the chain-link fence, a trail leads to Pauley Creek. This is a particularly pretty area of pocket water.

At Second Divide, identified by a sign, Second Divide Trail heads to Pauley Creek, but it is a 2-mile walk. At a Y in the trail, take the right-hand branch, which drops to the creek.

MIDDLE FORK OF THE YUBA RIVER

The Middle Fork of the Yuba begins in 6,200-foot-high Jackson Meadows Reservoir, south of Highway 49 and Yuba Pass, and flows southwest until it ends in Englebright Lake, west of Nevada City. There is limited access and only so-so fishing.

The upper river is accessible via Jackson Meadows Road, a 17-mile drive off Highway 89 north of Truckee, and is typical fishing for the high Sierra. The best fishing in this area is at **Milton Reservoir**, which is about 2 miles below Jackson Meadows Reservoir and can be reached by following the Henness Pass Road downriver from Jackson Meadows. This

Kenneth Susman

During late summer, a stealthy approach should be used to hook trout in low, clear water. Here an angler inspects a pool on the North Fork of the Yuba.

shallow lake sits at 5,690 feet and is ideal for float tubing. It is popular as a family camping and swimming spot during the summer, but doesn't get much fishing action because it is special-regulations water, requiring barbless lures or flies. The impoundment holds a number of rainbows and browns from eighteen to twenty-two inches, with a few even bigger. Plentiful hatches of midges, caddisflies and *Callibaetis* mayflies keep the fish fat and healthy. The preferred time for anglers is in the early spring, just after ice-out. As the summer wears on, weed beds line the edges, but anglers still can fish near the inlet of the Middle Fork of the Yuba and do well.

Recommended flies are dark Woolly Buggers, along with the standard Sierra nymphs such as Pheasant Tails, Hare's Ears, and Zug Bugs, size 12 to 14. A Z-Wing Caddis fished as a pupa or emerger also can be effective. For dries, caddis imitations are the best bet. An Elk Hair Caddis does fine in size 12 or 14, or perhaps a bit smaller late in the summer, as do generic midges in sizes 18 through 22 on long, light tippets.

The next access point is along Tyler Foote Crossing Road, which branches off Highway 49 several miles south of North San Juan. The last access is at the Highway 49 bridge across the Middle Fork, about a mile north of North San Juan. Between the Highway 49 bridge and Tyler Foote Crossing Road downstream, water from the Middle Fork is piped to

Bullard's Bar Reservoir, so while there may be plenty of water flowing at the upper end, the Middle Fork can be low below the Highway 49 bridge. During the early summer, enough water may be flowing for good fishing, but as the weather heats up, so does the water, and the fish drop down into long and narrow Englebright Lake.

SOUTH FORK OF THE YUBA RIVER

The upper section of the South Fork of the Yuba River near Donner Pass is easily accessible from Interstate 80 and is bordered by numerous campgrounds. As a result, it is heavily stocked and heavily fished early in the season, while the water is high and cold enough to sustain a good trout population.

Near the town of Washington, off Highway 20 via Washington Road, there are colder-water areas that can provide decent fishing. But there is a lot of private property, and the locals can be actively unfriendly, so the fishing just isn't worth the hassle. By the time this fork of the Yuba crosses Highway 49 and flows into Englebright Lake, it is too warm to be much good for anything but squawfish.

FLIES AND HATCHES

Every area seems to have its favorite flies (often for no particular reason, as far as I can see), and for those who fish the Yuba River, it's the Buzz Hackle. Locals swear by it, even while admitting they don't know why it catches so many trout.

The actual hatches are what you would expect—a variety of mayflies, caddisflies, and stoneflies, including Salmon Flies, Golden Stones, and Little Yellow Stones—and come off at slightly different times at different elevations. Since much of the angling is in pocket water, riffles, and pools, attractors do well. Here are some flies to use.

DRIES

Caddis imitations, including the Elk Hair Caddis all season long and the October Caddis in the fall; standard mayfly imitations, including Pale Morning Duns and the Parachute Adams; stonefly imitations for Golden Stones and Salmon Flies, which hatch from May sometimes into July; and attractors, including the Buzz Hackle and the Yellow Humpy. All are tied in sizes 14 to 18, except for the stonefly imitations, which can be larger, as big as size 6, but more commonly size 8 and 10.

NYMPHS

Pheasant Tails, Green Rock Worms for caddis larvae, and Zug Bugs, all size12 or 14. LaFontaine's Sparkle Emergers can be killers. Also effective are stonefly imitations as big as size 6, when the hatches are coming off.

TERRESTRIALS

Ant imitations always are effective, although they can be hard to fish because they are difficult to see in the changing light conditions of fast-moving Sierra streams. Try them anyway. A good pattern is a Parachute Black Ant, size 12 or 14, but early in the year, a larger carpenter ant look-alike also will work. Michael Fisher at Nevada City Anglers suggests fishing a regular dry fly with an ant as a dropper—that way you can watch the fly, but still should see any strike on the ant.

Later in the season, grasshopper imitations do well in some areas, but a lot of the Yuba is evergreen forest, rather than grass, so they aren't as effective as in meadowlands, where trout can key on them.

SUMMING UP

The best fly fishing clearly is on the **North Fork** and its tributaries. So why bother with the Middle and South Forks? North Fork fishing is what you make it—stocked hatchery fish at campgrounds and bridges, or wild rainbows and browns where hiking is involved. The only exception is the 4.7-mile special-regulations Wild Trout section from Sierra City downstream to Ladies Canyon Creek, where there is no planting. The fishing isn't noticeably better than on the rest of the river, but at least you're guaranteed wild trout. And don't forget the tributaries: the **Downie River, Lavezzola Creek,** and **Pauley Creek,** all accessible from the town of Downieville. There aren't many drive-up areas, and the dirt roads are narrow, but the fishing is fine, particularly if you've got the legs and the desire to do some hiking. There seem to be just about as many big fish in the tributaries as in the Yuba itself.

The usual ratio for the Yuba and its tributaries is about 30 percent brown trout and 70 percent rainbows. Expect to catch fish eight to ten inches long, with some going six or seven inches longer. There also are lunkers that measure into double digits. Browns of five or six pound aren't caught daily, but enough are picked up every season to remind us they are there. In the upper stretches of the tributaries, there also are brookies for fun fishing and—dare I say it—good eating.

✦ ✦ ✦ ✦ ✦

ADDITIONAL INFORMATION

FLY SHOPS
Nevada City Anglers, 417 Broad Street, Nevada City, CA 95959; (530) 478-9301. A full-service fly shop.
Bobs' Fly Shack, 488 W. Onstott Road, Yuba City, CA; (530) 671-9628. A full-service fly shop.
Sierra Hardware, Main Street, Downieville; (530) 289-3582. Some flies and basic gear is available.

HOSPITALS
Western Sierra Medical and Dental Clinic. Court House Square, Downieville; (530) 289-3298.

PUBLIC CAMPING
Information on campgrounds is available from:
The Downieville Ranger District, North Yuba Ranger Station, 15924 Highway 49, Camptonville, CA 95922; (530) 288-3231.
Tahoe National Forest Headquarters, 631 Coyote Street, Nevada City, CA 95959; (530) 265-4531.
The Sierra County Chamber of Commerce, P.O. Box 206, Loyalton, CA 96118; (800) 200-4949.
The Downieville Chamber of Commerce, P.O. Box 473, Downieville, CA 95936; (530) 289-3507.

MORE SOURCES
Other information is available from the Sierra County Chamber of Commerce and the Downieville Chamber of Commerce at the addresses and phone numbers listed above, and from the Nevada City Chamber of Commerce, 132 Main Street, Nevada City, CA 95959; (800) 655-NJOY or (530) 265-2692.

CHAPTER 6: THE LAKE TAHOE AREA
The Truckee is Famous, but There's Other Water, Too

Kenneth Susman

THE Lake Tahoe area is one of the most popular destination resort centers in California. It's easy to see why—gambling on the Nevada side, spectacular scenery, plenty of hiking, biking, and walking (not to mention skiing, snowboarding, and all the other winter sports), camping, boating, a plethora of motels and hotels, and food of all types.

It's even got fishing, much better fishing than one would expect, considering the huge number of visitors and thousands and thousands of summer homes that have brought this once-idyllic resort area citylike congestion and numerous ecological problems. While the fishing may be good, however, it also can be difficult, particularly on the Truckee River, Lake Tahoe's centerpiece for fly-line anglers. Except for a few stretches, it is a big, brawling river that holds its secrets well, demanding both fishing knowledge and the ability to wade aggressively and cast accurately. The expert can hook big rainbows and browns, mostly on nymphs, while the novice will go away convinced the river is barren.

Martis Creek Lake also stands out as an excellent fishery, but here again, matching the hatch and providing your fly with a perfect drift or action is the key to catching the big ones. Boca, Prosser, and Stampede Reservoirs provide easier pick-

Although access to the Truckee River is quite easy from Interstate 80, you can usually find a stretch where no one else is fishing.

ings, since they are much larger and have more stocked rainbows, while the Little Truckee River is smaller than the main Truckee and easier to handle for a less-experienced fly fisher. Lake Tahoe and Donner Lake offer good fishing, particularly for big Mackinaw trout, but they aren't noted as spots for fly fishing. Donner is planted heavily with rainbows, however, about 70,000 a year.

THE TRUCKEE RIVER

The Truckee River from Lake Tahoe to the Nevada border can be broken down into several sections, with the 12-mile special-regulations stretch from Trout Creek near the town of Truckee downstream to Boca Bridge the most popular area for fly fishers. The river actually begins at Tahoe City and is Lake Tahoe's only outlet. Flow is controlled by a small spillway in the center of town, near the intersection of Highways 89 and 28 at what is nicknamed "Fanny Bridge." That name comes from the upturned bottoms of spectators leaning over the railing of the bridge, watching trout twenty-five to thirty inches long slurping in insects washed from the lake or the bread and other edibles tossed at them by those hovering above. Of course this area—and for 1,000 feet downstream—is closed to fishing.

What can be considered the first section of the Truckee River runs 4.2 miles from Lake Tahoe to River Ranch at the turnoff to Alpine Meadows Ski Resort. It is mostly deep pools and fairly slow water that is better suited to bait and lure fishing than to flies. It also is exceedingly popular with rafters, since it is so slow-moving and safe that they can rent rafts at Tahoe City, float downstream on their own, and be picked up at the River Ranch takeout. I've seen days when the river is so full of blue-and-yellow rafts that they seem to form a sold, colorful stream that an angler could walk across. My best suggestion for this area is to stay away, although there are certainly plenty of fish, and in the evening (after the rafters have gone), hatches can provide decent dry-fly action.

Downstream from River Ranch to the city of Truckee is the best area for novice anglers who aren't afflicted with the wild-trout syndrome and are happy to ply their skills on stocked rainbows and a few smallish wild browns. Mostly riffles with a few runs, this 10-mile section of the Truckee is easily accessible from Highway 89 for almost its entire length, with numerous turnouts and campgrounds. When the water is high, there also is rafting in this area, but not nearly as much as upstream.

On a positive note, there are times when this section of the Truckee fishes very well, offering anglers a mixture of stockers, holdovers, and wild browns. Like most of the rest of the Truckee River, this is best fished by short-lining nymphs through slots and in likely holding areas, such as in front of and behind rocks—anyplace that could provide a trout with a slow spot in which to rest and feed. As for hatches, pretty much every type of bug is available—mayflies, caddisflies, midges, and stoneflies. In the early season, smaller mayflies do well, along with midges and caddis larvae and pupae. There also is a late-spring Golden Stone hatch that can be imitated with Stimulators.

Randy Johnson, who guides regularly on the Truckee, suggests using Gold-Ribbed Hare's Ears along with weighted marabou A.P. series nymphs in black, brown, olive, and green in sizes 10 through 16. For riffles and runs, Johnson prefers nymphing with caddis imitations and Little Yellow Stones from June through the rest of the summer. In the fall, the best bet are *Baetis* mayfly imitations, along with stonefly nymphs and caddis larvae.

Donner Creek flows into the river just before it reaches the town of Truckee. This is the last area planted with hatchery trout, and from here downstream it is essentially a wild-trout river, although regulations change depending on the section.

The river runs through the town of Truckee and can be reached from a number of residential roads. The problem is that the backs of houses and businesses line the river, and it isn't a very pleasant place to fish, particularly when less-than-friendly dogs are running loose.

Trout Creek empties into the river on the eastern edge of Truckee and marks the beginning of the official Wild Trout section. Regulations in this section call for barbless flies

and lures, no bait, and a two-trout limit of fifteen inches or more. To get there, take Highway 267 from Truckee toward Interstate 80 and turn to the right on Glenshire Drive, just outside town. Glenshire Drive parallels the river for the next 4 miles, with easy access all the way. The railway runs between the road and the river, but it doesn't present a problem—there are numerous parking areas alongside the tracks, and it is an easy walk to the Truckee.

This is the most popular part of the river because it is the easiest section for fly fishers, with open areas for casting and spots where wading is not difficult. There are plenty of trout here, including some big browns, but they are fished over regularly and can be difficult to hook. The insect populations here are pretty much the same as in the rest of the river. It offers fish a smorgasbord of bugs.

The end of this easier-fishing area is where Glenshire Drive crosses the old Highway 40 bridge just west of Glenshire. Downstream is a well-posted 3-mile stretch of the river that belongs to the San Francisco Flycasters and is restricted to members only. Court rulings provide that anglers can wade rivers and fish if they stay below the high watermark and thus keep off private land. However, this downstream stretch of the Truckee is difficult to wade. As a result, you probably can do better elsewhere and prevent a hassle if you run into the club's members or the guards who patrol the river. For the record, however, this is a fly fishing-only section from Glenshire Bridge downstream to 100 yards upstream of the Highway 80 bridge at Union Mills.

From the Highway 40 bridge, Glenshire Drive moves away from the Truckee, and there is no easy access for 4 miles, until Glenshire Drive intersects Hirschdale Road, which goes to the Boca Bridge area. Glenshire Drive continues another 3 miles and then dead-ends at an auto wrecking yard. From where it crosses the river along an old steel bridge to the yard is good fishing, although access involves a short hike into the canyon. Nymphing here can be excellent.

Hirschdale Road leads to I-80 and Boca Bridge, where the special-regulation Wild Trout section ends. Near Boca Bridge is a good area to fish, whether upstream in the Wild Trout section or downstream, where regulations permit all forms of angling, but allow only a two-trout take. This is excellent nymphing water for big trout. It can be tough wading—but it can be waded. Bring a wading staff and be prepared to take your time working into position to cast effectively to likely spots.

During the evenings, particularly late in the season, dry-fly activity picks up. Once again, it is a match-the-hatch situation, with numerous mayflies and caddisflies coming off the water. The trick is finding out what the fish are feeding on.

Johnson says streamers imitating the speckled dace and Lahontan redside shiners that are common throughout the area can be effective for big browns. He also notes that the

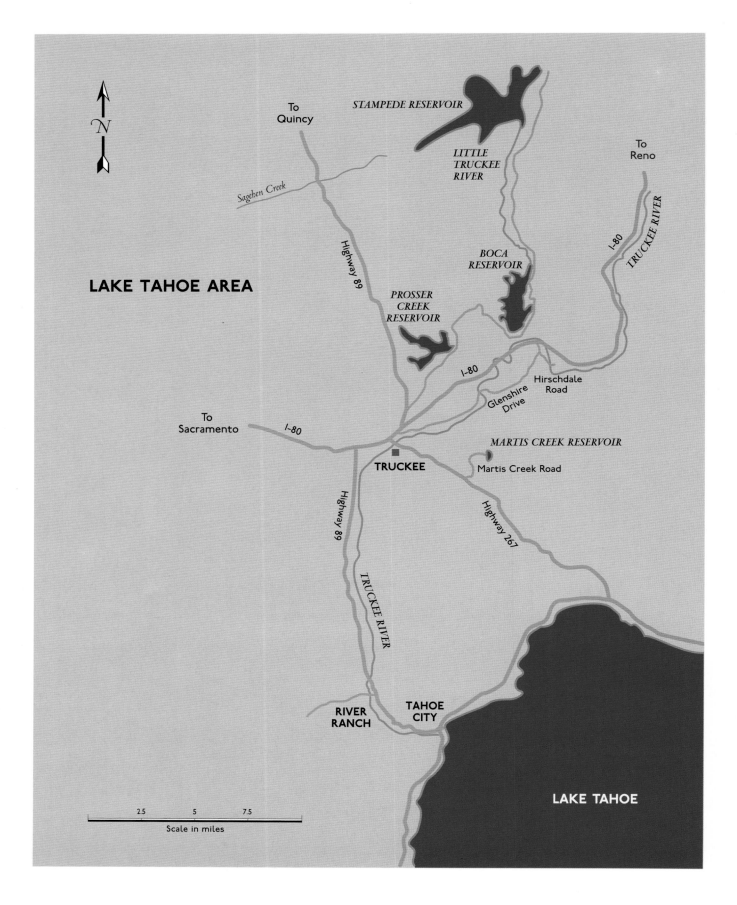

N

To Quincy

STAMPEDE RESERVOIR

LITTLE TRUCKEE RIVER

Sagehen Creek

To Reno

BOCA RESERVOIR

Highway 89

I-80

TRUCKEE RIVER

LAKE TAHOE AREA

PROSSER CREEK RESERVOIR

I-80

Hirschdale Road

Glenshire Drive

To Sacramento

I-80

MARTIS CREEK RESERVOIR

TRUCKEE

Martis Creek Road

Highway 89

Highway 267

TRUCKEE RIVER

RIVER RANCH

TAHOE CITY

LAKE TAHOE

2.5   5   7.5

Scale in miles

Rick E. Martin

Bill Sunderland shows off a rainbow caught on a yellow Woolly Bugger just above Boca Reservoir. The flat water there is perfect for wading, with lots of large fish.

river is open to night fishing, which is when big browns feed.

Anglers who want to fish upstream from Boca Bridge can backtrack by using the I-80 on-ramp at Boca Bridge and follow I-80 west toward Truckee as it crisscrosses the river. Use any of the turnoffs that allow roadside parking, but don't park on the highway—the California Highway Patrol polices the area and you'll get ticketed.

For fly-fishing purposes, the Truckee ends 10 miles downstream from Boca Bridge at Gray Creek. There are some deep pools with big trout, but they are more suited to bait fishermen.

The 3-mile stretch of deep water from Hirschdale to Floriston flattens out as it goes into the Floriston area. Although the dirt road along the river at the Floriston exit of I-80 is blocked off, it is possible to use it to walk to the river.

From Floriston downstream, a flume takes some of the water out of the river for several miles. The trout are still there, but the water can be low enough to make fishing difficult.

MARTIS CREEK LAKE

This little reservoir, one of the most famous small fly-fishing lakes in California, is perfect for float tubing or small boats. It is catch-and-release only, restricted to barbless artificial flies

and lures. It is 3 miles southeast of the town of Truckee on Highway 267, toward Kings Beach. The Martis Creek Reservoir turnoff is clearly marked, and the paved road leads 2 miles to a campground that is just above the reservoir.

There are big browns and the Eagle Lake strain of rainbows, and to catch them involves more than tossing out a generic attractor or trolling a black Woolly Bugger from a float tube (although occasionally that works, too). To be regularly successful means studying the bugs and determining what is tickling a trout's palate.

During the early season, when the fish are beginning to feed strongly after the winter, stripping streamers can trigger hits by large browns. Johnson uses size 4 to size 10 olive Flashabuggers and green sunfish patterns during this period, then switches to blood midges as the temperature begins to warm up a bit. A key, he says, is long, long leaders in 6X or 7X. That's tough going with big fish, but whoever said fly fishing was easy?

During the summer, *Baetis* mayfly hatches are common, so use standard patterns such as the Adams, both parachute and otherwise, along with Pheasant Tail and Hare's Ear Nymphs. Damselflies hatch in June and July and can be imitated both as nymphs and adults.

BOCA, STAMPEDE, AND PROSSER RESERVOIRS

These three major reservoirs all are easily accessible on paved roads—Prosser from Highway 89 leading north from Truckee, and Boca and Stampede from the Boca exit off I-80.

Stampede is heavily planted with rainbows, along with occasional stockings of browns and kokanees. Mackinaws were

Ken Morrish

put into the lake in the mid-1980s, and some of them are still around, huge fish that generally are caught only by deep trolling. They help keep the populations of nongame fish, such as tui chubs, Tahoe suckers, and red-sided shiners, under control.

Boca Reservoir used to be noted as a brown trout fishery, but there has been a steady decrease in numbers, probably because of sharply fluctuating water levels. Now it mostly contains planted rainbows. Prosser Reservoir also is planted regularly and it has a self-sustaining brown trout population.

All three lakes can be fished from float tubes or small boats. For the fly fisher, working along the banks or near the dams in the evening is the most effective tactic, particularly for anybody seeking dry-fly action. The one time these areas are really good is during ice-out, usually in mid-March to mid-April, when the fish that have been trapped all winter go on a feeding spree. Even fishing from the banks is effective during this period. Use big streamers and nymphs on a sinking or sink-tip line, along with a slow retrieve.

THE LITTLE TRUCKEE RIVER

The Little Truckee River between Boca and Stampede Reservoirs is a good-news, bad-news 4-mile stream. The good news is that is has good fishing for browns, rainbows, and, in the fall, kokanees. The bad news is that flows yo-yo up and down because they depend on water released from Stampede, and that in turn is determined by what is needed in Nevada. I've been fishing the Little Truckee and doing well when suddenly the water turns off-color and fills with moss and other debris being washed downstream. A look at the bank shows the river is steadily rising—and that's the end of the fishing for that day.

Although this stretch of the Little Truckee was planted in the past, the DFG undertook habitat improvements and discontinued putting in hatchery trout, in effect turning it into a self-sustaining wild-trout stream. There currently are no special regulations on the Little Truckee. This could change, so be sure to check, even though the Tahoe area is one of the better-posted sections in California.

Insects are more or less the same as found on the main Truckee—caddis, *Baetis*, Sulfur mayflies, and dark stoneflies. Short-line nymphing is the most effective way to fish this stream, although in the evenings and on cloudy days there can be good dry-fly fishing with mayfly imitations.

Just above Boca Reservoir, the Little Truckee slows and spreads out in a wide, shallow stretch that becomes a holding area for many of the lake's big fish, particularly early in the season. It is shallow enough in many areas to be easily waded. Streamers such as Matukas, Woolly Buggers, or

The Desolation Wilderness offers more than one hundred lakes, and many creeks, for fly fishers seeking an alpine angling experience.

Woolly Worms in black, brown, olive, and yellow can be effective—cast them out, let them swing, and then retrieve them with a slow strip.

The Little Truckee above Stampede Reservoir offers good early-season fishing for resident fish and for spawning fish that have come out of the lake. Access is along Highway 89 north of Truckee and along Jackson Meadows Road, but much of the land is private, so be careful about trying to get to the river without permission. Hatches are the same, and black ant and grasshopper imitations also are effective.

SAGEHEN CREEK

This pretty little creek is accessed by a bridge on Highway 89 that crosses it 8 miles north of the town of Truckee. Miniature pockets and pools, riffles characterize the stream, which abounds with rainbows, brookies, and browns, although few of them are large.

About 2 miles of Sagehen Creek, upstream from the Highway 89 bridge to the gauging station—which isn't on any map I can find, but which is obvious when you get there—is now a Wild Trout, catch-and-release section. Only barbless flies and lures are permitted. From the gauging station upstream is closed to fishing. Downstream from the Highway 89 bridge there are no special regulations. It is good fishing, but also is a very popular area for creekside hikers.

Mayfly and caddis hatches are plentiful, and this is an area where attractor dries—with the Yellow Humpy probably the best bet—will work in fast-moving water. Try nymphs and dries a size or so smaller than on the Truckee River. An Adams, Little Yellow Sally, or Elk Hair Caddis in size 14 or 16 works well, and your stock nymphs—Pheasant Tails, Zug Bugs, Hare's Ears, and Green Rock Worms, all a size larger—do well for nymphing. The stream is small enough that generally nymphs can be fished without any extra weight, although a strike indicator can help detect subtle takes in some of the larger pools. The entire stream can be fished from the bank, although hip waders, or shoes you don't mind getting wet and muddy, are a plus in crossing from one side to the other.

Although there are open areas, the larger fish tend to be found in protected areas that are hard to get at because of brush or trees. If you spot a working fish, dapping can be a very effective way to get a fly into the right spot.

THE DESOLATION WILDERNESS

There are myriad backcountry lakes and creeks in the mountains around Lake Tahoe, many with a worthwhile trout population. Perhaps the best-known area is the Desolation Wilderness, located on the eastern edge of the lake and north of Highway 50. This federal wilderness area created in 1966 encompasses about 100 square miles and just about as many lakes. Many of them have fish, including rainbows, brookies, browns, and even goldens.

Rick E. Martin

This is a nice-sized brown trout given the narrow creek it came from.

There is one major negative for most anglers (and a major plus for some)—these lakes, with very few exceptions, can't be reached except by hiking. Those few lakes that can be fished within a hike-in, hike-out day suffer enough pressure to make them second-rate fisheries.

This area is complicated enough so that hikers need topo maps and U.S. Forest Service maps. It also helps to talk to folks who know the area. Not all of the way-back lakes have good fishing, although many of them do. Either the Forest Service or the California DFG is a good source of information on current conditions. There also are a number of specialized books about hiking and fishing the Desolation Wilderness.

And yes, there really are golden trout in the area, most of them stocked at one time or another. **Cup Lake,** at 8,600 feet, probably is the best bet for goldens, and it is reasonably accessible from Highway 50. A strong hiker probably could make a go of it in one day, but fishing time would be limited. Neighboring **Saucer Lake** also has goldens, but they are much smaller.

SUMMING UP

The **Truckee River** has plenty of fish, including big ones, but fishing it is tough going and generally difficult for the inexperienced fly fisher. Short-line nymphing is effective if backed by aggressive wading that puts the angler in a position to get a proper drift into holding spots. For those who know the river and fish it regularly, it is first-rate. For those who are unfamiliar with its waters, it is a test of skill.

Martis Creek Lake, just outside the town of Truckee, long has been famous as a stillwater fishery. It has demanding, match-the-hatch angling, but the big ones are there to be caught. Use a float tube or a pram.

The **Little Truckee River** between Stampede and Boca Reservoirs and **Sagehen Creek** are two small-stream well-known trout fisheries, and they accordingly get a fair amount of pressure from anglers. Sagehen is strictly a small-trout stream, but lots of them in a lovely setting. Two miles of the creek has been declared Wild Trout, catch-and-release fishing. The Little Truckee has fishing good enough that planting has been suspended, and there now is a natural population of rainbows and browns, some of them big. Look for this section between the reservoirs to become an official Wild Trout stream with special regulations. With any luck, it soon will offer as good as or better fishing than the main Truckee River.

♦ ♦ ♦ ♦ ♦ ♦

ADDITIONAL INFORMATION

FLY SHOPS

Mountain Hardware and Sports, 11320 Donner Pass Road, Truckee, CA 96151; (530) 587-4844. Although this is a general-purpose hardware store, it has a good fly-fishing section with knowledgeable staffers.

Truckee River Outfitters, 10200 Donner Pass Road, Truckee, CA 96161; (530) 582-0900. This California outpost of the Reno Fly Shop is open from April to October.

Kiene's Fly shop, 2654 Marconi Avenue, Sacramento, CA 95821; (916) 486-9958, (800) 4000-FLY. Web site: http://www.kiene.com. This is a full-service fly fishing store not far off I-80.

Tahoe Fly Fishing Outfitters, 3433 Lake Tahoe Boulevard, Highway 50; (530) 541-8208. Web site: http://www.sierra.net/fly-fishing. E-mail: flyshop@sierra.net.

Reno Fly Shop, 294 East Moana Lane, #14, Reno, NV 89502; (702) 825-3474. A full-service fly shop with the latest information on the Tahoe area.

American Fly Fishing Company, 3523 Fair Oaks Boulevard, Sacramento, CA; (800) 410-1222 or (916) 483-1222. Web site: http://www.americanfly.com.

Fly Fishing Specialties, 6412 Tupelo, suite C, Citrus Heights, CA 95610; (916) 722-1055. Located just off Highway 80.

Bud's Sporting Goods, 10108 Commercial Row, Truckee, CA 96151; (530) 587-3177 Some fly-fishing equipment.

Swigard's True Value Hardware, 200 N. Lake Boulevard, Tahoe City, CA 95730; (530) 583-3738. Some fly-fishing equipment.

HOSPITALS

Truckee: Tahoe Forest Hospital, 10955 Donner Pass Road, Truckee, CA 96160; (530) 582-3554.

South lake Tahoe: Barton Memorial Hospital, 2170 South Avenue, South Lake Tahoe, CA 96150; (530) 542-3000.

PUBLIC CAMPING

There are numerous campgrounds, both public and private, in this area. For Forest Service campgrounds, contact the Truckee Ranger District, 10342 Highway 89 N., Truckee, CA 96161; (530) 587-3558. For private campgrounds or for lodging, contact the Truckee Chamber of Commerce, 12036 Donner Pass Road, Truckee, CA 96161; (530) 587-2757.

MORE SOURCES

Contact the Truckee Chamber of Commerce at the above address and phone number for additional information. For hiking anglers who want to fish in the Desolation Wilderness, Jerome Yesavage's *Desolation Wilderness Fishing Guide* gives helpful details on specific lakes. It costs $12.95 and is published by Frank Amato Publications, P.O. Box 82112, Portland, OR 97282; (803) 653-8108.

CHAPTER 7: THE AMERICAN RIVER
Rafting Paradise, Fun Fishing.

Bill Sunderland

RAFTING, not fly fishing, is the most popular outdoor sport associated with the American River—the South Fork is home to one 22-mile run that alone draws 200,000 people annually to its rapids and cascades. Still, there is a lot of fishing; you just have to look for it and be willing do some hiking .

Considering how close the American is to Sacramento and its burgeoning environs, it doesn't get that much fishing pressure. What pressure there is tends to be from bait and lure anglers at the few points it can be accessed by vehicle. There's a good reason for this—the North and Middle Forks of the American River tumble along the bottoms of deep, rocky canyons that are not inviting for anybody but the avid hiker.

On the other extreme, much of the South Fork, which parallels Highway 50 to South Tahoe, is easily reached. The result is lots of private land, stocked trout, and fishing that could be termed mediocre at best.

All this means that there aren't that many fly fishers who call the American River their home water. Those who do tend to be a hardy lot who love the isolation and are willing to spend the physical effort necessary to make the most of the river.

You may have to work hard to catch a rainbow of this size on the Norh Fork of the American, but such fish are definitely there.

Charles Von Geldern is among these. A long-time California Department of Fish and Game biologist who was one of the original heads of the Wild Trout Program after it was initiated in 1972, he retired in 1989, but still regularly fishes the Forks of the American.

He describes it as a "wonderful trout stream," with rainbows running from eight to sixteen or seventeen inches and occasional larger browns. He also has a theory that I haven't heard before, but that anglers might keep in mind: when mergansers, a duck that eats fish, are in the area, they scare fish enough to put them down for hours.

"I keep a fishing diary, and in an area where one day I caught thirty-eight fish on a dry fly, on another day, the fish seemed to be scary and spooked, although there was nobody around. I rounded a bend and found mergansers," Von Geldern says. "It also happened to me in other areas—they were full of fish, but spooked, and in each case I saw mergansers."

THE NORTH FORK OF THE AMERICAN RIVER
The North Fork originates at 7,900-foot-high Mountain Meadow Lake 4 miles northwest of Squaw Valley Ski Resort and flows westward to Folsom Lake. It is a state and national Wild and Scenic River from Palisade Creek, several miles below its headwaters, for 37 miles downstream, to the

bridge at Iowa Hill Road near Colfax. This 37-mile stretch also is in California's Wild Trout Program, which means no fish are planted. It is not part of the state Catch-and-Release Program, however, and there are no special regulations, either on tackle or keeping fish.

The only drive-in access to the Wild Trout section of the North Fork is at the Iowa Hill Bridge, which can be reached best from Interstate 80. Take the Colfax exit, then turn right. Iowa Hill Road is the second left, past the California Department of Forestry fire station. It is about 3 miles to the river by way of a paved road that drops sharply into the canyon. There is a campground with day parking at the bridge, and fly fishers can go either upstream or downstream. This area is worked heavily by gold miners, some of whom stay at the campground for extended periods, and anglers need to be careful while wading so as not to step into holes left from suction dredging.

Iowa Hill Road crosses the bridge and continues 19 miles to Forest Hill Road, a major artery that follows the ridge-line between the canyons of the North and Middle Forks of the American River. Upstream there are several hike-in accesses to the North Fork, none of them easy. Once you are on the water, however, the American River Trail parallels the south side of the river for nearly 10 miles, from Mumford Bar to Sailor Flat. This is Von Geldern's favorite stretch of river, a wild and unruly cascade he describes as "a wonderful thing to have."

Sailor Flat Trail, which leads to the upper (eastern) end of the American River Trail, branches north from Forest Hill Road a couple of miles before it reaches Robinson Flat Camp. There is a 4x4 road 1.5 miles to the trailhead, and then it is a another 3 miles to the river. This is a steep trail, something to remember if you're planning on hiking out.

Trails to Mumford Bar can be reached either from I-80 or from Forest Hill Road. From I-80, take the Emigrant Gap exit, turn right, and follow Forest Service Scenic Road 19 (called Texas Hill Road on some maps). After 7 miles it crosses the North Fork of the North Fork of the American, a lovely little stream offering good small-trout fishing throughout the early season. There is a campground there, and anglers can rockhop their way upstream or downstream. It gets low in the fall, but anglers who want to fish pools can do pretty well with small trout. The fall scenery and the privacy make up for the lack of big fish.

Another 7 miles along the road, which becomes gravel, there is a fork. Go left half a mile to a gate. From there, a trail winds about 2.5 miles to the North Fork of the American at Mumford Bar. From Forest Hill Road on the south side of the river there is a parking area and trailhead that leads 3.5 miles to the river. Both the north and south trails are steep. Downstream from Mumford Bar to Colfax, several other trails lead to the river, but once an angler is on the water, moving along the bank involves scrambling or wading, which can be difficult unless the water is very low.

From Colfax downstream—out of the Wild Trout Area—there are a couple of drive-in accesses that are good starting points for working the North Fork. The first is reached by following Ponderosa Way from the West Paoli Lane exit from I-80. Turn right at the exit. About halfway to the river, the 5-mile-long road turns to gravel and becomes bumpy, although family sedans will have no problem. The Auburn State Recreation Area is on the south side of the one-lane bridge. Ponderosa Way continues up the southern side of the canyon 3.2 miles to Forest Hill Way.

The big hole under the bridge isn't much good for fly fishers, but upstream or downstream there are riffles or gravel bars that offer excellent opportunities when the water is low. There are trails to the river on either side of the road. An alternative is to go to where Shirttail Creek enters the Middle Fork, between Ponderosa Way and Colfax. This road also can be reached via the West Paoli Lane exit—go left, instead of right, at the exit, then right on Yankee Jim Road, which drops 4.5 miles to the river. After crossing the North Fork, it climbs 8.5 miles to the town of Foresthill on Forest Hill Road. There is an Auburn State Recreation Area picnic ground at the bridge. It's big water here, not the easiest fly fishing.

The DFG's 1979 Wild Trout Program management plan for the North Fork noted that its studies showed the growth of wild rainbows was slow because of the lack of nutrients in the water, with the number of fish reaching more than ten inches extremely low. "A twelve-inch fish would be over five years old, a rarity in a river like the North Fork," the report states. Von Geldern says his fishing experiences in this area, which are extensive, have shown fish bigger than that, running up to seventeen or eighteen inches.

THE MIDDLE FORK OF THE AMERICAN RIVER

Like the North Fork, the Middle Fork flows through a deep canyon. There are, however, a few drive-in access points, either from Forest Hill Road, to the north, or from French Meadows Road, to the south.

Von Geldern's favorite area is from Oxbow Reservoir, sometimes called the Ralston Afterbay, upstream all the way to French Meadows Reservoir, more than 15 miles of stream. He suggests going to the river at Oxbow and then working upriver. Access to Oxbow is at the town of Foresthill from Mosquito Ridge Road. This road first crosses the North Fork of the Middle Fork, which also offers some good fishing possibilities. Although the bridge is high above the river here, there is a gated road that leads down to the water, and rockhopping over big boulders upstream or downstream isn't that difficult. It is nice pocket water with occasional riffles.

Mosquito Ridge Road continues to Oxbow, then climbs back onto the ridge and goes east to French Meadows Reser-

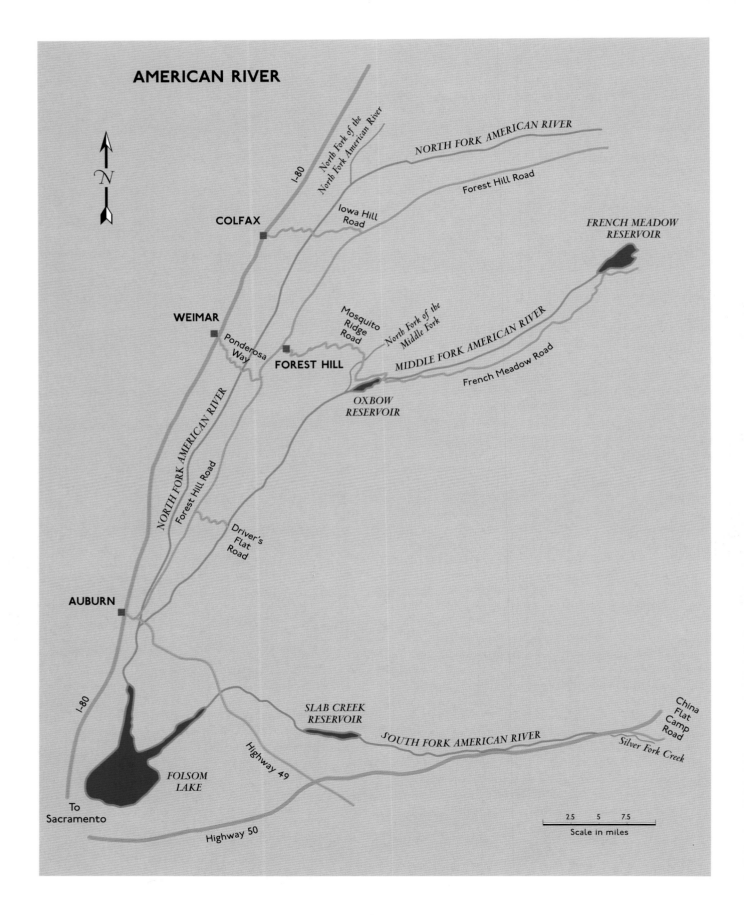

AMERICAN RIVER

N

North Fork of the
North Fork American River

I-80

NORTH FORK AMERICAN RIVER

Forest Hill Road

Iowa Hill
Road

COLFAX

FRENCH MEADOW
RESERVOIR

Mosquito
Ridge
Road

North Fork of the
Middle Fork

WEIMAR

Ponderosa
Way

MIDDLE FORK AMERICAN RIVER

French Meadow Road

FOREST HILL

OXBOW
RESERVOIR

NORTH FORK AMERICAN RIVER

Forest Hill Road

Driver's
Flat
Road

AUBURN

I-80

SLAB CREEK
RESERVOIR

China
Flat
Camp
Road

SOUTH FORK AMERICAN RIVER

Highway 49

Silver Fork Creek

FOLSOM
LAKE

To
Sacramento

Highway 50

2.5   5   7.5

Scale in miles

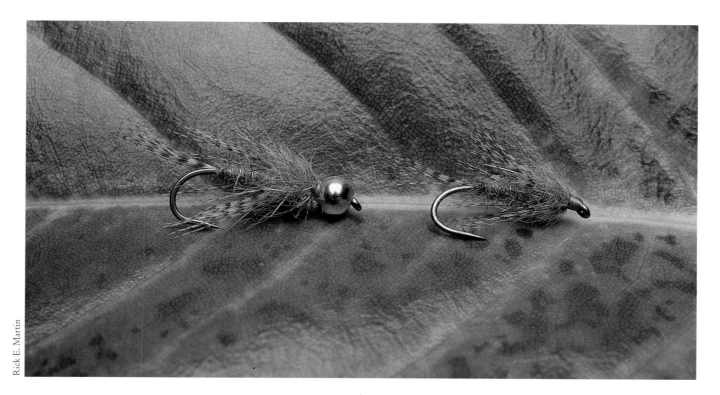

Rick E. Martin

Bird's Nest nymphs, both with and without bead heads, are an effective fly throughout the Sierra Nevada. These flies were tied by Jeff Yamagata.

voir. One other river access is at the Interbay Reservoir, about halfway between Oxbow and French Meadows. A steep road turns south from Mosquito Ridge Road and drops 2 miles to the reservoir. There is little parking and only difficult access to the river here.

French Meadows Reservoir is a popular camping, boating, and fishing area that probably is better left to bait and lure anglers. Above French Meadows, there are accesses to the upper Middle Fork by way of dirt roads on either side of the river. There also are several campgrounds. Pools, pocket water, and riffles can be productive for fly fishers here, since the fish see mostly bait and lures.

For anglers who want to fish big water at a lower elevation, there is Driver's Flat Road, which turns south from Forest Hill Road near Lake Clementine. The 3-mile drive is on a some-times bumpy gravel road that leads to a popular rafting put-in downstream from the infamous Ruck-a-Chucky Rapids, a tough stretch of water that must be portaged. There is plenty of parking, and anglers can fish downstream or walk upstream along a gated road for about three-quarters of a mile to where it ends on a sandy beach beside a big pool that can pro-vide excellent evening action on dry flies.

To go farther upstream, follow the Western States Trail and look for ways to get down to the river. This whole stretch is a popular mining area, and in the summer, where there is access there also may be miners.

Canyon Creek and **Otter Creek** feed into the river from

the south in this area and both are good small-trout fishing if you can cross the river to get to them. Wading depends on the time of year and the flows.

THE SOUTH FORK OF THE AMERICAN RIVER

The lower section of the South Fork, from Chili Bar Reservoir downstream, is the stretch of the river that gets those 200,000 white-water types each year, 100,000 of them making the trip with commercial rafting companies, the rest private rafters, kayakers, and even canoers.

The fishing doesn't really start for most fly-line anglers until the area above the slow-moving waters leading into Slab Creek Reservoir. Just upstream from the reservoir, **Silver Creek** flows into the river from the north and offers good fishing for medium-sized trout, a mixture of planted rainbows and wild rainbows and browns. Access to Silver Creek is by way of Forebay Road, which branches north from Highway 50 at Riverton, near Pollock Pines. This area was hit hard by the January 1997 floods, which closed Highway 50 until the following fall. It will take a bit of time to recover, but in the long run, fishing should not be affected.

From Riverton to the headwaters of the South Fork, not far from South Lake Tahoe, Highway 50 crisscrosses the river or is within easy walking distance all the way. However, access itself is somewhat limited because of homes and pri-vate property.

The DFG does a lot of stocking here, but anglers who want to go for wild fish, even if they are small, can work feeder streams. Some of the better fishing is on the Silver Fork, which flows into the South Fork from the south at Kyburz.

Bill Sunderland

The road to China Flat Camp and Silver Fork Camp parallels the Silver Fork for more than a dozen miles, offering plenty of access and fishing. There are numerous feeder creeks that flow into the Silver Fork, and the higher upstream you go, the better the wild-trout fishing becomes, although most of them are small. You can fish the Silver Fork all the way to where it begins with the merger of Silver Creek (not the one farther downstream) and Caples Creek.

Another area that can provide good fishing is the extreme upper end of the South Fork, not far from South Lake Tahoe. There are a number of homes in the area, but they are on leased U.S. Forest Service property, which means anglers should be able to access the river. There are wild browns and rainbows in this section.

One lake in this area worth exploring is **Wrights Lake**, reached via Wrights Lake Road, which goes north from Highway 50 about 15 miles west of South Lake Tahoe. Float tubing is the best way to catch its rainbows and browns.

SUMMING UP

The **North and Middle Forks of the American River**, although close to the Sacramento area, with its large population, don't get much fishing pressure for the simple reason there is little access. Anglers who want to enjoy what these rivers have to offer have to work for it by hiking steep trails. The most popular hike-in stretch of American River is the section between Mumford Bar and Sailor Flat on the North Fork. Although anglers need to make a steep hike into the canyon to get to either place, once there, they can follow the American River Trail along the river. For small-stream fishing, try the North Fork of the North Fork—it has small trout in a beautiful setting.

◆ ◆ ◆ ◆ ◆ ◆

ADDITIONAL INFORMATION

FLY SHOPS

Kiene's Fly Shop, 2654 Marconi Avenue, Sacramento, CA 95820; (800) 4000-FLY. A full-service fly shop.

American Fly Fishing Company, 3523 Fair Oaks Boulevard, Sacramento, CA; (800) 410-1222 or (916) 483-1222. Web site: http://www.americanfly.com.

Auburn Outdoor Sports, 858 High Street, Auburn, CA 95603: (800) 205-9201 or (530) 885-9200. An outdoor-sports store with a large fly-fishing section.

HOSPITALS

Auburn: Sutter Face Hospital, 11815 Education Street, Auburn, CA 95603; (530) 888-4500.

Placerville: Marshall Hospital, Marshall Way, Placerville, CA 95667; (530) 622-1441.

Truckee: Tahoe Forest Hospital, 10955 Donner Pass Road, Truckee, CA 96160; (530) 582-3554.

PUBLIC CAMPING

At Auburn State Recreation Area Campground in the North and Middle Fork rafting areas, camping permits are required. Call (530) 885-4527 for information and permits.

MORE SOURCES

An excellent fishing map for the American River is produced by StreamTime, P.O. Box 991536, Redding, CA 96099; (530) 244-0310. This map, which costs $9.95, also shows rafting access points and rapids.

A typical stretch of the American River, running deep in its canyon. Good fishing if you can get to it.

CHAPTER 8: HIGHWAY 4
The North Fork of the Stanislaus and the Mokelumne Rivers

Paolo Marchesi

HIGHWAY 4, from Angels Camp through Murphys, Arnold, and Dorrington, past Alpine Lake, and over Ebbetts Pass to Markleeville on the eastern slope of the Sierra Nevada, is one of the prettiest drives in California. My folks had a home at Hathaway Pines near Arnold, so I fished the area a lot over the years—the closest I've ever had to home water.

The highway runs southeast, mostly through the Stanislaus National Forest, while at the crest high on the spine of the Sierra, the Mokelumne Wilderness lies to the north and the Carson-Iceberg Wilderness to the south. Only recently has this huge wonderland become popular—for years, it was a wilderness paradise coveted and used by a few hikers, campers, and anglers. It still is not crowded, but more and more vacationers are flocking to the area, and Angels Camp, Murphys, and Arnold are growing to meet their needs.

There are two rivers accessible from Highway 4 on the western slope of the Sierra, the North Fork of the Stanislaus and sections of the Mokelumne. (That's pronounced moe-CALL-uh-me, but the locals just call it "the Moke." "Umna" was the local Miwok Indian suffix for "river,"

Dan Leichty fishes the North Fork of the Stanislaus. Much of the river consists of riffles and pocket water.

hence the Anglicized Mokelumne, Tuolumne, and Consumnes Rivers.) There also are lakes, including Spicer Reservoir, Lake Alpine, Mosquito Lake, the Highland Lakes, and a variety of walk-in waters that sometimes offer good fishing. On the eastern slope, the twisty, two-lane blacktop winds down to the East Carson River and its tributaries, which are covered in the Carson River chapter.

Trout fishing here is what you make of it. There aren't many easy access points, and those that exist are planted with hatchery trout and pounded heavily, mostly with Power Bait, crickets, and worms. My formula is simple: the more rugged the country and the tougher the hike to get to the water, the better the fishing.

The best I can do is tell you where to access the rivers and streams and occasionally whether it is better upstream or downstream. But Mother Nature does have a way of changing things—some areas that provided good fishing during the drought years of the early 1990s lost their luster when the heavy rains returned and the 1997 floods reconfigured sections of Stanislaus River. People also have a hand in this—logging roads that offer access points are constantly being built and old access roads closed.

This is not trophy trout country, nor is much of it prime water offering thirty-fish days. No matter—it is spectacularly beautiful, the fish are wild and wily, and the fly-line angler should be proud to catch a dozen trout during a fishing day. There are occasional big ones, mostly browns from sixteen to nineteen inches and even larger, but the norm is more in the range of six to eleven inches, predominantly rainbows. There are brookies, too, but not as many as in some other Sierra streams.

When you find them, the trout tend not to be selective. I rely heavily on a Royal Wulff or Red Humpy in fast waters and on more accurate imitations such as a Parachute Adams or Elk Hair Caddis in slower runs. Also very effective are imitations of black ants and, in the mid to late summer, grasshoppers. More important than having a varied selection is having a number of different sizes, generally from 12 to 18.

The same holds true with nymphs. Old-timers favor the Zug Bug, but Pheasant Tails, Princes, Bird's Nests, and Gold-Ribbed Hare's Ears, either with and without bead heads, will pretty much cover any situation you'll run into. These are mostly fast-flowing streams with riffles, pools, and lots of pocket water, and the trout don't have much time to decide whether to take a fly.

If the trout are there, and you offer them a reasonable presentation, they'll grab it. The fly fisher's difficulty is picking likely holding spots and getting to them without breaking a leg or becoming tangled in bankside bushes and trees. And yes, there are rattlesnakes, bears, and mosquitoes, along with some poison oak.

To sum up, what you have is tough hiking, rugged country, and pretty good fishing. Is it worth it? You bet!

NORTH FORK OF THE STANISLAUS RIVER

This lovely mountain river became a tailwater fishery with the construction of Spicer Reservoir in the late 1980s and has been improving steadily, despite several setbacks. The Stanislaus took a beating from the floods early in 1997. However, the scouring of the streambed probably improved spawning habitat and in the long run will be a bonus for the Stan.

Highway 4 is the access road for the North Fork of the Stanislaus pretty much all the way upstream from New Melones Reservoir near Angels Camp to the headwaters near Lake Alpine. The trouble is, the highway runs high on the heavily wooded mountainside, and the river is at the bottom of a deep canyon, with only occasional roads or trails providing access to the water. For the most part, those accesses are the starting points for an angler, although they can be destinations, if you don't mind company and hatchery trout.

For fly fishers, **New Melones Reservoir** deserves a few words, since at certain times and places it offers good fishing. When it was filled, New Melones destroyed what was then probably the most popular white-water run in the United States, one that drew an amazing 50,000 rafters and kayakers annually. From the original authorization in 1944 to when it actually was finished in 1979, conservationists

fought New Melones tooth and nail. Even then, it wasn't filled to its capacity of 12,500 surface acres until 1983.

The reservoir now is a major playground for water skiers, personal-watercraft enthusiasts, and power boaters, not to mention people with houseboats. However, the lake is 23 miles long and has about 100 miles of shoreline, including numerous coves and inlets that can shelter anglers. There are rainbow, German brown, and Eagle Lake trout, including some trophy-sized monsters, along with largemouth bass, catfish, crappies, and bluegills. It is open to fishing twenty-four hours a day, all year.

For fly fishers, winter is best time to go because threadfin shad, a key food for larger trout, are in the coves and along the shore from about November to February. The shad draw rainbows and browns to the surface, and anglers can use boats or float tubes to get to them with streamer baitfish imitations. The rest of the year, the fish are deeper, and trolling with lures or bait is much more effective.

The first access to the Stanislaus River upstream from New Melones is via the old Camp Nine Road from Vallecito, just east of Angels Camp on Highway 4. This was where the popular Camp Nine Run began before New Melones was built and now is the high watermark of the reservoir when it is full. There generally is a lot of water coming into the lake at this point, but anglers can follow a trail upstream and find some runs that hold big trout, including spawners that move out of the lake. It is more popular as a bait and lure area, however, because of the deep holes.

Although there are several access roads in the Murphys and Hathaway Pines areas, they don't offer much in the way of decent fly fishing. It's best to follow Highway 4 east and drop into one of the more isolated access points.

CALAVERAS BIG TREES STATE PARK

The first major access to the river, and one of the most popular areas for family fishing, is Calaveras Big Trees State Park, 3 miles east of Arnold on Highway 4. From the park entrance, where visitors must pay to enter, a paved road leads 6 miles to the Stanislaus. At the bridge crossing the river, the Department of Fish and Game stocks rainbows, making it a popular put-and-take fishing area. There are two major state-run campgrounds in Calaveras Big Trees. Both are popular and fill quickly on holiday weekends, but neither of them is on the river.

Fly fishers can make their way up or down the river from the bridge area and get into wild trout, but there is better fishing from some of the access points upstream. This road also leads to Beaver Creek, described below.

SOURGRASS AND BOARDS CROSSINGS

Sourgrass Crossing is reached by following Board's Crossing Road from Dorrington, 3 miles east of Calaveras Big Trees State Park on Highway 4. The paved, two-lane road winds

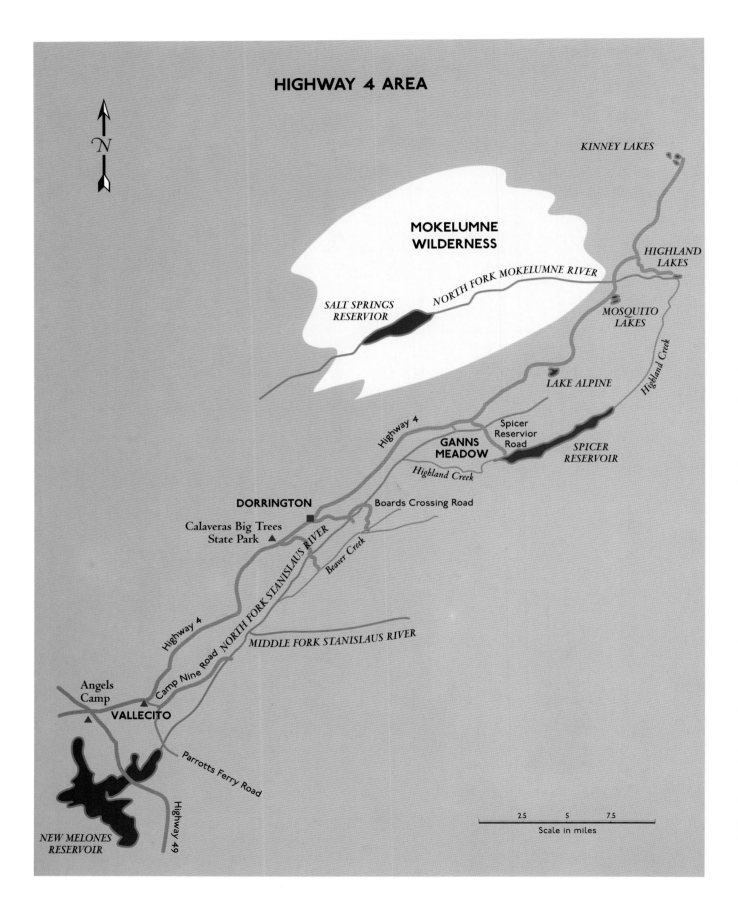

HIGHWAY 4 AREA

N

KINNEY LAKES

MOKELUMNE
WILDERNESS

*HIGHLAND
LAKES*

*SALT SPRINGS
RESERVIOR*

NORTH FORK MOKELUMNE RIVER

*MOSQUITO
LAKES*

Highland Creek

LAKE ALPINE

Highway 4

Spicer
Reservoir
Road

*SPICER
RESERVOIR*

GANNS
MEADOW

Highland Creek

DORRINGTON

Boards Crossing Road

Calaveras Big Trees
State Park ▲

NORTH FORK STANISLAUS RIVER

Beaver Creek

Highway 4

Camp Nine Road

MIDDLE FORK STANISLAUS RIVER

Angels
Camp

▲

VALLECITO

Parrotts Ferry Road

Highway 49

2.5   5   7.5

Scale in miles

*NEW MELONES
RESERVOIR*

deep into the canyon, where a single-lane bridge crosses the river. In January 1997, a major slide took out the bridge and campground, along with part of a new campground under construction. The bridge was quickly replaced (this is a heavily logged area, and the bridge was crucial to get to timberland), but the campgrounds took a bit longer to restore. There was a major fish kill below the slide because of the mud and debris washed into the river, but nature replenished the trout, and fishing returned to normal. The river at the bridge is stocked with rainbows, but it is a good jumping-off area for anglers working upstream or downstream to get away from stocked fish.

From the old campground on the south side of the river, a jeep road parallels the Stanislaus upstream for a mile or so before it disappears in a washed-out gully. From there on, it is nothing but a primitive trail, but the fishing is worth it. The farther you walk, the better the chance that you won't be sharing the river with others. There are any number of riffles, runs, and pools, and it's up to the angler to pick a likely spot and work it properly. The fish are where they are supposed to be, but getting to them can be difficult. Dredging some of the deeper pools with large nymphs can produce chunky browns, but for the most part, rainbows are the common catch, with a fish of twelve inches a good-sized prize.

Fishing downstream from Sourgrass Crossing is easier going. The first few hundred yards are unfishable rapids, and rather than walk down from the bridge, drive another quarter of a mile along the road after it crosses the bridge, park anyplace you can find enough room off the road, and then work your way down to the river along one of the many paths.

Although it isn't stocked, this is a fairly heavily fished area, so the trout that have survived are more sophisticated than wild fish in some more isolated sections of the Stanislaus. A trail parallels the river all the way to Board's Crossing, a mile or so downstream. Although there are a few spots where the river can be crossed late in the year, fishing from the bank is just about as good. Wading allows anglers to get into a better position to work some likely fish-holding spots, but proficient casters can pretty well cover the water from the bank without getting their feet wet.

Board's Crossing is reached via a bumpy dirt road that leaves Board's Crossing Road (the paved road known as Board's Crossing Road actually goes to Sourgrass Crossing) just as it begins to work its way down into the canyon from Dorrington. It isn't clearly marked, but is the only other road going to the river. Although the 4-mile drive down is steep, four-wheel drive is not necessary.

Another way in is to follow Board's Crossing Road across the Stanislaus and up the other side of the canyon, where an unmarked dirt road to the right drops down to Board's Crossing. This road actually is in better shape and is easier on the family sedan.

There are private homes at Board's Crossing near the bridge across the river, which limits access. Just downstream on the south side of the river is a Forest Service campground.

There are big holes in this stretch of the river, both upstream and downstream from the bridge. They are not only fished heavily, but also serve as swimming pools during hot weather. On the other hand, I took the biggest fish I ever caught in the Stanislaus out of a hole just upstream from the bridge, an eighteen-inch brown caught at midday on a size 12 Pheasant Tail.

BEAVER CREEK

Beaver Creek, a good early-season, small-fish stream, is reached from either Calaveras Big Trees State Park or Sourgrass Crossing Road. During the drought years of the late 1980s and early 1990s, I almost always spent opening day here—the water was in perfect shape, and the small rainbows that inhabited Beaver Creek were avid in chasing dry flies.

I always caught dozens of rainbows. The negative was that a couple of times I ended up fishing in a snowstorm that made me wonder if I would be able to get out before the road became impassable.

To get to Beaver Creek through Calaveras Big Trees State Park, follow the paved road to the Stanislaus River and then continue for another 3.5 miles to the creek, where there is a picnic area, but no overnight camping. The DFG stocks rainbows here and at several other nearby spots on the creek, but trails follow the creek, so working upstream or downstream is easy for those who want privacy and wild trout.

To get to Beaver Creek by way of Sourgrass Crossing, a better area for most fly fishers, continue along the paved road up the south side of the canyon after crossing the river. Near the crest of the canyon, the paved road ends, and the dirt road that continues splits. To the left is the road to **Rattlesnake Creek,** which has some nice camping spots, but offers only mediocre fishing. (I've had a couple of blue-ribbon days on small browns on Rattlesnake Creek, but for the most part have worked hard for only a few small fish.)

The right fork leads 5 miles to Beaver Creek. This area belongs to Louisiana Pacific Lumber Company and is heavily logged. LP keeps it open for fishing in the summer and even maintains a small campground on the creek. It also controls a gate a mile down the dirt road, which is locked in the off-season to prevent visitors from taking firewood.

The dirt road splits again at Beaver Creek, with the right fork crossing the creek and winding up into the backcountry. To the left, it parallels Beaver Creek for another 5 miles, allowing access at just about any point. Only a hundred yards down the road there is the pretty meadow campground set up by Louisiana Pacific, with flat campsites and toilets. Otherwise, visitors can camp at just about any open spot along the creek—there are plenty of them.

Along the first mile or so of Beaver Creek after the road forks, the DFG stocks rainbows. Anglers continuing upstream find a more defined canyon, with riffles and pocket water where

Paolo Marchesi

small trout abound. In the spring and early summer, they will readily take just about any fly offered. Size 14 or 16 Black Ants almost always are a winner.

Five miles upstream, shortly after crossing a small bridge where Little Beaver Creek joins the main creek, the road forks again at a large, grassy meadow just made for camping. Past the meadow, the right fork of the road moves away from the creek, while after half a mile the left fork also begins to climb and easy access is lost. The left fork follows the ridgeline to make a 15-mile loop and becomes Rattlesnake Creek Road going back to the paved Sourgrass Crossing Road.

There are a lot of rainbows in Beaver Creek, feeding on caddisflies, stoneflies, and mayflies, but most are in the six-to-ten-inch range. There also are some small brookies. As on the Stanislaus River, an angler can work along the creek far enough to guarantee private fishing, but there is enough streamside brush that the going occasionally can be tough.

RAMSEY

A jeep road leads from Highway 4 at Cottage Springs to the Stanislaus River at an area called Ramsey, but you'll do your vehicle a big favor by taking the hour to walk it, instead. As Dan Leichty of White Pines Outdoors in Arnold put it, "There are $50,000 in broken jeep parts scattered along that road. It is nasty." Ramsey has the longest section of flat water in the entire river, a beautiful stretch lined by alders. Although there are rainbows, this is a prime area for big browns

GANNS MEADOW

A walk-in access to the Stanislaus is down a trail at Ganns Meadow on Highway 4. Ganns Meadow is about two-thirds of the way from Dorrington to Spicer Reservoir Road and is marked by several old cabins on the north side of the highway—the side opposite the trail. It's a 2-mile walk to the river and a tough hike coming back out, but there is some excellent fly fishing on this section of the river.

BIG MEADOW

A drive-in access to the river is at Big Meadow Campground just before Spicer Reservoir Road. The road leads to the Boy Scout camp at Sand Flat and at times can require a four-wheel drive because of loose gravel. This section of the river is upstream from Highland Creek, the major tributary that flows out of Spicer Reservoir, so late in the year it doesn't hold much water. The best bet when the water is low is to work downstream to where Highland Creek comes in (see below) and fish from there on down. On the other hand, early in the season, when the Stanislaus downstream is running too high for effective fly fishing, this section is in excellent shape.

Rocky river beds invariably lead to lost flies. But as a plus, trout in fast water aren't too selective toward fly patterns.

SPICER RESERVOIR ROAD

This two-lane paved road crosses the North Fork and then goes on to Spicer Reservoir, where anglers can fish Highland Creek below the dam. Both places offer some of the best fishing in the area. Since the Stanislaus at this point is above Highland Creek, it is much smaller than below and is very fishable early in the season.

There is a campground at the river, 4 miles from Highway 4, that has toilets, water, and several dozen campsites set among the tall conifers. Anglers can fish for planters within a few hundred yards of the crossing or work their way along the Stanislaus. Downstream there are some deep pools, but it takes more than an hour's hiking to get to the first of them. Away from the campground, anglers need to wade because the best way to get downstream is to cross from one side of the river to the other as the terrain demands.

An alternative is **Highland Creek** below Spicer Reservoir, reached by following Spicer Reservoir Road to its end just below the dam. The first-half mile or more of water looks good, but doesn't produce as many trout as would be expected in such a tailwater fishery. A better bet is to hike thirty minutes or so downstream and begin working likely holes. This isn't as easy as it sounds because there is no clear trail through the heavy brush and big rocks.

How fishable this area is depends on how much water is being released from Spicer. During the spring, and often well into the summer, the releases can be high enough to make fishing difficult. Try checking one of the sports stores in Arnold (listed below) to find out how much water is being released before making the trek to Spicer.

SPICER RESERVOIR

What could have been an excellent fishing area is at best mediocre thanks to the greed of some anglers and the unwillingness of the Department of Fish and Game to do anything about it .

Spicer was built in the 1980s to replace a smaller dam, cutting off the main spawning area for trout in the lake. The trout tried to spawn in a canal from nearby Utica Reservoir to Spicer Reservoir. The canal, Hobart Ditch, became known as Slaughter Gulch because the big spawners were trapped and became prey to anglers who killed them by the hundreds. Some locals called on the DFG to institute special regulations, but the state agency didn't take action, and within a few years, most of the big fish in Spicer were dead, carted off to somebody's freezer instead of being allowed to spawn.

So now all Spicer has to offer is so-so fishing for planted rainbows, Kamloops, and cuttbows—a cross between cutthroat and rainbow trout. For fly fishers, working the shoreline, either in small boats or with float tubes, is the most productive way to ply this long, narrow lake.

LAKE ALPINE

Lake Alpine is one of the prettiest of the lakes in the high Sierra, with deep, blue waters and wooded hillsides. It sits at 7,350 feet right alongside Highway 4 and is a popular destination for campers, hikers, and anglers. There are a number of lakeside campgrounds, along with a store and restaurant.

For the fly-line angler, it's a great place to visit, but not at the top of the fishing list. Since much of Lake Alpine is deep, most of the time, trolling with lures or fishing with bait is the best way to go. However, there generally is an evening hatch at the lower end of the lake that can bring big trout to the surface for an hour or so before dark. At that time, using a small boat or a float tube near the dirt dam at the lower end of the lake can get a fly fisher into trout. Since the hatches generally are various-sized mayflies, a Parachute Adams is the preferred pattern.

MOSQUITO LAKES

From Lake Alpine, Highway 4 narrows and twists its way up to Pacific Grade Summit, where there is a popular campground at Mosquito Lakes. These two shallow lakes are heavily planted and are fun family fishing—anglers sitting in plastic lawn chairs and tossing Power Bait into the lakes are the norm. There are a few resident browns caught very occasionally. Fly fishers can pick up stockers, particularly during the evening, when they are feeding on the surface.

MOKELUMNE RIVER

While the North Fork of the Stanislaus lies to the southwest of Highway 4, the Mokelumne River is in the drainage to the northeast. The first access from Highway 4 is by way of Summit Level Road, which leads to Railroad Flat. This gravel two-lane can be accessed either at White Pines, near Arnold, or from Camp Connell, outside Dorrington.

This is country for the more adventurous angler—the entire area is honeycombed with logging roads and private land, and finding your way to fishable water is strictly trial-and-error. In addition, the Georgia Pacific Lumber Company owns much of the land, and many areas are fenced off. There are just about as many small creeks as there are roads, some big enough to hold fish throughout the season, but many too small to sustain a year-round population of trout.

Buy the latest Stanislaus National Forest map at the ranger station in Hathaway Pines and spend a day or two exploring the area. There are plenty of fish, even some bigger ones. There also are bears, rattlesnakes, and a lot of poison oak.

HERMIT VALLEY

From Pacific Grade Summit, Highway 4 drops sharply down into Hermit Valley, a pretty meadow bisected by the North Fork of the Mokelumne River. There are campgrounds,

A float tuber plies the waters of Upper Highland Lake near Ebbetts Pass.

plus some fencing to keep cattle from wandering too much.

The Mokelumne in the meadow is a little-fished resource and is particularly attractive for anglers who aren't up to strenuous hiking. Fly fishers can walk the undercut banks and toss flies, including grasshoppers, into likely spots. There aren't

Rick E. Martin

many big trout here, but it still is an easy, fun spot to fish, mostly for planted rainbows.

Also worth mentioning is Pacific Valley, a small valley with a campground just west of Hermit Valley. There is a clearly marked turnoff from Highway 4 as it drops down from Pacific Grade Summit. **Pacific Creek** meanders through the valley and offers fishing for small trout.

If you want to do some hiking, follow the trail along the North Fork of the Mokelumne downstream out of Hermit Valley and into the Mokelumne Wilderness. After a couple of miles, a major tributary, **Deer Creek,** flows into the river, almost doubling its size. Deer Creek itself has plenty of rainbows in its many plunge pools. There's also a jeep road of sorts, Forest Service Road 8No2, which leads from

Hermit Valley across the Mokelumne and up Deer Valley and Clover Valley to Lower Blue Lake. This road also can be accessed from the Blue Lake side via Highway 88.

HIGHLAND LAKES

A mile before Highway 4 reaches Ebbetts Pass, a dirt road leads 5 miles south to Highland Lakes, a pair of snow-fed, high-altitude lakes that are the headwaters for both Highland Creek and the North Fork of the Mokelumne. The 5-mile road to the lakes goes through a narrow valley cut by the Mokelumne, which flows out of Lower Highland Lake. This is pretty fly-fishing water, particularly in June or July, after the first rush of snowmelt and before it becomes so low and clear that the fish are extremely spooky. Because of the altitude and heavy snowfall, Highway 4 over Ebbetts Pass generally isn't opened by Caltrans until late April or early May, and during heavy snow years, it may take a month longer for the road to Highland Lakes to clear.

When the water drops to a fishable level, fly anglers will find this section of the Mokelumne is loaded with rainbows—including some large holdover stockers—along with brookies and an occasional brown. I "discovered" the area by accident many years ago. I had been fishing Highland Lakes and stopped in the valley to have a luncheon sandwich. Since I could eat with one hand, I grabbed a fly rod with the other and tossed a Royal Wulff into the water, where it immediately was gobbled by a twelve-inch rainbow. Lunch forgotten, I became serious. The result was a forty-fish afternoon, with dozens of brookies in the seven-to-ten-inch class and a scattering of rainbows that ran up to fourteen inches. I've never had as good a day since, but I've still caught plenty of fish there.

At that point I had fished Highland Lakes a dozen times and never had stopped to fish the Mokelumne because every time I asked a bait or lure angler "How's the fishing?" I got a negative reply. This proves that bait and lure anglers might not be catching fish, but sometimes fly-line types can hit a jackpot—and also that you should never trust what another angler tells you.

Highland Lakes themselves are tough fishing, but the trout are there, including stocked rainbows. Since the little lakes sit high in the Sierra and are not protected, they are constantly swept by wind. A float tube is about the only way to work the lakes properly, and in one you're constantly battling with the wind. At times I've had to put in on the upwind side, let myself be blown across the lake, then walk back along the bank and start again.

Upper Highland Lake is the headwaters of Highland Creek, which feeds Spicer Reservoir, and an avid angler can follow a steep creekside trail downstream into the Carson-Iceberg Wilderness and all the way to the reservoir, about 5 miles away. It is fun fishing, but not easy going, so don't try to do it in one day if you want to get plenty of fishing time.

KINNEY LAKES

Just to the east of Ebbetts Pass is Kinney Reservoir, a stocked, roadside fishery that can be fun if you can get there during ice-out. Less than a mile to the north along a path that leads from the reservoir are Upper and Lower Kinney Lakes, which have more wild trout than the reservoir. Although I've had some luck on the two lakes, I've also had days when I would swear there wasn't a fish there.

RAYMOND, NOBLE, AND BULL LAKES

If you're trying for a miniature grand slam of brook, cutthroat, and golden trout, the Pacific Crest Trail where it crosses Highway 4 near Ebbetts Pass offers the opportunity. To the north, the Pacific Crest Trail winds by Upper Kinney Lake and another few miles to Raymond Lake, which is above 9,100 feet and has golden trout. To the south of Highway 4, the trail leads 4 miles to Noble Lake, which has big brookies. A trail from there leads another 4 miles to Bull Lake, located in Bull Canyon, where cutthroat can be found. So this mini grand slam is strictly for the avid hiker. You can buy detailed U.S. Forest Service maps for the Carson-Iceberg Wilderness and the Mokelumne Wilderness at the ranger station in Hathaway Pines or in Markleeville.

THE MOKELUMNE WILDERNESS

The Mokelumne Wilderness is a 105,165-acre area between Highways 4 and 88 in portions of the Stanislaus, El Dorado, and Toiyabe National Forests. In addition to gaining access from Highway 4 along the Pacific Crest Trail, hikers can enter from Highway 88, either from Caples Lake or from the road to Upper and Lower Blue Lakes. The North Fork of the Mokelumne River flows through the wilderness deep inside a rugged canyon, but there are trails that lead to the water, including one from Mount Reba, near the Bear Valley Ski Resort.

Like most ventures into wilderness areas, a hiking trip here needs to be planned and will take several days. Mokelumne Wilderness maps and wilderness permits are available from a number of National Forest Service stations, including the Hathaway Pines Stanislaus National Forest Ranger Station and the Alpine Ranger Station near Bear Valley, as well as from the Alpine County Visitors Bureau in Markleeville (see below for details). Mokelumne Peak, 9,334 feet high, and the neighboring Mokelumne Tetons dominate the landscape in this area.

Other ways to enter the wilderness area are through Hermit Valley (see above) or by driving to Salt Springs Reservoir and then hiking upstream along the North Fork. The road to Bear River Reservoir and Salt Springs Reservoir branches off from Highway 88 on the way to Jackson.

SUMMING UP

The closest thing I have to home turf is one of the most beautiful sections of the Sierra Nevada—rugged, conifer-covered mountains, myriad streams and rivers, and enough fishing so that you can go for days without encountering other anglers. It's not easy fishing in any sense. Strong hikers willing to explore can have a field day working their way upstream or downstream from access points on the **North Fork of the Stanislaus.** An alternative is to fish the **Mokelumne River** northeast of Highway 4. And although there also are a few lakes that offer good fishing, the best are hike-in waters such as **Noble Lake, Bull Lake,** and **Raymond Lake.** For really serious hikers, there is the Mokelumne River Canyon, which cuts through the Mokelumne Wilderness on the spine of the Sierra.

Personally, I like to start the season as far up as I can get on **Beaver Creek.** It is easy wading, and although the trout aren't big, there are a lot of them and they are hungry. In June or so, when the snowmelt eases, the **North Fork of the Mokelumne** coming out of Highland Lakes can be a blast, particularly if you can get in before the DFG has begun stocking.

The North Fork of the Stanislaus and **Highland Creek** below Spicer Reservoir have plenty of fish, but you need to work these waters properly. In other words, pick your spots, and if they don't produce, move on.

✦ ✦ ✦ ✦ ✦ ✦

ADDITIONAL INFORMATION

FLY SHOPS

White Pines Outdoors, 2182 Highway 4, Arnold, CA 95223; (209) 795-1054. A full-service fly-fishing shop with some other fishing gear.

Ebbetts Pass Trading Post, Arnold Plaza, 925 Highway 4, Arnold, CA 95223; (209) 795-1686. A general sporting-goods store with a good stock of fly-fishing equipment.

The Bear's Lair, 18880 Highway 88, Lockford, CA 95237; (209) 727-0200. A fishing and gift shop with a good selection of fly-fishing gear.

HOSPITALS

Arnold: Arnold Medical Clinic, 2182 Highway 4, Suite A100, Arnold, CA 95223; (209) 795-4193. Arnold Family Medical Center, 2037 Highway 4, Arnold, CA 95223; (209) 795-1270.

San Andreas: Mark Twain St. Joseph's Hospital, 768 Mountain Ranch Road, San Andreas, CA 95249; (209) 754-3521.

Sonora: Tuolumne General Hospital, 101 Hospital Road, Sonora, CA 95370; (209) 533-7100. Sonora Community Hospital, 14540 Highway 108, Sonora, CA 95370; (209) 532-3167.

PUBLIC CAMPING

Most of the campgrounds in this area are in the Stanislaus National Forest Calaveras Ranger District on Highway 4 in Hathaway Pines. Their address is P.O. Box 500, Hathaway Pines, CA 95233 and their phone is (209) 795-1381. Campfire permits are not required in most developed campgrounds, but are necessary in other camping areas and can be obtained from the ranger station. If you know where you want to stay, call MISTIX at (800) 280-2267 for reservations.

For information on camping in Calaveras Big Trees State Park, write them at P.O. Box 120, Arnold, CA 95223, or call the park at (209) 795-2334.

NEW MELONES RESERVOIR

The Bureau of Reclamation, the U.S. government agency that handles the reservoir, can be reached at (209) 536-9094.

New Melones Lake Marina, 6503 Glory Hole Road, Angels Camp, CA 95222; (209) 785-3300. This is a full-service marina and rents fishing and patio boats, along with houseboats.

A source for fishing information on New Melones Reservoir is Glory Hole Sports, 2892 Highway 49, Angels Camp, CA 95222; (209) 736-4333.

MORE SOURCES

The Calaveras Lodging and Visitor's Association, P.O. Box 637, Angels Camp, CA 95222; (800) 225-3764. Web site: www.calaveras.org/visit.html.

The Alpine County Visitor's Information Bureau, #3 Webster Street, Markleeville, CA 96120; (530) 694-2475. Fax: (916) 694-2478. E-mail: alpcnty@telis.org.

Alpine Station, Highway 4, 1.5 miles east of Bear Valley; (209) 753-2811.

CHAPTER 9: HIGHWAY 108

Great Pickin's in the Mother Lode

Paolo Marchesi

THE Highway 108 corridor winding east to Sonora Pass abuts a series of canyons and gorges offering limited access to water, but where you can get to streams and rivers, it is a fly fisher's bonanza. In fact, it has a stretch of arguably the best water on the western side of the Sierra Nevada, the Wild Trout section of the Stanislaus River's Middle Fork below Beardsley Reservoir.

Wait, there's more! Fly-line types are just beginning to discover the variety of streams here, and the scenery is spectacular. Unlike Highway 4 along the North Fork of the Stanislaus, Highway 108 passes through a series of small towns geared for tourists. There's a good choice of hotels, motels, eateries, and other amenities stretching from the town of Sonora 30 miles up the road to Strawberry. Camping areas abound, and Kennedy Meadows boasts a pack station that caters to anglers who want to ride horses into any of the prolific fishing lakes that dot this section of the high Sierra, including some in Yosemite National Park. Kennedy Meadows, about 10 miles west of Sonora Pass, also is the jumping-off point for hardy backpackers who ply backcountry lakes and streams. Highway 108 should go on any fly fisher's "I've got to try it" list. But hurry, because other folks are discovering it, too.

The stalk: Dan Leichty works his fly through prime holding water on the Middle Fork of the Stanislaus River.

As is true in so much of the western Sierra Nevada, the angling here is what you make of it. Where you can reach a river or stream is just the beginning of the journey—hiking is necessary to get to better areas and away from stocked fish. Some hiking is easy going, along well-defined, bankside trails; other places demand more stamina and rock-scrambling ability.

THE MIDDLE FORK OF THE STANISLAUS RIVER

Let's start with the best first, the stretch of the Middle Fork below Beardsley Reservoir, an impoundment that sits at an elevation of 3,405 feet. This tailwater Wild Trout fishery stretches about 17 miles, down to where the North and Middle Forks of the Stanislaus join as they feed into New Melones Reservoir. (See the Highway 4 chapter for details on the North Fork and New Melones.)

Regulations vary on this piece of water. The small afterbay just below Beardsley Reservoir has a two-trout limit, fourteen inches and larger, and requires barbless flies and lures. It can be fished all year. For about 3 miles downstream, from the afterbay to the U.S. Forest Service footbridge at Spring Gap, the regulations are the same, but the season is from the last Saturday in April until November 15. Downstream from the footbridge to New Melones there is a two-trout limit, but all methods of taking fish can be used. The

Middle Fork is not planted along this entire stretch, so it holds only wild trout, with a fifty-fifty split between rainbows and browns.

This part of the Stanislaus Middle Fork can be broken into three sections defined by access points—the afterbay and river 3 miles downstream to the Spring Gap footbridge, the river from the footbridge 3 miles to the access at Sand Bar Flat Campground, and the river from Sand Bar Flat 11 miles to New Melones Reservoir.

BEARDSLEY AFTERBAY AND STANISLAUS RIVER TO SPRING GAP FOOTBRIDGE

This is the best-known and most heavily fly fished section of the Stanislaus, and for good reason. Big rainbows and browns ply the waters, slurping up insects and generally enjoying themselves like any tailwater trout that can count on a steady, year-round supply of cold water. The afterbay is only a few hundred yards long and moves like a slow-flowing river. When flows are low, it is slow enough that it can be safely navigated in a float tube, an excellent way to fish what is essentially a long slick. Trout sometimes can be seen cruising the water looking for dinner or holding along the banks. Both in the afterbay and the river below it, an angler should cast to specific fish whenever possible, rather than just tossing out a nymph or dry fly and hoping for the best. Sometimes this is easy, but, if you're afoot, more often it involves creeping into a concealed position where you won't scare the fish. These trout are big and smart, and they see a lot of anglers.

The road to Beardsley branches north from Highway 108, 4 miles east of Strawberry. It is an excellent, two-lane paved road that winds 9 miles deep into the canyon to the big reservoir. Near the bottom, a turnoff to the right goes to Beardsley Point, where there is a boat ramp, while the main road continues to the earthen dam.

A paved road drops down the face of the dam to a parking area on the afterbay. This road used to follow the afterbay and river for about half a mile, but the January 1997 floods washed out a 100-yard section, leaving a jumble of big boulders that anglers must scramble across to get to the road on the downstream side. From where the road ends, a path on the north side of the river goes downstream.

Access also is possible on the south side of the river by walking along a gated road that leaves from the top of the dam and goes all the way to Sand Bar Flat. This actually is tougher access because the road for the most part is above the river, and anglers must bushwhack their way down to the water, not necessarily easy going.

Many local anglers believe the washout will help the river here. They feel it was getting too much pressure, even with the special regulations, and that the need to clamber over boulders to go downstream will cut the number of visitors.

Below the afterbay are slicks interspersed with rapids and a few small waterfalls. It is big enough water, even at minimum flows, so that wading is limited. As in the afterbay, browns and rainbows can easily be seen in the flat water, and casting to specific fish can be the way to a thirty-trout day. Working rapids and other fast water also can be effective, but the fish tend to be smaller.

The best fishing here usually begins in mid-June, after the major part of the runoff is over and the reservoir slows its releases to a maximum of 200 cubic feet per second. It tapers off a bit after September because as the weather turns colder, there are fewer hatches to stir up the fish. And let's face it, the fish become smarter as the year goes on and they see more fur and feathers floating over them.

As in most of the rest of the Sierra, caddisflies and mayflies are the main bugs, along with some stoneflies. A good early-season pattern is a Golden Stone in about a size 8. As the year progresses and the fish get wiser, it pays to drop from size 12 or 14 to 16 or smaller in caddis and mayfly imitations. Midges also are in the river's makeup, and there are times when the trout key on them and it is hard to get fish to take anything else.

But you never know about trout. Pat Twohig, owner of the Mother Lode Fly Shop in Sonora, tells of the angler who wanted something "big and ugly" and ended up buying some red-and-silver Lefty's Deceivers on a 2/0 hook, a fly used mostly to imitate baitfish in the ocean.

"He caught some big browns, and now he comes back a couple of times a month and usually catches some nice fish," Twohig laughed. "And he doesn't use anything but Deceivers."

This same stretch of water can be fished by working upstream from the Spring Gap footbridge. To get to Spring Gap—and to Sand Bar Flat—take the Spring Gap Road turnoff from Highway 108, just west of Cold Springs. At Fraser Flat, 2.5 miles from Highway 108, the road crosses the South Fork of the Stanislaus. This is a popular river campground, and the area is hard hit by bait and lure anglers, but can be fished upstream or downstream.

The dirt road eventually forks, with Spring Gap to the right and Sand Bar Flat to the left. It is about 13 miles from the South Fork to either of these Middle Fork accesses. To get to Sand Bar Flat, stay left at the various intersections—some are marked, some aren't—until you reach Forest Service Road 4N85, which, if vandals have been active, may also be unmarked. This road leads over the hill and dale to Sand Bar Flat. The road to Spring Gap doesn't go all the way to the river, but anglers can park and follow a gated PG&E gravel road a scant .8 miles to the footbridge.

SPRING GAP FOOTBRIDGE TO SAND BAR FLAT

An alternative to walking to the river at Spring Gap is to drive to Sand Bar Flat along the same road. Sand Bar Flat is a popular campground and heavily used by lure anglers. Hiking upstream is easy along a trail on the south side of the

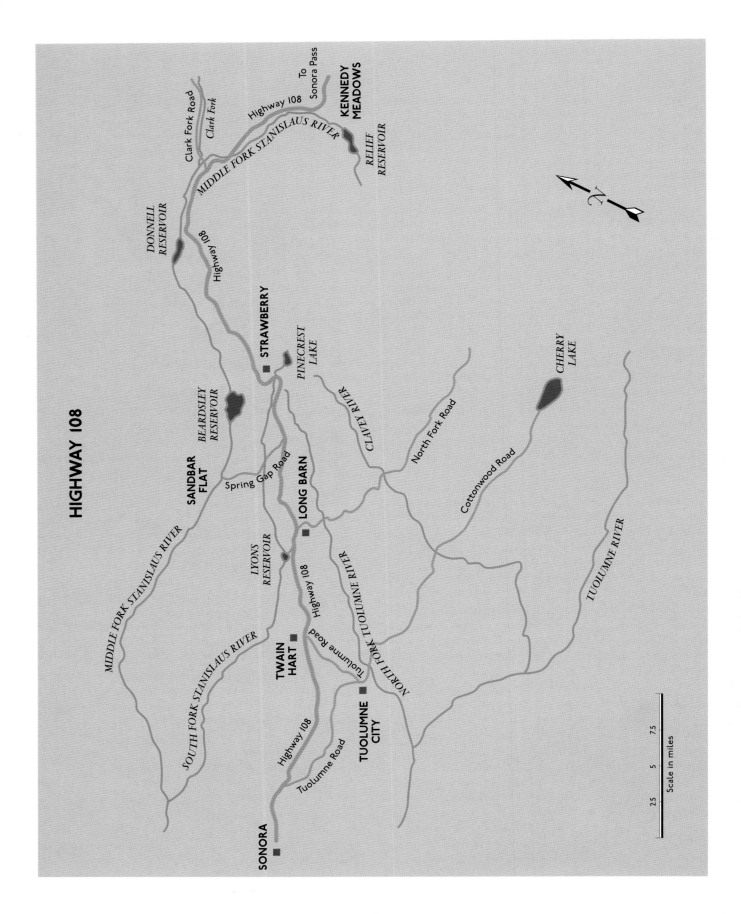

Paolo Marchesi

The hookup: Fish on!

river, and a twenty-minute walk gets anglers away from most competition.

SAND BAR FLAT TO NEW MELONES RESERVOIR

This area, accessed from Sand Bar Flat, is described by local fly-line anglers as "a little secret" that offers great fishing as far as a fly fisher wants to walk. What passes as a trail actually is on the south side of the river, but anglers need to cross the river at Sand Bar Flat (there is a bridge), then walk downstream and recross the river over a small plank bridge.

There are plenty of fish from eight to eighteen inches, and the hiking angler can have a field day. As with the rest of the river, caddis imitations such as the Z-Wing Caddis, Elk Hair Caddis, and Goddard's Caddis work well, along with the Adams and other mayfly varieties, including Pale Morning Duns and Light Cahills. For nymphs, Bird's Nests, Pheasant Tails, Zug Bugs, and big stonefly imitations are favored.

ABOVE BEARDSLEY RESERVOIR

The Middle Fork of the Stanislaus from Beardsley Reservoir upstream to Donnell Lake flows deep in a rugged gorge with no direct access except at Hells Half Acre, just above the reservoir. To get to this starting point, follow Forest Service Road 5N06, which turns off Beardsley Road a couple of miles from Highway 108.

For those who want real adventure, Forest Service Road 5N09Y parallels the river, but to get to the water involves some major scrambling down the hillside. This is for strong, experienced bushwhackers only. Once on the river, it is difficult to move upstream or downstream because of large rocks, dense vegetation, deadfalls and other obstacles. Not surprisingly, though, the fishing can be quite good.

A couple of miles above Donnell Lake, a reservoir that sits at almost 5,000 feet, the Middle Fork joins Highway 108 and is easily accessible all the way to Kennedy Meadows. If you're going that way, take a few minutes to stop at the Donnell Vista, which offers a beautiful view of the lake and the river canyon.

The stretch of the Stanislaus along Highway 108 is a favorite playground for camping, hiking, and fishing. It is pretty water, a typical Sierra freestone stream tumbling down the mountain. And it does contain fish, although most of them are stocked rainbows. There are a number of campgrounds along this 9-mile stretch of river. On the positive side, fly fishing sometimes can produce multifish days, even if most are hatchery rainbows.

Kennedy Meadows, with a summertime grocery store, private campground, and horse packing operation, is a mile off Highway 108. The Stanislaus flows through the meadow and for 4 miles to **Relief Reservoir,** the headwaters of the Middle Fork. The road is closed to vehicular traffic from Kennedy Meadows, but anglers can walk upstream and fish the meadows if they don't mind rubbing shoulders with a couple of hundred head of cattle and fishing for mostly stocked trout. Hikers can fish the river all the way to the reservoir by following the trail that leads out of Kennedy Meadows.

Kennedy Meadows is the jumping-off point for fishing a series of excellent high-country lakes. Backpackers with time and legs of steel can do it on foot, but for old folks like me, a better bet is to use horses from the Kennedy Meadows Pack Station. They have a variety of programs, including a one-day ride-and-fish expedition to **Kennedy Lake,** which is 7 miles each way. Or you can go top-of-the-line and spend a week in the backcountry with everything provided by the pack station, including a cook. Another reason for using horses is so you can take in a float tube, a key to fishing many of the lakes.

Prime destinations, whether by horse or foot, are the **Emigrant Lakes** and **Huckleberry Lake.** The two Emigrant Lakes are about 15 miles from Kennedy Meadows and Huckleberry is 21, sitting on the edge of Yosemite National Park. There are numerous other small lakes around Huckleberry that offer fine fishing. These lakes in the Emigrant Wilderness, which makes up the eastern section of the Stanislaus National Forest, offer big browns and brookies, many in the twenty-inch range.

An alternative is the Carson-Iceberg Wilderness, which can be accessed from north of Kennedy Meadows. There are a number of lakes there that offer good fishing, not to mention a variety of streams. Some of these are named in the Highway 4 chapter.

Since this is high country, it's best to wait until July to trek in, and early October is pretty much the end of the season.

THE CLARK FORK OF THE STANISLAUS

The Clark Fork of the Stanislaus joins the Middle Fork several miles above Donnell Lake, flowing in from the north. The Clark Fork road from Highway 108 follows the river for nearly 10 miles before it dead-ends in Iceberg Meadow, where the Carson-Iceberg Wilderness begins.

The Clark Fork is a pretty stretch of small-stream water, with riffles, runs, and rapids. It also offers lots of access and because of this mostly provides put-and-take hatchery rainbows. There are a number of heavily used roadside campgrounds and picnic areas that draw families from all over.

Wild-trout aficionados can park at the end of the road and follow a well-marked trail upstream into the Carson-Iceberg Wilderness and all the way to Sonora Pass. This trail is a favorite with horse packers and backpackers. There also are a number of other trails worth exploring for the angler. One leads from the Clark Fork Horse Camp on Clark Fork Road north to Spicer Reservoir on the North Fork of the Stanislaus. It crosses a number of small streams that have good fishing, including **Highland Creek,** which is the main source of the North Fork. (See Chapter 8.) Backpacking anglers should buy detailed U.S. Forest Service maps of the Stanislaus National Forest and the Carson-Iceberg Wilderness before starting a backcountry trip.

The Clark Fork is a better fishery early in the year, when snowmelt keeps it flowing. Late in the season it becomes low, and the fish are spooky and hard to catch.

SOUTH FORK OF THE STANISLAUS

There are only a few access points to the South Fork of the Stanislaus, but they can lead to productive fishing. One of the best is at Lyons Reservoir, 2 miles from Highway 108. The Lyons Reservoir Road goes north from Highway 108 just past Sierra Village, which is between the towns of Mi-Wuk Village and Long Barn. It is at the end of a little-used California Highway Patrol truck checkpoint and is clearly marked.

Also clearly marked is the fact that this road is closed at sundown, so don't overstay your welcome, or you won't be able to get back on Highway 108 through the gate at the end of the road. There are signs to this effect both at the beginning of the road and at Lyons Reservoir.

From Lyons Reservoir, walk across the dam to the north side, then follow the trail upstream from where the South Fork flows in. The trail is an old railroad bed and is ideal for mountain bikers, whether they are there for the angling or the exercise. The fish here are mostly browns, including some decent-sized ones. Just pick your spot and fish it thoroughly. Below the dam, the South Fork has little water in it and isn't worth fishing, except very early in the season.

An alternative way to reach the upstream section and the old railroad bed is via Forest Service roads that honeycomb the area and that are accessible from the road to Sand Bar Flat. You'll need a map, some time, and a willingness to explore.

The same piece of water, which stretches for about 5 miles, also can be reached by way of a downstream trail from Fraser Flat, which is a popular campground on the South Fork reached by way of Spring Gap Road (see the Middle Fork of the Stanislaus section above). From Fraser Flat, anglers also can fish upstream 4 miles to Strawberry on Highway 108, where the South Fork crosses the road after flowing out of Pinecrest Lake. Forest Service Road 4N13 from Fraser Flat goes close to the river for most of the way.

From the Highway 108 crossing, anglers can fish upstream to Pinecrest, a mile-long stretch of water. Above Pinecrest, there is no access to the South Fork except by hiking.

The South Fork is smaller than the Middle Fork, and as a result is a better early-season trout stream. It is planted at access points, but otherwise holds a good wild-trout population.

A WORD ABOUT LYONS RESERVOIR AND PINECREST LAKE

There is no boating, float tubing, or swimming allowed in Lyons Reservoir because it supplies drinking water for the area. It is stocked with trout and is popular with bank anglers, but it also holds a solid population of bass, even though it is at 4,228 feet.

Pinecrest Lake is very popular for boating and fishing and is heavily stocked with rainbows. Occasionally, local fly fishers will float tube it just before the season closes, when there aren't as many boats or vacationers as during the summer. At this time, the lake is well below its highest level, and the fish are concentrated.

LOWER STANISLAUS RIVER

A section of the Stanislaus River worth mentioning, even though it is pretty much out of the Sierra Nevada and into the San Joaquin Valley, is near Knights Ferry on Highways 108/120 below Goodwin Dam. It has a Wild Trout designation.

This stretch of water is reached either from the turnoff to the south shore of Tullock Reservoir (at the end of a stretch of four-lane highway if you're going west, the beginning if you are traveling east) or from Knights Ferry. It is a tailwater fishery with big trout and is open from January 1 until October 31, which makes it particularly popular during the early part of the year, when other rivers are closed. When releases from Tullock are high, it is tough to fish, but when water flows are low, it can be very productive with both nymphs and dries.

Regulations vary. From Goodwin Dam downstream to the covered bridge near Knight's Ferry, they dictate catch-and-release, barbless hooks, and no bait; from the covered bridge downstream to Orange Blossom Bridge, two trout, twelve inches or longer, can be kept, and only flies or lures with barbless hooks can be used; from Orange Blossom Bridge downstream, there are no tackle restrictions, and two legal-sized trout can be kept.

THE NORTH FORK OF THE TUOLUMNE AND THE CLAVEY RIVER

To the southwest of Highway 108, the North Fork of the Tuolumne and the Clavey River flow through narrow canyons. Both are accessible at a couple of spots on paved roads that turn off from the highway. The Tuolumne is planted near the road, but offers wild trout for hikers. The Clavey is one of California's original Wild Trout rivers and has only wild fish.

The first access to both rivers is on the road that goes to Tuolumne City, which branches off from Highway 108 just north of Sonora or from the highway at Twain Harte about 10 miles east. From Tuolumne City, this road—which leads to Cherry Lake—drops into a canyon and crosses the Tuolumne at River Ranch Campground, a private camping area. You can fish for planters here or work upstream or downstream for wild trout.

Another 13 miles along the road it crosses the Clavey River. The bridge is high above the river, and it is tough to get to the water, but once there, anglers can fish either upstream or downstream. It isn't easy going, with plenty of big boulders impeding progress.

Cherry Lake, part of the Hetch Hetchy water system that serves San Francisco, is 30 miles from the Highway 108 turnoff, and the road is paved all the way. Cherry Lake itself is popular with boaters, and bait and lure fishing is more effective than fly-line angling.

The second access to the Tuolumne North Fork and the Clavey is through the town of Long Barn along Merrill Springs / North Fork Road. A bridge crosses the Tuolumne 3 miles from Highway 108, and it is another 12 miles to the Clavey.

Both rivers offer better early-season fishing, since they tend to become little more than trickles late in the year. Another early-season alternative is **Trout Creek,** reached by way of a clearly signed Forest Service road that turns off shortly before you cross the Clavey.

Two other possibilities are **Jawbone** and **Reed Creeks,** both of which cross the road to Cherry Lake between the Clavey River and the reservoir. For those who want to explore, Forest Service and logging roads crisscross the entire area and lead to a variety of small streams, all of which have fish in them. They aren't big trout, but fishing attractors when the water is flowing can be a fun way to spend an early-summer day.

SUMMING UP

The **Middle Fork of the Stanislaus** downstream from Beardsley Reservoir provides some of the best fishing on the western slope of the Sierra Nevada, offering plenty of big brown and rainbow trout. It is officially designated a Wild Trout, catch-and-release stream by the DFG, although in this case "catch-and-release" means you can keep two trout fourteen inches or longer. There are several access points, but then you have to use foot power to get to the best water. The prime time to fish this area begins in June after the spring runoff and lasts through the summer.

For early-season fishing, try the **South Fork of the Stanislaus** above Lyons Reservoir, a drive-in, hike-upstream destination. There are plenty of fish in this pretty stretch of water, including some big browns.

Anglers who aren't fanatics about catching only wild trout have a variety of planted waters to sample. The **Middle Fork** from a few miles above Donnell Lake to Kennedy Meadows has roadside access and is a pretty, freestone Sierra stream. The same holds true of the **Clark Fork of the Stanislaus,** which flows into the Middle Fork from the north. Both have multiple U.S. Forest Service campgrounds and are popular summer destinations.

Backpackers and serious hikers have a choice of excellent fishing destinations. Each of Forks of the Stanislaus accessible from Highway 108, not to mention the **North Fork of the Tuolumne** and the **Clavey,** has miles of water that offer good wild-trout fishing for the angler willing to scramble upstream or downstream from a handful of roadside access points. In addition, there is the Emigrant Wilderness, reached

Paolo Marchesi

from Kennedy Meadows, an area that offers fishing for big trout in lakes high in the Sierra. **Huckleberry** and **Immigrant Lakes** are the most noted destinations, but there are plenty of lesser-known lakes that are just as good. Most of the lakes are far enough into the wilderness to require multiday backpacking trips. An exception is **Kennedy Lake,** which is 7 miles from Kennedy Meadows and can be fished in one day. An alternative is to take advantage of one of the horse-packing trips offered by the Kennedy Meadows Pack Station. An added plus, apart from making it easier on your legs, is that you can bring along a float tube, an excellent way to have a thirty-fish day on some of the lakes.

Flies are the usual Sierra collection of dries and nymphs, along with terrestrials such as black ant and grasshopper imitations. On the Wild Trout section below Beardsley, use size 12 to 14 dries early in the season, going down to size 16 and smaller later in the year.

◆ ◆ ◆ ◆ ◆

The Landing: Dan Leichty shows why it's sometimes wise to carry a net.

ADDITIONAL INFORMATION

FLY SHOPS

Mother Lode Fly Shop, 14841 Mono Way, Sonora, CA 95370; (209) 532-8600. Fax: (209) 532-1519. A full-service fly shop.

Sierra Angler, 3600 Sisk Road, Modesto, CA 95356; (209) 545-9555. A full-service fly shop.

HOSPITALS

Tuolumne General Hospital, 101 Hospital Road, Sonora, CA 95370; (209) 533-7100.

Sonora Community Hospital, 14540 Highway 108, Sonora, CA 95370; (209) 532-3167.

PUBLIC CAMPING

There are numerous U.S. Forest Service campgrounds in the area, but because this is a popular vacation corridor, they can fill up quickly during summer holidays such as Memorial Day, the Fourth of July, and Labor Day. For a list of campgrounds, contact the Mi Wok Ranger District, Highway 108, P.O. Box 100, Mi Wuk Village, CA 95346; (209) 586-3234, or the Stanislaus National Forest, 19777 Greenley Road, Sonora, CA 95370; (209) 532-3671. If you know what campground you'll stay at, reservations can be made by calling (800) 280-2267.

MORE SOURCES

The Tuolumne County Visitors Bureau, P.O. Box 4020, 55 West Stockton Street, Sonora, CA 95370; (800) 446-1333 or (209) 533-4420. They will provide free brochures on places to stay, eat, and other services available in the area.

Kennedy Meadows Resort and Pack Station, P.O. Box 4010, Sonora, CA 95370; (209) 965-3900.

CHAPTER 10: THE YOSEMITE PARK AREA
Tourist Mecca, Fly-Fisher's dream.

Bill Sunderland

YOSEMITE National Park's spectacular natural beauty is a thing of wonder, bringing in tourists from all over the world. Well, it's got good fishing, too, much better than would be expected, considering the millions of visitors who jam its roads, scenic overlooks, and hiking trails.

Not all that many serious anglers fish in the park, particularly fly-line types. Hikers walk the banks of the Tuolumne River (pronounced two-ALL-uh-me) at Tuolumne Meadows, high on the eastern end of the park, but not many of them dip a bit of fur and feathers into the water. Big mistake! The Tuolumne offers fine small-stream fishing.

Much the same can be said about the Merced River as it flows between jam-packed roads in Yosemite Valley. Picnickers, hikers, and just plain scenery lookers grace its banks from dawn until dusk all summer long. Only a few of them, mostly lure anglers, try their luck, usually without much success. There are big fish here, and they'll respond well to a fly, mainly because they don't see many of them. They are most used to lures and kids swimming and splashing in the cool, clear water.

Then there is the backcountry, featuring lakes high in the Sierra, some easy to get to, many involving long hikes along the park's trails. This is a gray area for anglers because the lakes in the park no longer are stocked, and many have become barren of trout.

Tuolumne Meadows, high in Yosemite National Park.

The Yosemite Valley, long inhabited by Indians, was first seen by non-natives when General Joseph Walker crossed the Sierra Nevada in 1833. The valley wasn't entered by whites until March 27, 1851, when the Mariposa Battalion commanded by James D. Savage descended into the area. It was christened "Yosemite" because they believed that was the name given by the Indians who lived there. In fact, the Indians were Miwoks who called it "Ahwahnee."

Only four years later, the first tourists visited Yosemite, predecessors of hordes that have numbered more than 50 million. Yosemite became a park during the Civil War, when Abraham Lincoln signed a bill on June 30, 1864 deeding the valley and the Mariposa Grove of trees to California. It had a checkered history until it was made a national park on October 1, 1890.

Today, the park covers 758,123 acres and has 318 lakes and 1,361 miles of flowing water within its boundaries. Access from the north is via Highway 120, known as Tioga Road in the park, which splits Yosemite more or less west to east and climbs over Tioga Pass to Highway 395 on the eastern slope of the Sierra. At 9,945 feet, this is the highest Sierra road pass and is closed in winter.

From Merced, Highway 140 enters the park at El Portal, while from Fresno, Highway 41 crosses the boundary at the South Entrance. The road to Hetch Hetchy, the big reservoir located inside the park, branches north from Highway

120 just outside the park entrance at Big Oak Flat. Few other roads are within the park, but there are 800 miles of excellent trails—this is a premier Sierra Nevada hiking destination.

Rainbows were the native trout here, and because of the spectacular falls on both the Tuolumne and Merced Rivers, they inhabited only the lower stretches of water. More than 100 years of planting put brown, rainbow, brook, and golden trout into most of the streams and lakes. There also were several unsuccessful attempts to stock graylings. Then, in the 1970s, the National Park Service cut back on stocking and completely halted the practice in 1991, which has led to the demise of fish in many lakes that do not provide natural spawning areas for trout.

The Tuolumne River in the park has no special restrictions. Not so on the Merced, where from the Happy Isle Footbridge in Yosemite Valley downstream to the Pohono Bridge, five brown trout can be kept and fishing is with barbless flies and lures. Rainbows must be released, a regulation aimed at restoring the river to native-trout status.

From the Yosemite Park boundary downstream to Foresta Bridge, no rainbow trout can be kept, although two brown trout may be taken. Fishing, which is open all year, is only with barbless hooks and flies. Below Foresta Bridge to Lake McClure there are no restrictions during the normal season, from the last Saturday in April to November 15, but from November 16 until the general season begins again in the spring, only two trout can be kept.

THE TUOLUMNE RIVER

The Tuolumne River begins at Tuolumne Meadows, 10 miles west of Tioga Pass, where the Lyell Fork and the Dana Fork converge near the Tuolumne Meadows Visitor Center. Tuolumne Meadows sits at 8,600 feet and is the largest subalpine meadow in the Sierra Nevada.

Both the Dana Fork, which parallels Highway 120 from Tioga Pass, and the Lyell Fork, which can be reached by a trail from the visitor's center, offer great small-stream fishing. The trail along the Lyell Fork, called the John Muir Trail in the park, is part of the Pacific Crest Trail, which stretches the length of the Sierra Nevada—and from the Canadian to Mexican borders. It follows the Lyell Fork or is nearby for the entire 10 miles to its headwaters.

It's not a difficult trail and gets heavy hiking traffic. Still, this stretch of water is not fished much and is a great area for a day hike. The trout are brookies and browns, with the brookies more prevalent at the higher elevations. Most are small, with occasional larger browns. Attractors such as Yellow Humpies or Royal Wulffs work just fine in size 12 or 14. As in most of the higher Sierra streams, the hatches are few, and the fish are hungry.

The Dana Fork, which gets its name from its headwaters on 13,053-foot-high Mount Dana just west of Tioga Pass, has less water, but easier access. The stream flows through Dana Meadows, near Highway 120, then turns into pocket water alongside the highway until it joins the Lyell Fork. Fish here are browns, brookies, and some rainbows, but are smaller than in the Lyell Fork.

From the inception of the Tuolumne River at the beginning of Tuolumne Meadows until it drops into the Tuolumne Canyon 3 miles later, the river meanders back and forth across a green-and-gold landscape surrounded by granite peaks that take your breath away. You can't fish here without stopping occasionally to gaze at the beauty that is one of nature's wonders.

Tuolumne Meadows is a popular spot in Yosemite, and there is a constant traffic of cars creeping along Highway 120 and hikers walking along the trails on day trips or on their way to the backcountry. The river, wide and shallow, with little bankside vegetation, is within a few hundred yards to a half a mile from the road all the way.

With so much activity, it is surprising how little of it involves fishing. To begin with, this isn't a river for lures—fly fishing is the way to go. Late in the summer and into the fall, the river is low and clear and the fish, mostly brookies and browns, are spooky. But they also are preparing for a long, cold winter, so they'll grab anything that looks like food as long as they aren't scared away. Fish the undercut banks and any other area that seems to offer protection.

You have to present a low profile and make your casts light and long to be successful. What you offer isn't that important—attractors, ants, and hoppers are all you need for a thirty-fish day. The trout aren't that big, but they fight like mad and have colors so spectacular you'll be reaching for your camera with even an eight-inch fish.

Before following the Tuolumne out of the meadows, it might be worthwhile to mention some lakes and streams in the Tioga Pass area, both inside and outside the Yosemite National Park boundaries. Hike-in lakes within the park that definitely have fish are the **Gaylor Lakes** and **Granite Lakes**, just northwest of the pass. These five lakes are an easy day hike from Highway 120, with Middle Gaylor Lake probably the best because of its hefty population of brook trout, some of which reach fourteen inches. Outside the park, fish still are stocked in many lakes, so there is more choice. **Tioga** and **Ellery Lakes** are right beside Highway 120 east of the park entrance. They are popular with bait and lure anglers, and although they can be fly fished, they probably aren't the top choice for those who want wild trout. Another drive-up lake that contains mostly hatchery rainbows is **Saddleback Lake**, reached via a paved 2-mile road just outside the park. A resort at Saddleback rents boats and has fishing gear.

From Tuolumne Meadows downstream, the Tuolumne River is hike-in water. It drops quickly into the Grand Canyon of the Tuolumne, which stretches 25 miles to Hetch Hetchy Reservoir. A trail from the meadows follows the river and provides access either for the day hiker or the angler who wants to spend a night or two camping and fishing.

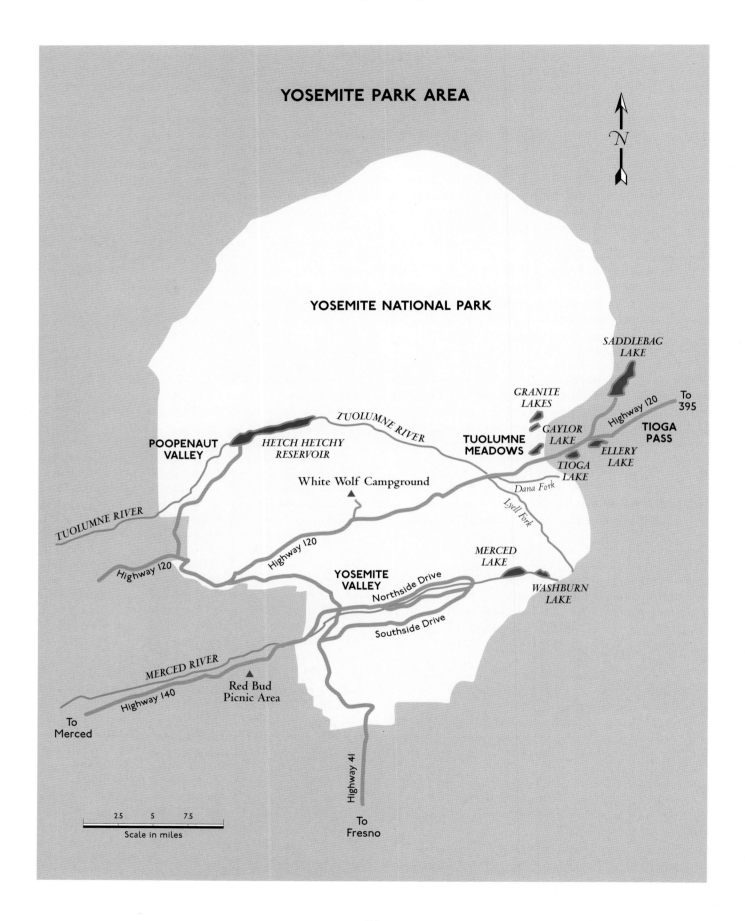

The first 10 miles of the downstream hike offer views of a number of spectacular waterfalls, culminating with Waterwheel Falls. If you don't want to hike all the way down, you can get into the lower part of the canyon by hiking the 7 miles from White Wolf Campground off Highway 120. Be warned—it is a steep trail down and a lot steeper coming back up. As is to be expected when there is not much pressure, the angling is excellent for rainbows, browns, and brookies. This stretch of water in the canyon probably provides some of the best fishing in Yosemite.

Below Hetch Hetchy Reservoir, the best fishing is at Poopenaut Valley, reached via a road that turns off Highway 120 just outside the park entrance. There is a mile-long trail from the Hetch Hetchy road dropping steeply down into the valley, a one-hour walk down, two or more coming back up. It's also prime habitant for rattlesnakes and poison oak. This is a tailwater fishery that can provide big trout; the trouble is, they are tough to get because most of them hold in deep pools. Decide for yourself if it is worth it. From Hetch Hetchy downstream to the Early Intake Diversion Dam only artificial lures with barbless hooks can be used, and the limit is two trout of twelve inches or more.

About 6 miles of the river below Hetch Hetchy is in the park, and about double that from Poopenaut Valley to the Early Intake Powerhouse downstream. From there, it is 27 miles to Don Pedro Reservoir—a total of 83 miles from the headwaters of the Lyell Fork. This entire stretch of the Tuolumne became a federal Wild and Scenic River in 1984.

THE TUOLUMNE OUTSIDE YOSEMITE NATIONAL PARK

There's good fishing (and lots of white-water rafting) on the sections downstream from Yosemite, but it is mostly rugged hiking country with only a few access points. The first way in is from the Kirkwood Trailhead, which can be reached on a paved road that goes to the Early Intake Powerhouse. This road branches off from National Forest Road 17, which is between Highway 120 and Cherry Lake. From the Early Intake Powerhouse, hike the Preston Falls Trail upstream. There are large browns on this stretch of river.

Below that, the river stretches through Jawbone Canyon to Lumsden Bridge and is a favorite white-water section for experienced rafters and kayakers. Note that the water level can fluctuate rapidly because of releases from the powerhouse. Go into the canyon from the lower end, at Lumsden Bridge. A trail upstream is on the opposite side of the river from the Lumsden Bridge Campground (not to be confused with the Lumsden Campground at Meral's Pool).

Downstream from Lumsden Bridge, the road follows the river for about 3 miles, although access is difficult until it reaches Lumsden Campground at Meral's Pool, a popular put-in for rafters. A better way to fish the area between the bridge and the campground at Meral's Pool is via the trail downstream from the campground at Lumsden Bridge.

From Meral's Pool downstream it is strictly hike-in (or raft-in) country, but this stretch has excellent big-trout fishing. There is a trail from the Lumsden Campground at Meral's Pool that runs 6 miles to Clavey Falls where the Clavey River enters the Tuolumne. There also are several trails off Ferretti Road, which goes from Groveland to Smith Station roughly parallel to Highway 120.

According to those who fish it regularly, this entire stretch of river is first-rate water for those who want to backpack and camp along its shores. There are lots of good-sized rainbows, with even bigger browns. From Lumsden Bridge to the Clavey River Falls, only artificial lures with barbless hooks can be used. Two fish can be kept, twelve inches or smaller.

Although for the most part rafting and fishing come during different seasons, anglers should know that the Tuolumne is very popular with white-water types when the water is high in the spring. From Cherry Creek to Meral's Pool is Class V—that's experts only—and as a result doesn't get that much pressure. But from Meral's Pool 18 miles to the Ward's Ferry takeout it is Class IV and is used heavily by commercial rafters. This stretch of river is regulated and the number of rafters controlled, so there shouldn't be that much conflict.

THE MERCED RIVER

About 30 miles of the Merced River is in Yosemite National Park, dropping 9,000 feet from its headwaters on 11,726-foot-high Merced Peak until it leaves the park at the 2,000-foot level. Along the way, it topples over two spectacular falls—Nevada Falls and 317-foot-high Vernal Falls, which marks the entrance of the Merced into Yosemite Valley. Vernal Falls, the lower of the two falls, stopped the upstream migration of trout until people planted them above the falls a century ago.

ABOVE YOSEMITE VALLEY

Trails go past Vernal and Nevada Falls, through Little Yosemite Valley, and upstream to **Merced** and **Washburn Lakes,** near the headwaters of the river. There are fish—and people and bears—all the way. This is popular hiking country, and campgrounds, particularly the one at Merced Lake, always are full. The fishing is good for brookies, browns, and rainbows, with most of them in the small category, although there are a fair share that stretch above the twelve-inch range.

Merced Lake is heavily fished, mostly by bait and lure anglers. Throwing flies can be an advantage, but is becoming less so as more people find out about the old bubble-and-fly setup that can be tossed with a spinning rod. Washburn also has fish, but not as much heavy pressure. Above Washburn, the fish are smaller (mostly brookies), and the fishing pressure is nearly nonexistent, making it excellent territory for an angler who enjoys easy casting to six-to-nine-inch nonselective trout.

YOSEMITE VALLEY

Most of the fishing inside Yosemite National Park takes place on this stretch of water, much of it by inexperienced anglers. The river runs through what is the busiest, most populated section of the valley, where campgrounds abound and where day-trip buses pour in and out in steady streams. ("Streams" is plural because the Southern and Northern Drives are one-way.) As noted above, there are special regulations here—only brown trout can be kept, and rainbows must be released. It's up to the angler to know the difference between the species.

The Merced flows for 7 miles through the valley, winding placidly through the trees. For anglers, it is easy to wade, and there is plenty of space for casting. Since most of those fishing this area do it with spinning gear, fly fishers have an advantage, particularly those who know enough to work undercut banks, downed trees, and other areas where there are spots for trout to hide.

This also is the area that took a major hit from the January 1997 floods, which wiped out half of the campgrounds in the valley (they were rebuilt outside the flood plain) and ripped the river to pieces as it flowed over the banks and crashed into the canyon below. The trout population suffered, but Mother Nature has a way of doing her own restocking program, and fishing is back to normal. Still, my suggestion for this area is to enjoy the scenery and then go someplace else to fish.

BELOW YOSEMITE VALLEY

Coming out of Yosemite Valley, the Merced drops into a gorge alongside Highway 140 (called El Portal Road inside the park). This area isn't fished much because it is tough going, clambering over rocks. That's a shame because there are plenty of fish here, including big ones, split fifty-fifty between browns and rainbows. For anglers in the know, this is the best stretch of the Merced River, both inside the park and just outside the park boundary.

If you have the legs and the desire, go to it—you can have an excellent multifish day. Because of snowmelt, the fly fishing doesn't begin here until July, which means that even though the Salmon Fly hatch extends up to this area, it comes in the spring, when the river is too high to be productive. During the period that it can be fished, there is the usual Sierra assortment of caddisflies and mayflies. Since it isn't fished much and there is a lot of pocket water, it is more a question of getting the fly into the right place than of getting the right fly.

BELOW YOSEMITE NATIONAL PARK

The Merced River is paralleled for most of its fishable length downstream from Yosemite by Highway 140. The first section is the 4-mile stretch to Foresta Bridge at the Red Bud Picnic Area, which is open to fishing all year. Only flies and lures with barbless hooks can be used, and two browns and no rainbows can be kept. Red Bud also is a major rafting put-in for the popular 29-mile run to Bagby. This is strictly a spring run, and the rafting is finished by mid-June.

Because it is open during the winter, this stretch can be a productive area in February and March, before the snowmelt begins. It is pocket water, with riffles and some rapids. Trout are of a respectable size, but not big. There are the usual Sierra bugs, plus a Salmon Fly hatch that may or may not be fishable due to water levels, along with a population of October Caddis.

From Foresta Bridge downstream to where the South Fork of the Merced enters, the main stem also provides excellent fishing, and the water is pretty much the same as upstream. There are no special restrictions below Foresta Bridge. There is a trail that follows the South Fork a couple of miles upstream to Hite Cove.

Below the South Fork to Briceburg, which is pretty much the end of the good fly fishing for trout, the river has more runs and slicks, along with deeper pools, and Highway 140 follows it all the way. By using a dirt road from Briceburg, anglers also can fish for a few miles downstream, an area that gets less pressure than those beside the highway.

SUMMING UP

The **Tuolumne River** flowing through Tuolumne Meadows in Yosemite National Park is about as pretty a place to fish as you'll find anywhere. It may not be lunkerland, but there are enough fish that you can have a multitrout day without working too hard at it. If you want to do some easy hiking, walk up the **Lyell Fork of the Tuolumne** from the Visitors Center at Tuolumne Meadows. Even easier to reach is the **Dana Fork of the Tuolumne**—it pretty much parallels Highway 120 from Tioga Pass to Tuolumne Meadows. It's a trade-off, though: easier access, smaller fish.

Another lovely place is the **Merced River** in Yosemite Valley. Unfortunately, most of the fishing pressure in the park is centered there, with most of the anglers doing more to scare the fish than to catch them. Serious fly fishers, if they have the legs, should go into the gorge below the valley. It is by far the best section of the Merced to fish, but huge boulders make it tough going to reach much of the pocket water that holds decent-sized fish. For backcountry fishing, anglers can work their way up the Merced above Yosemite Valley. It is easy hiking, although the lakes, including **Merced** and **Washburn Lakes,** and the river itself get a fair amount of pressure. To get away from the crowds, fish upstream from **Washburn Lake**—almost no anglers go that far.

✦ ✦ ✦ ✦ ✦ ✦

ADDITIONAL INFORMATION

FLY SHOPS

Sierra Angler, 3600 Sisk Road, Modesto, CA 95356; (209) 545-9555.

Yosemite Angler, 49er Shopping Center, Highways 49 and 140, Mariposa, CA 95338; (209) 966-8377.

HOSPITALS

Yosemite Park: For emergency medical care twenty-four hours a day, call (209) 372-4637. Otherwise, appointments can be made from 8:00 A.M. to 5:00 P.M., weekdays.

Sonora: Tuolumne General Hospital, 101 Hospital Road, Sonora, CA 95370; (209) 533-7100, or Sonora Community Hospital, 14540 Highway 108, Sonora, CA 95370; (209) 532-3167.

Fresno: St. Agnes Medical Center, 1303 Herndon Avenue, Fresno, CA 93720; (559) 449-3000. Also, Kaiser Permanente, 7300 N. Fresno Street, Fresno, CA 93720; (559) 448-4500. Valley Children's Hospital, 9300 Valley Children's Place, Madera, CA 93638; (559) 353-3000.

PUBLIC CAMPING

Camping in Yosemite is mostly by reservation only, year-round, and fills up well in advance. For information and to make reservations, call or write DESTINET, 9450 Carroll Park Drive, San Diego, CA 92121; (800) 436-7275. Information also may be obtained on-line at http://www.destinet.com.

For wilderness permits and for backcountry camping, contact the Wilderness Management Office, Yosemite National Park, P.O. Box 577, Yosemite National Park, CA 95389; (209) 372-0285, or for wilderness permit reservations, (209) 372-0740.

MORE SOURCES

There are excellent books on Yosemite National Park. For anglers, Steve Beck's *Yosemite Trout Fishing Guide* not only covers accessible areas, but also gives details on a number of backcountry lakes. It costs $14.95 and is published by Frank Amato Publications, P.O. Box 82112, Portland, OR 97282; (503) 653-8108.

Another book useful for hiking anglers is *Yosemite National Park,* by Jeffrey P. Schaffer, which details just about every hike within its boundaries, but doesn't say anything about the fishing. This book, which is updated regularly, costs $19.95 and is published by Wilderness Press, 2440 Bancroft Way, Berkeley, CA 94704; (800) 443-7277.

An excellent waterproof topo map of the park is published by Trails Illustrated, P.O. Box 3610, Evergreen, CO 80439.

The Tuolumne County Visitors Bureau, P.O. Box 4020, 55 West Stockton Street, Sonora, CA 95370; (800) 446-1333 or (209) 533-4420.

The Yosemite Junction Visitor Center, Highways 120 and 108; (209) 984-4636.

The Yosemite Sierra Visitors Bureau, 41729 Highway 41, Oakhurst, CA 93644; (559) 683-4636.

The Coulterville Visitor Center, 5007 Main Street, Coulterville, CA 95311; (209) 878-3074.

Mariposa Town Center, 5158 Highway 140, Mariposa, CA 95338; (800) 208-2434 or (209) 966-2456.

The Lee Vining Chamber of Commerce and Mono Lake Visitor Center, Highway 395 and 3rd Street, Lee Vining, CA 93541; (760) 647-6629 or 6595.

YOSEMITE PARK INFORMATION TELEPHONE NUMBERS

Recorded general information (weather, etc.): (209) 372-0200.

General information, live operator. This is a toll call, $1.95 for the first minute, $.95 for each additional minute: (900) 454-YOSE, 8:00 A.M. to 4:30 P.M.

Lodging reservations: (209) 252-4848.

Camping Reservations: (800) 436-7275.

CHAPTER 11: THE SAN JOAQUIN RIVER
Water and Power, and Trout

Rick Bean

THE San Joaquin, north of Fresno, between Yosemite and Kings Canyon National Parks, is an example of how California's water politics have decimated some of the state's rivers. Gene Rose, a Fresno journalist who wrote the book *San Joaquin: A River Betrayed*, says the federal government "has taken this river and diverted it to its virtual destruction. During a typical year, 98.5 percent of the water production is diverted to drainages that have little or no water." Rose describes what has happened to the San Joaquin as "an indictment of our stewardship of the rivers that should be our arteries of life." Still, there is fly fishing in the San Joaquin high in the Sierra, between the many dams and reservoirs that control its course down the western slope.

The best-known part of the San Joaquin is reached from the eastern slope of the Sierra Nevada—the Devil's Postpile section of the Middle Fork, near Mammoth Lakes. That stretch of the river is covered in the Owens River chapter.

Otherwise, there are only a few good fly-fishing sections that can be accessed without backpacking or horse packing. Although the area is dotted with lakes and myriad feeder streams that hold a good supply of trout, there seems to be

Rancheria Creek, which feeds into Huntington Lake, can offer fine fishing for large brown trout in the autumn. As the power lines imply, many impoundments in the San Joaquin River drainage were built to generate electricity.

little angling pressure, except by a handful of hikers. Most visitors to the Sierra National Forest, where these waters are located, concentrate on a handful of big reservoirs, such as Huntington Lake, Shaver Lake, and Bass Lake, which are at lower elevations and aren't noted for fly-line angling. They are stocked, have campgrounds and other amenities, and are aimed more at the Power Bait trade.

However, the Pineridge Ranger District of the Sierra National Forest says there are over 190 miles of streams and rivers and 350 lakes or reservoirs in this area—a cornucopia for the exploring angler. For those who love to hike and fish, grab some good maps, talk to the Forest Service about conditions, and go to it! Chances are you'll find numerous backcountry trout that have never seen a fly.

THE SOUTH FORK OF THE SAN JOAQUIN

The best accessible fishing is on the South Fork of the San Joaquin, which originates at Martha Lake, high in the mountains of Kings Canyon National Park, and flows into Florence Lake, one of the many impoundments created to control the river's water. Below the lake, the South Fork works its way through rugged country until it hits the main stem of the San Joaquin—the Middle Fork, which comes from the Devil's Postpile area—just before the river flows into Mammoth Pool Reservoir.

One of the better-known areas on the river is Mono Hot Springs. It is on the South Fork, at the crossroads from Florence Lake and Thomas A. Edison Lakes. The resort, which has cabins, a restaurant, and natural hot springs for bathing, is at 6,500 feet, deep in the Ansel Adams Wilderness, and is an 18-mile drive along Kaiser Pass Road from Huntington Lake. Huntington Lake and Shaver Lake are reached via Highway 168 from Fresno and are family resort areas with fishing, boating, camping, and other outdoor activities.

The river is stocked at Mono Hot springs and at Jackass Meadows, where the South Fork flows out of Florence Lake. Jackass Meadows can be reached by way of a four-wheel-drive road from the hot springs. Apart from the stocked rainbows, the entire stretch of river holds a population of wild browns in the ten-to-eighteen-inch range, along with some brookies at higher elevations.

Although the South Fork provides some of the best fishing that is easily accessible on the San Joaquin, releases from Florence Lake can mean low water late in the season. It also is rugged country and home to numerous rattlesnakes. Caddisflies and mayflies are plentiful, and in the late summer, from early August on, hopper imitations also are effective. Pocket water can be fished with Royal Wulffs or Humpies.

Some local anglers consider the fishing better just above Florence Lake. To get above the lake is either a 5-mile hike around the lake or a dip into your pocket to pay for a ride on a ferry that makes the trip once a day from a campground near the dam. Above the lake, anglers can hike upstream for about 4 miles before they run into a ranch, which is private property. The first mile or so above Florence Lake has the best fishing, with the trout becoming smaller upstream. If you are into backpacking, it is possible to hike around the ranch and rejoin the river upstream. At higher elevations, the San Joaquin also holds golden trout, but none of the fish are very big. The Pacific Crest Trail parallels the river for about 5 miles of the upper section of the South Fork.

This entire part of the Sierra is dotted with high-country lakes, some of them with good fishing. Three of the best are **Dutch Lake, Hidden Lake,** and **Crater Lake,** all west of Florence Lake. They can be reached via a trail that leaves from the Florence Lake Campground, and although it is only 3 miles, it is a steep, uphill grind. Crater Lake is the longest hike, but it has big brookies and rainbows.

A major feeder stream to the South Fork is **Mono Creek,** the main water source for Thomas A. Edison Lake. It also flows out of the lake and joins the South Fork at Mono Hot Springs. Mono Creek offers good fishing, both above and below the lake.

THE MIDDLE FORK OF THE SAN JOAQUIN

After it leaves the Devil's Postpile area, the Middle Fork is accessible only by hiking until it nears the Mammoth Pool Reservoir, a long, narrow impoundment that is a major control reservoir for the river. The best fishing is the mile or so above the reservoir. Upstream from that section is Hells Half Acre and the Ansel Adams Wilderness, and anybody who wants to fish the river will have to do some serious rock scrambling.

THE NORTH FORK OF THE SAN JOAQUIN

The North Fork of the San Joaquin originates in a series of lakes at the spine of the Sierra and flows south into the Middle Fork. There is no road access, but Minarets Road from near Shaver Lake leads to Clover Meadow Station and a four-wheel-drive road goes on to Soldier Meadows. It is about a 3-mile hike from there to the river at Sheep Crossing. Fishing for browns is good either upstream or downstream.

OTHER AREAS

For off-highway-vehicle enthusiasts, the Forest Service recommends a series of roads in the Red Mountain area south of Huntington Lake. OHV roads lead to a number of lakes, including **Mirror, West, Strawberry, Coyote,** and **Red Lakes,** all of which have rainbows and/or brookies. Small boats or float tubes can be used, although no motors, either electric or gasoline, are permitted on Coyote, since it is in the Dinkey Lakes Wilderness. For beginners, easier OHV routes lead to **Brewer, Beryl,** and **Tocher Lakes.** Information on these OHV routes can be obtained from the Pineridge Ranger Station (see below).

SUMMING UP

This is a good river drainage for backpacking anglers who want to do some high-country exploring. Apart from the Devil's Postpile stretch of the Middle Fork of the San Joaquin, which is accessible from the eastern slope of the Sierra near Mammoth Lakes and is covered in the Owens River chapter, good fly fishing is hard to come by unless your chosen pattern is Power Bait. There are a large number of lakes and streams that can be reached only by hiking or horseback, and these get very little pressure. Grab a topo map and/or a map of the Sierra National Forest and go to it! You'll probably find fish in just about every stream and lake you explore.

◆ ◆ ◆ ◆ ◆

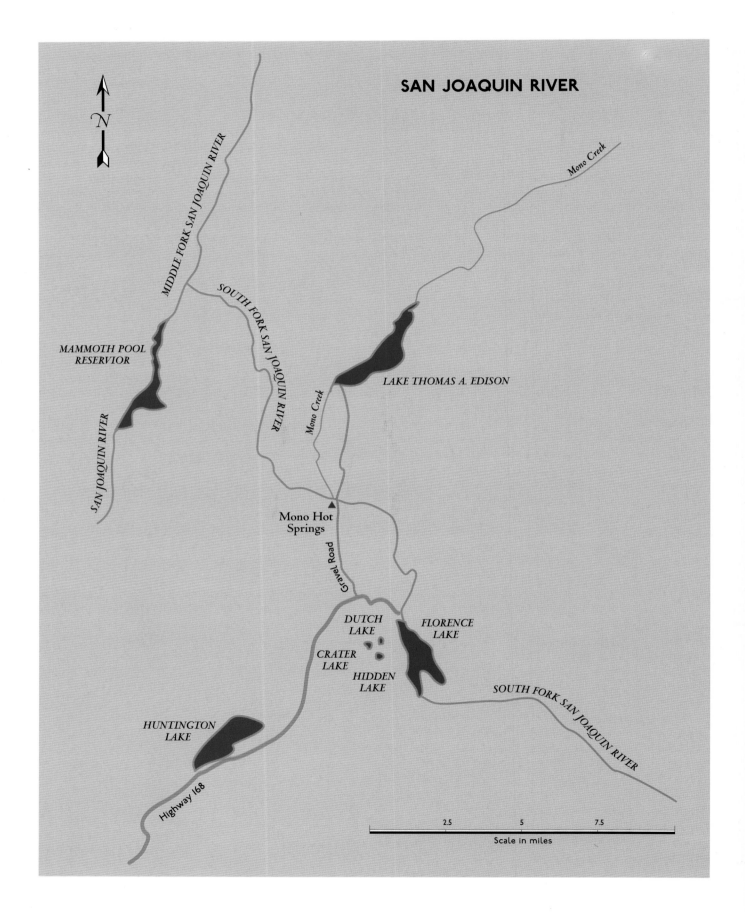

SAN JOAQUIN RIVER

N

MIDDLE FORK SAN JOAQUIN RIVER

SOUTH FORK SAN JOAQUIN RIVER

Mono Creek

MAMMOTH POOL RESERVIOR

SAN JOAQUIN RIVER

Mono Creek

LAKE THOMAS A. EDISON

Mono Hot Springs

Gravel Road

DUTCH LAKE

CRATER LAKE

HIDDEN LAKE

FLORENCE LAKE

SOUTH FORK SAN JOAQUIN RIVER

HUNTINGTON LAKE

Highway 168

| | 2.5 | 5 | 7.5 |

Scale in miles

Paolo Marchesi

Scott Milener tries to find trout below Rainbow Falls, Middle Fork of the San Joaquin River.

ADDITIONAL INFORMATION

FLY SHOPS

The Golden Trout, 618 4th Street , Clovis, CA 93612; (559) 322-9477.

Mel Cotton's Sports, 6511 N. Blackstone, Fresno, CA 93710; (559) 432-4649. Carries some fly-fishing gear.

Herb Bauer's Sports, 6264 N. Blackstone, Fresno, CA 93710; (559) 435-8600. Carries some fly tackle.

HOSPITALS

St. Agnes Medical Center, 1303 Herndon, Avenue, Fresno, CA 93720; (559) 449-3000.

Kaiser Permanente, 7300 N. Fresno Street, Fresno, CA 93720; (559) 448-4500.

Valley Children's Hospital, 9300 Valley Children's Place, Madera, CA 93638; (559) 353-3000.

PUBLIC CAMPING

Pineridge Ranger Station, P.O. Box 559, Prather, CA 93651; (559) 855-5360.

Clovis Ranger Station, 1600 Tollhouse Road, Clovis, CA 93612; (559) 297-0706.

MORE SOURCES

Mono Hot Springs Resort, General Delivery, Mono Hot Springs, CA 93642; (559) 325-1710. Their web site at http://www.monohotsprings.com includes a fishing report. The resort is open from mid-May to November 1.

Also call or write the Pineridge Ranger Station or the Clovis Ranger Station at the addresses and phone numbers given above.

CHAPTER 12: THE KINGS AND KAWEAH RIVERS
Great Winter Fishing, Great Summer Fishing.

Paolo Marchesi

THE Kings River for most California fly fishers is an unknown quantity, seldom fished except by Central Valley locals from Fresno or Visalia who aren't about to advertise how good some of it is and draw in crowds of outsiders. There's even a bigger fly-fishing secret, the nearby Kaweah River (that's pronounced ka-WEE-ah) in Sequoia National Park.

The Kings really is three rivers, the first starting high in the Sierra Nevada and tumbling through Kings Canyon National Park. Then there's the Kings above Pine Flat Reservoir, a Wild Trout stretch that is one of the few blue-ribbon fisheries in this state open year-round. Last is the Kings below Pine Flat Reservoir, where it flattens out to make its final trip into the Central Valley near Fresno. Years ago, this was prime trout water that drew fly-line anglers from all over. Today, it is a much-abused stretch of river pounded by bait anglers, who have trashed the area so badly that it looks like an urban slum. Still, there are plenty of big fish in this 12-mile section of the river, and there are times when it can be excellent fishing—weekdays during the winter, when few people are around, for example. Let's take this area as the first section and work upstream.

A hike up the Middle Fork of The Kings River will provide the adventurous fly fisher with spectacular scenery and trout-filled water.

THE KINGS RIVER BELOW PINE FLAT RESERVOIR

To get to the Kings River directly below and above Pine Flat Reservoir, follow Highway 180 from Fresno, then turn east on Trimmer Springs Road or Piedra Road, which parallel the Kings on either side of the river. Both roads lead to the little town of Piedra, where a bridge crosses the Kings and where most of the public fishing ends, since the river then moves onto private property. Trimmer Springs Road continues around the northern side of the reservoir and is the access to the Wild Trout area above Pine Flat. There isn't much access to the first part of the lower Kings because of orange groves and farms with "No Trespassing" signs. But at the upper end, below Piedra Bridge, there is easy access—so easy that there are signs telling visitors not to wash their vehicles in the river.

This is worm and salmon-egg country, where just about any method, legal or not, seems to be used to take fish. On sunny weekends, forget it and go somewhere else. On weekdays, fly fishers can have some fun and perhaps attract the attention of the big trout that still lie in deep water. There are evening hatches, particularly on a number of long slicks, that bring big fish to the surface and can provide excellent action.

Behind Avocado Park, which is on the southern bank a couple of miles downstream from Piedra Bridge, is one of those places. In the park there is a stocked pond where fishing pressure is heavy. A hundred feet behind the pond, the Kings can be reached by way of a dirt road that leads from either end of the park to the river and the back side of the pond. Here there is a large slick that as dusk approaches often is dimpled with rising trout. In the winter, when releases from Pine Flat are low, it can be waded.

Caddisflies are the main food, and the Kings River Caddis, particularly the parachute version, is effective in sizes12 through 16. In the winter months, the caddis hatch slows, but there is almost always a heavy midge hatch that calls for flies in the size 20 to 24 range.

For the record, this part of the Kings was an excellent fly-fishing river until the mid-1980s, cherished by the few people who knew about it. It was decimated by the drought of the late 1980s and early 1990s and a reduction of flows from the reservoir. There is some talk of negotiating steady flows from Pine Flat Reservoir that could put this once-great tailwater fishery back into action. Keep an eye on what happens in coming years—things could change for the better.

ABOVE PINE FLAT RESERVOIR

It is a curvy, 25-mile drive on Trimmer Springs Road around Pine Flat Reservoir to where the Kings enters it. One of the many arms of the reservoir on the way is fed by **Big Creek,** which early in the season can be fished upstream from where the road crosses it.

Although the Kings River can be productive anyplace there is access, the most popular area is the Wild Trout section, starting at Garnet Dike (or Dyke, as it is sometimes spelled). This begins 7 miles upstream from where Trimmer Springs Road crosses the river at a one-lane Bailey bridge. The paved road doubles back and climbs into the mountains, but upstream access is available on dirt roads on either side of the river. The road on the northern side of the Kings, that is, on the far side of the bridge coming from Pine Flat Reservoir, dead-ends after 7 miles at Garnet Dike Campground, where there are toilets, water, and campsites. Undeveloped riverside camping areas also abound along the road to Garnet Dike Campground. The road on the south side is shorter, not going as far as Garnet Dike.

Since it became a Wild Trout area in 1991, from Garnet Dike upstream is the favorite section for fly-line anglers. But from Garnet Dike downstream to the reservoir, the river has not been stocked for decades and offers almost as good fishing. From Garnet Dike Campground there is an easy, bankside trail that goes 3 miles upstream. Above that, the river enters a canyon and becomes almost impassable if the water is high.

Garnet Dike also is a favorite put-in spot for spring and early-summer rafters, who in high-water years make this stretch of the river a busy spot during the day. In reality, when the water is high enough for rafting, it isn't the best time for fly fishing, so the two water sports don't clash that much. If you want to fish and there are rafters putting in, just walk upstream. This entire stretch of river offers riffles and runs, along with a few big holes.

The best time to fish here is before the snow begins to melt in the spring. From April through June, snowmelt makes the river too high and too cold for good fishing, although fishing picks up again in the summer. The main problem then is that it is too hot for most anglers.

This isn't an easy place to fish, and novice fly-line anglers probably won't do well. Although many people use dry flies, it is much more productive to fish nymphs, which yields rainbows and browns averaging twelve to fourteen inches, with many even bigger. Larry Goates of the Buz Buszek Fly Shop in Visalia, who is a native of the area, says his preferred rig for this stretch of water is a two-nymph setup—a size 12 Beadhead Prince Nymph on top and a size 14 or 16 Z-Wing Caddis on the bottom. The trick is to make certain your flies are scraping the bottom, which involves constantly adjusting the split shot or whatever weight you use. If you aren't getting hangups, you aren't deep enough.

From Garnet Dike, the Kings is not accessible by road until it reaches Highway 180 near Boyden Cave, in the Sierra National Forest, nearly 10 miles upstream. From Pine Flat Reservoir to Garnet Dike there is a two-trout limit, but there are no restrictions on tackle. From Garnet Dike upstream to Boyden Cave it is barbless flies and lures only, with a zero-trout limit.

If you're willing to hike, or better yet, backpack, the Middle Fork of the Kings River offers fine angling for smallish trout in a wilderness setting (the Monarch Wilderness, to be precise). It's confluence with the main stem of the Kings is about a mile's hike north of Trimmer Springs Road.

THE UPPER KINGS RIVER

Access to the upper Kings River in the Sierra National Forest and the Kings Canyon National Park is via Highway 180, which drops into the canyon and picks up the river (which at this point is actually the South Fork of the Kings) at Boyden Cave. From there to the end of the road at Copper Creek is about 17 miles, with Cedar Grove Village at the 10-mile mark.

This entire section of the Kings is not stocked and has about an equal number of wild rainbows and browns. Anglers can keep only two trout, with no restrictions on tackle. The river is open to fishing all year, but because the road is closed by snow in the winter, it is something of a moot point. Upstream from Copper Creek there are no special angling restrictions.

From Boyden Cave to Cedar Grove, the river tumbles through the canyon, although for the most part there is easy access. The first 7 miles of this stretch is pocket water with deep pools, large-river fishing that gets good only as the flow drops. The upper 3 miles to Cedar Grove is easier water for anglers, offering slower pools and runs.

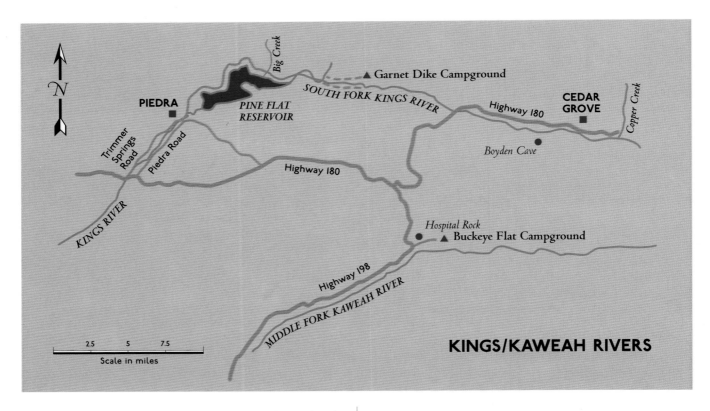

KINGS/KAWEAH RIVERS

From Cedar Grove to Copper Creek, where the road ends, the river slows considerably, and the fishing is easier. Copper Creek is a major trailhead, with long-term parking for hikers headed into the backcountry. It also is an excellent jumping-off spot for anglers to work upstream to where Bubbs Creek enters the Kings, an easy 2-mile hike.

Between Zumwalt Meadows, about half a mile downstream from Copper Creek, all the way to Bubbs Creek, there is mostly flat water, with occasional stretches of light pocket water. Early in the season, when some lower stretches are too high for effective fishing, this can be productive for small fish. Hikers can continue up the trail past Bubbs Creek high into the wilderness or follow another trail up Bubbs Creek.

About the only feeder stream that offers good fishing is **Roaring River,** which joins the Kings halfway between Cedar Grove and Copper Creek. Less than a mile upstream from the intersection is Roaring River Falls, well worth the walk, even if you're not fishing. The fishing is downstream from the falls and can be good in the spring, when the water is high.

For this upper section of the Kings, the biggest fish are in the first 6 or 7 miles above Boyden Cave, averaging ten to twelve inches. Upstream, they get progressively smaller, although there still are plenty of them.

Caddisflies are the primary food, followed by mayflies and stoneflies. Stimulators and Elk Hair Caddises work well in size 12 and 14. Any beadhead nymph is effective, although Bird's Nests and Princes are preferred by local anglers.

THE KAWEAH RIVER

The Kaweah River, which flows from Sequoia National Park to Lake Kaweah, near Visalia, is a little-fished jewel that deserves a place in the sun. Most of the river from the lake up to Sequoia National Park is on private land with no access. But once you are in the park, from the Ash Mountain entrance upstream, it offers great fly fishing.

Larry Goates, who learned to fly fish on the Kaweah, said the drought affected the river, but with the return of wet years it has blossomed into a consistent fishery—"I tell people the Kings gets more pressure than it needs, and the Kaweah doesn't get as much as it can handle." Since the river is in Sequoia National Park, it contains wild trout, a mixture of browns and rainbows, most of them bigger than those in the upper Kings. The average size runs between ten and twelve inches.

Highway 198 from Visalia pretty much follows the Kaweah to Hospital Rock, 6 miles into the park. A road branches south to Buckeye Flat Campground, a good jumping-off point for anglers who want to hike up the river. In the canyon alongside Highway 198, anglers need to do some serious boulder hopping to fish the river, which is mostly large pools and deep runs, with only a few pocket-water stretches. There also is a lot of poison oak.

From Buckeye Flat Campground, a trail follows the river upstream, but is high above the water. Anglers can make their way down to the river, but the first easy spot to get to the Kaweah is at Burton Creek, which requires about a 6-mile hike. At that point, a switchback trail leads down to the water.

Other easy access points farther along the trail are at Buck Creek and River Valley. The trail from Buckeye Flat is fairly level, with little elevation gain, but it faces south, so it can be hot in the summer. The best fishing for this part of the river comes as early as May, a month or so before the Kings River in Sequoia National Park hits its peak

SUMMING UP

Both the **Kings** and **Kaweah Rivers** offer excellent fishing, with the added incentive that the Kings can be fished in the winter, when most prime rivers in California are closed to angling.

The best big-trout section is on the Kings, the Wild Trout water above Garnet Dike. This is Wild Trout water, with barbless hooks and catch-and-release required, and isn't easy fishing, but with nymphs, effective fly-line anglers can have multifish days with browns and rainbows running up to eighteen inches. The upper section of the Kings in the Kings Canyon National Park has smaller fish, but lots of them. And it is beautiful country.

The Kaweah River in Sequoia National Park is the well-kept secret here. There is reasonably easy access, and it produces the biggest fish inside the park, bigger even than those in the upper Kings River.

♦ ♦ ♦ ♦ ♦ ♦

ADDITIONAL INFORMATION

FLY SHOPS
Buz Buszek Fly Shop, 400 N. Johnson, Visalia, CA 93291; (559) 734-1151. A full-service fly shop that has been around for half a century and is probably the oldest fly shop in California.

HOSPITALS
St. Agnes Medical Center, 1303 Herndon Avenue, Fresno, CA 93720; (559) 449-3000.

Kaiser Permanente, 7300 N. Fresno Street, Fresno, CA 93720; (559) 448-4500.

Valley Children's Hospital, 9300 Valley Children's Place, Madera, CA 93638; (559) 353-3000.

Kaweah Delta Health Care District, 400 West Mineral King, Visalia, CA 93291; (209) 625-2211.

PUBLIC CAMPING
Information on the many campgrounds in the Kings Canyon / Sequoia National Parks is available through the Visitor Information Center, Three Rivers, CA 93221; (559) 565-3134.

MORE SOURCES
The Kings Canyon / Sequoia National Parks Visitor Information Center listed above provides information on everything from road conditions to backcountry permits.

For information on the Visalia area, contact the Visalia Convention and Visitors Bureau, 301 E. Acequia, Visalia, CA 93291; (800) 524-0303 or (559) 738-3435. Fax: (559) 730-7024.

For information on the Fresno area, contact the Fresno Visitors Bureau, 808 M Street, Fresno, CA 93721; (800) 788-0836 or (559) 233-0836.

CHAPTER 13: GOLDEN TROUT COUNTRY
High Sierra Paradise

Bill Sunderland

THE southern end of the Sierra Nevada is a dramatic climax to California's premier mountain range, dropping sharply from peaks over 11,000 feet to the Joshua trees and creosote brush of the Mojave Desert. It also is the home of one of the most beautiful fresh-water fishes in the world and California's state fish since 1939, the golden trout.

For many Southern Californians, a trek into golden-trout country is handy because it is close to Los Angeles, San Diego, and all the satellite cities that turn the area into a megalopolis. It can be a quick weekend getaway for anglers, not to mention campers, hikers, backpackers, and four-wheel-drive enthusiasts.

The truth be told, it isn't the best fly fishing in the Sierra. There are few waters that regularly produce big trout, and the handful of streams and river sections that are accessible without hiking are stocked by the Department of Fish and Game. In this aspect it is no different than much of the rest of the Sierra Nevada—there are hatchery rainbows at easy access points, along with a few wild trout and bigger holdovers, and most wild trout are available only by using your feet and stamina. But there are golden trout here in abundance, and that alone makes the Kern River drainage worth the trip.

The Golden Trout of the High Sierra are rarely large, (this fish is typical) but they're unsurpassed in beauty.

GOLDEN TROUT

First, a bit of detail on golden trout and where they came from. According to biologists, goldens evolved from rainbow trout that repopulated the high Sierra after the last Ice Age ended some 10,000 years ago. Why these trout took on such spectacular colors isn't known, but the predominant theory states it is protective coloration, making them hard to see against the light-colored sandy stream bottoms of the region. A second theory is that this coloration helps them deal with the high levels of solar radiation that living organisms receive at higher altitudes.

There are three subspecies of golden trout—the Little Kern golden trout, the Volcano Creek golden trout, and the Kern River rainbow trout. To complicate matters, in most areas, rainbows have interbred with goldens, and finding a genetically pure golden is difficult.

The Little Kern River golden trout inhabited most of the Little Kern River drainage, but interbred with rainbows introduced into the area in the 1930s and 1940s. It is a threatened species, and brood stock are being reared at the DFG's hatchery near Kernville. In an effort to save this small trout and keep it as genetically pure as possible, a program has been underway since 1975 to rid streams and lakes in the area of other fish.

Volcano Creek golden trout are native to Volcano Creek (renamed Golden Trout Creek) and the South Fork of the

Kern River. This is the fish that most golden-trout anglers will catch, since it has been transplanted into many streams and lakes in the southern high Sierra.

Kern River rainbow trout genetically are golden trout and once lived in the Kern River, from the Kern Canyon north of Bakersfield upstream to the headwaters of the river in Sequoia National Park. They are the least colorful of the golden trout and for the most part are small, rarely over ten inches. They are no longer believed to be in the Kern River below Johnsondale Bridge.

Biologists can't tell them apart without taking them to a laboratory, so an on-stream angler should be happy just to identify one as a golden. Color is what distinguishes a golden for the angler. They all have light-olive backs with numerous small spots and sides that become colored gold below the lateral line. The sides are marked by a bright, reddish-orange stripe and by par marks that continue into maturity. Their lower belly also can be a bright, reddish orange. All this coloration isn't present in all fish—there can be a good deal of variation, even within one subspecies.

THE KERN RIVER DRAINAGE

The Kern River drainage is home to a number of wilderness areas, including the Golden Trout Wilderness, the Dome Land Wilderness, and the South Sierra Wilderness. All three are accessed only by hiking or horseback and are watered by streams and honeycombed by lakes that hold goldens and other species of trout. However, there are a number of streams with goldens that can be reached without hiking. For the most part, the fish aren't big—ten inches is a large one. But that is the nature of fishing for goldens. It is their beauty and feistiness, and not their size, that draws the angler.

The heavier populations of golden trout are found in streams to the east of the Kern River, including the South Fork of the Kern. West of the Kern River is a much more accessible and therefore more popular area, with myriad streams and roads that crisscross the mountains. The larger, more popular streams are stocked with hatchery rainbows, although there are plenty of wild trout still to be found by the angler willing to walk.

THE KERN RIVER

The 80-mile-long main fork of the Kern River above Lake Isabella is divided into four sections—22 miles upstream to Johnsondale Bridge, the 4-mile stretch of Wild Trout water upstream from Johnsondale bridge, 27 miles upstream from the Wild Trout area to the boundary of Sequoia National Park, and the Kern in the park, 27 miles to its origin at 11,800-foot-high Lake South America.

For many fly fishers, only the 4-mile Wild Trout section is going to be of major interest, unless they want to do some serious hiking. Downstream to Lake Isabella is roadside fishing and is heavily planted, while the river from the Wild Trout section upstream, both in and out of Sequoia National Park, has only hike-in access.

This 80-mile stretch of the Kern River is the focus of the Upper Kern Basin Fishery Management Plan put together in 1995 by the California Department of Fish and Game, Sequoia National Forest, and Sequoia National Park. The main goals, carried out as part of a five-year plan, are to "protect and enhance native fish populations and their habitats, restore, protect and enhance the native Kern River rainbow trout populations so that threatened or endangered listing does not become necessary, [and] provide for recreational fishing."

From Lake Isabella 22 miles upstream to Johnsondale Bridge, the Kern River parallels Mountain Highway 99, which provides numerous access points, along with campgrounds and resorts. It is the favorite area for bait and lure anglers and annually is stocked with almost 100,000 hatchery trout. Although this was once prime water for the Kern River rainbow, biologists say there probably are no longer any native trout in the river due to interbreeding with other rainbows. This section of the river is open to fishing all year, and there are no special restrictions on the method of take. Limits are five per day, ten in possession. It also has a heavy population of coarse fish, particularly Sacramento squawfish and suckers. It isn't pristine wilderness fishing—as one area fly fisher put it, "I don't fish it because I don't like wading through dirty diapers and beer cans."

The upper 3 miles of this stretch, from the Fairview Dam to Johnsondale Bridge, may one day become part of the Wild Trout section. The DFG hopes to close the fish ladder at the dam, get rid of as many squawfish and suckers as possible, and then introduce Kern River rainbows.

The Wild Trout section, from Johnsondale Bridge 4 miles upstream to where U.S. Forest Service Trail 33E30 heads east to join the Rincon Trail, also requires a hike in, but a riverside path on the east side of the Kern makes walking easy until it ends about a quarter of a mile above the Wild Trout section. At Johnsondale Bridge there is plenty of parking, along with a good map of the river and the trail and clearly stated regulations for this section—artificial barbless flies and lures and a two-trout limit, fourteen inches or larger, from the last Saturday in April through November 15. This part of the river also is open to fishing the rest of the year, but no trout may be kept, and barbless lures and flies are required.

The Wild Trout section of the Kern and much of the water upstream is a fall fishery. There are no dams or obstructions, and it runs high and fast well into August, or even later. For the best fishing, it should be flowing at or below 500 cubic feet per second, although there are a few fly-line anglers who do well using nymphs and streamers during higher water.

As in most of the Sierra, caddisfly and mayfly patterns work well for dries, along with nymphs such as the Pheasant Tail, Prince, Bird's Nest, and Zug Bug. And don't hesitate to use a Muddler Minnow or some other streamer of your choice—there are bigger fish, up to seventeen or eighteen inches,

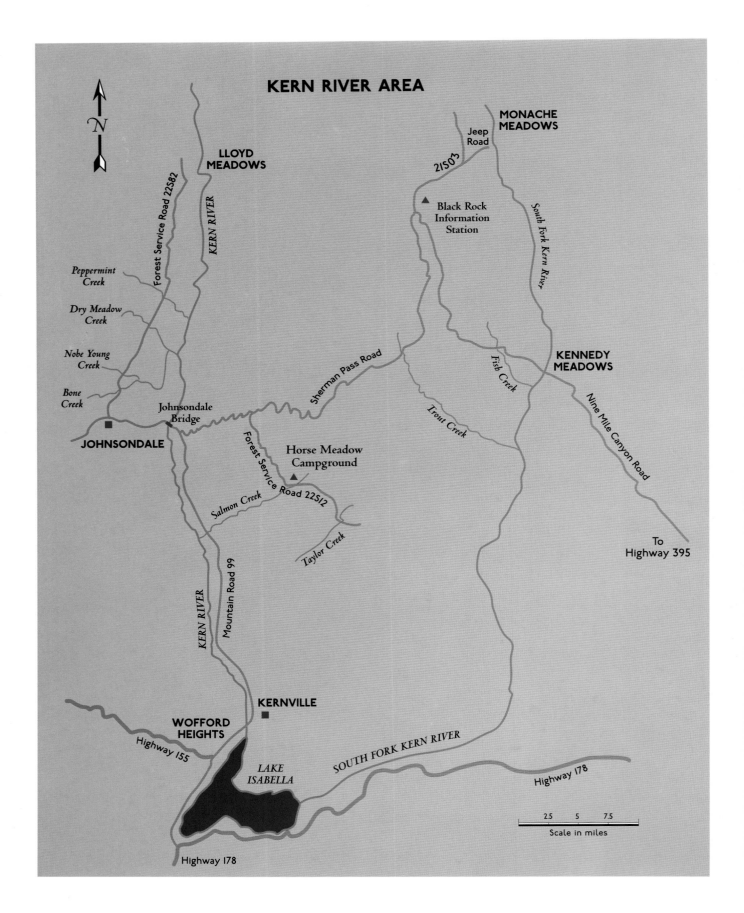

KERN RIVER AREA

N

MONACHE MEADOWS

Jeep Road

21S03

LLOYD MEADOWS

Black Rock Information Station

Forest Service Road 22S82

KERN RIVER

South Fork Kern River

Peppermint Creek

Dry Meadow Creek

KENNEDY MEADOWS

Nobe Young Creek

Sherman Pass Road

Fish Creek

Bone Creek

Johnsondale Bridge

Trout Creek

Nine Mile Canyon Road

JOHNSONDALE

Horse Meadow Campground

Forest Service Road 22S12

Salmon Creek

To Highway 395

Taylor Creek

KERN RIVER

Mountain Road 99

KERNVILLE

WOFFORD HEIGHTS

Highway 155

SOUTH FORK KERN RIVER

LAKE ISABELLA

Highway 178

2.5   5   7.5

Scale in miles

Highway 178

that can be enticed with the right dinner offering. DFG surveys of the Kern show more large fish in this section of the river than anyplace else. If anything, it seems to be improving, and hopes are that it will become a first-rate fishery with more and larger trout in coming years.

Although there are some browns, most of the fish are rainbows, including a few Kern River rainbows. The DFG does not stock the Kern River here, but part of its management plan is to put hatchery-bred Kern River rainbows into some of the tributaries of this section of the river, including Nobe Young, Bone, and Dry Meadow Creeks. Accessible sections of these creeks have long been stocked with hatchery rainbows.

From the boundary with Sequoia National Park to the Johnsondale Bridge, the Kern River runs through a rugged canyon, and above the Wild Trout section, a limited number of trails lead to the water, none of them a stroll through the meadow. On the positive side, there is a lot of good fishing, both in the Kern and in the Little Kern River, which joins the main stem at Forks of the Kern, 14.5 miles upstream from Johnsondale Bridge.

You'll need the latest U.S. Forest Service map of the area, but there are several well-trodden trails that lead to the Kern. The shortest is at Lloyd Meadows, which can be reached on Forest Service Road 22S82 from Johnsondale. It is only 2 miles in to the Forks of the Kern, but the elevation drop is 1,000 feet—something you'll become more aware of on the way out.

This access allows you to fish either the main Kern or the Little Kern. It also is a jumping-off spot for white-water rafters, including a few commercial companies that have permits for the area. They use pack animals to bring in their gear, and since there are Class IV and V rapids (that's dangerous, expert water) it is strictly for experienced river runners. The Little Kern, home to the Little Kern golden trout, is a much smaller, calmer river, with more runs and flats than the main stem.

Other accesses are via the Trout Meadows Trail, which starts at Trout Meadows, north of Lloyd Meadow, and reaches the river at Kern Flat, or the Ninemile Creek Trail, off Sherman Pass Road.

In the Sequoia National Forest itself there are 27 miles of the Kern, and none of them are easy to get to. All the trails are long and difficult, and the fishing can be good. Volcano Creek golden trout are the main species, and some of them have been planted in tributaries that initially were barren. There also are brookies, browns, and non-native rainbow trout that were planted in the past and still exist in the area. This section of the Kern is designated a Wild and Scenic River, and in addition to being in Sequoia National Park, is part of the Golden Trout Wilderness. Access is from Mineral King, east of Visalia, or from Independence, in the Owens River Valley. In all cases, it is a multiday trip.

Lake Isabella provides some good fly fishing, although not of the trout variety. There are large bluegills and crappies and bigmouth bass up to fourteen or fifteen pounds. The best area is where the South Fork of the Kern comes into the lake, particularly in the morning and evening. In high-water years, this section, as well as where the main stem of the Kern enters the lake, is dotted with trees that have grown big during the drought, and when the lake is full have only their upper sections out of the water. These trees are perfect protection for bass. They also tend to keep boaters and personal watercraft hotshots out of the area, making it safer for anglers who want to float tube. You can ease in here with a boat, as well, but be careful of brush and trees that are just under the surface of the water.

During the summer, bass will take poppers, hair mice, and Zonkers or Matukas tied on a size 6 hook. Crappies run up to sixteen inches and will smash a Zonker. A locally popular fly is the Double Grey, something like a mosquito, but with a heavier hackle, tied on a size 12, 3X-long hook. It can be fished either dry or wet, using short strips to give it some action.

SALMON, TAYLOR, FISH, AND TROUT CREEKS

These creeks to the east of the Kern River all offer good fishing for small golden trout and can be reached by car. They are perfect spots for anglers who are intent on adding a golden trout to their "I've caught" list or for those who enjoy catching beautiful small trout in beautiful small streams.

The first thing an angler needs to do is get maps of the area, including the Sequoia National Forest map and the Golden Trout Wilderness / South Sierra Wilderness map. In addition, the ranger stations for the various districts (see below for addresses) have mimeographed sheets that are free and that provide large-scale maps of specific areas, along with details of campgrounds and just about anything else you might want to know. These are invaluable, unless you have eyes like a hawk, or a magnifying glass to read some of the small print on the larger maps. A bonus is that the various roads and trails are well signed, and the maps are accurate, which isn't always the case in the various national forests that make up the Sierra Nevada.

Salmon Creek can be reached via Sherman Pass Road east from Mountain Highway 99, just before it reaches Johnsondale Bridge. Then follow U.S. Forest Service Road 22S12 south to Horse Meadows, where there is a campground. Salmon Creek runs through the campground and can be fished either upstream or downstream. Forest Service Road 22S12 also continues to Big Meadow, which offers further access to the creek.

With brushy, overhung banks, Salmon Creek isn't easy fishing. There are numerous small goldens, but getting to them is a problem. Often, dapping—poking your rod through the brush and using only the leader to drop the fly on the

Paolo Marchesi

water—is the only way to go. For the most part, these aren't selective trout, so attractors such as Royal Wulffs or Humpies will work just fine. The key is not to scare the fish into hiding before it sees the fly.

Taylor Creek, which is similar to Salmon Creek, both in size and topography, but is somewhat more open, is farther along road 22S12. There is no developed campground, and it has even fewer visitors. Again, lots of small, eager goldens inhabit the creek.

Fish Creek, another gem for goldens, crosses Sherman Pass Road after it goes over the pass and drops toward Kennedy Meadows. Just west of the Rodeo Flat sign on the road is a pullout into a "Fire Safe" area that allows parking. A trail leads several hundred yards to Fish Creek, where Trout Unlimited and local cattle ranchers teamed up in 1996 to fence off a section of the creek to keep cattle from breaking down the banks. Anglers can work up or down the creek. Fish Creek Campground is nearby. There also is a road at the upper end of Troy Meadows that leads to the creek, or you can park on the roadside and walk across the meadow to the creek. Troy Meadows is about a mile from the intersection of 22S05 and 21S03, where the U.S. Forest Service Blackrock Information Station is located. The station is an excellent source of information for the area.

Trout Creek crosses Sherman Pass Road just east of Sherman Pass, and anglers can use a trail to follow it upstream or down. It also can be accessed via a dirt road from Paloma Meadows, 22S20. It, too, has small goldens and brushy banks that make for tough angling.

There are numerous other creeks in this section of the Kern River drainage that hold small goldens. If you like to hike, just pick one and start walking—you won't be disappointed, either with the scenery or with the fishing.

THE SOUTH FORK OF THE KERN RIVER

There are two drive-up access points to the South Fork, at Kennedy Meadows, where the highway crosses the river, or at Monache Meadows, where a jeep road allows four-wheel-drive vehicles to make their way to the water.

In the 6,100-foot-high Kennedy Meadows area, which has a campground, store, and two restaurants, the South Fork is stocked with both browns and rainbows and gets a lot of fishing traffic. At one point, the DFG stopped putting in hatchery rainbows because of the fear they would crossbreed with native goldens, but bowed to complaints from anglers that the browns were too hard to catch.

Coming from Southern California, Kennedy Meadows is about 25 miles off Highway 395 along Nine Mile Road, which branches west not far from the intersection of Highways 395 and 14. Coming from the other direction, this is the Sherman Pass Road. Where the highway crosses the road is

The Kern River provides approximately 80 miles of trout water.

a popular starting area for anglers, who can follow trails either up or down the river. Upstream it is about 4 miles to the Kennedy Meadows Campground and is fishable all the way.

Other drive-up access points are three dirt roads that branch west from the paved road that leads to the campground. There are both browns and rainbows in this area, and it can be nymphed effectively during the day or fished with dries during hatches, particularly in the evening. An alternative is to park at the campground and work upstream as far as your feet are willing to take you. This gets you away from most of the stocked fish. Since the Pacific Crest Trail goes through the campground, it is easy to follow this path and then drop down to the river wherever you want. There also are walk-in access points to the Kennedy Meadows section of the South Fork that will get anglers away from crowds and provide much better wild-trout fishing.

The road to the so-called Rockhouse area of the river turns west from the highway near the southern end of Kennedy Meadows, opposite the fire station. It used to lead 11 miles to the river, but the last 4 miles has been blocked off at the boundary of the Dome Land Wilderness. It is all easy downhill hiking going in, but that means it is uphill coming out. A number of creeks, including Fish Creek and Trout Creek, flow into the South Fork of the Kern in this area, which adds to the angling possibilities.

Fly selection includes Pheasant Tails, Gold-Ribbed Hare's Ears, and Chamois Nymphs, usually with bead heads, in size 12 or 14. Favored dries are the Parachute Adams, Elk Hair Caddis, and Little Yellow Stone in size 14 to 16, or later in the summer, hoppers in about size 12. Since there are no special regulations here, fly fishers will run across bait and lure anglers, but they tend to gather at the larger holes and don't work the runs and riffles that often produce the best fish.

Monache Meadows is reached by following 21S03 from the Blackrock Forest Service Information Station to the Monache Meadows Jeep Road. It is 2.4 miles to Snake Creek on the jeep road, and then about another 3 miles to the meadow and the river. Anglers can drive a ways upstream to Bakeoven Meadow or cross the river and drive another 2 miles south to where the road ends. It is about a 100-yard walk from the end of the road to the South Fork, which winds through the meadow. Note that this is indeed a four-wheel-drive road, although not a particularly tough one for 4x4 aficionados, so don't even think of trying it in a family sedan.

There are rainbows, browns, and golden trout throughout the river here. The DFG says the goldens are rainbow/golden hybrids, but they are extremely colorful and easy to catch. Just drop a dry fly or hopper under any likely overhang and chances are it won't be on the water for a second before a golden hits it. They may even come out of the water to grab it on the way down, particularly if you put a hopper in the bankside grass and pull it gently, so it drops into the steam.

Grazing is heavy here, and there are hundreds of cattle throughout the meadow. They have trampled the banks and muddied the river throughout, but it doesn't seem to have affected the fishing as badly as it might have. Catching forty or fifty trout a day is possible, and some of the goldens are ten or eleven inches long, although most are smaller.

To get away from the cattle, anglers can drop into a canyon downstream of Monache Meadows or work the water as it flows into the meadows upstream. Either way will provide good angling and better access to bigger browns or rainbows than is available in the meadow itself. Upstream is the favored way for anglers who fish here regularly.

In 1997, the California Fish and Game Commission added 200 miles of the South Fork of the Kern and all its tributaries to the Wild Trout Program, an act that will help protect the Volcano Creek golden trout. Monache Meadows is an area that is particularly vulnerable due to the heavy grazing, and this Wild Trout designation could move ranchers and conservationists toward a compromise, such as fencing off some of the river to keep cattle from destroying it. Discussions are under way, but don't hold your breath. At present, there are no special fishing regulations for the South Fork of the Kern, but this could change, so be aware of current DFG restrictions.

WEST OF THE KERN RIVER

A popular fishing area of the Kern River drainage is the crisscross of creeks and roads that lie to the west of the main fork of the Kern in the Johnsondale, Camp Nelson, Pine Flat, and California Hot Springs areas. For the most part, access is easy, and the streams are stocked with rainbows. This means there aren't many goldens and puts it in a class with much of the rest of the Sierra Nevada—pretty country, easy access, stocked fish for the most part, but good wild-trout angling for those who are willing to do some walking.

The best-known of the streams in this area is **Peppermint Creek.** Lower Peppermint Creek crosses 22S82, which parallels the Kern River north, while upper Peppermint Creek can be reached where it crosses the Western Divide Highway that leads to Camp Nelson.

Just to the south of Peppermint Creek is **Dry Meadow Creek,** another fishing favorite. **Nobe Young** and **Bone Creeks** are a bit farther south, but follow the same eastward path as they flow downhill to the feed the Kern River. All are stocked, and all offer good small-stream angling.

Nobe Young, in particular, can be good in the upper reaches, but the hiking is difficult, sometimes dangerous. The best entry point is at Last Chance Bridge, where Forest Service road 22S02 to Last Chance Meadow crosses the creek. This road branches north off the road to Lloyd Meadow.

There are lots of bears and rattlesnakes in this part of the forest, and deadfalls, poison oak, and nettles can making bushwhacking difficult. Although you really need to go only about three-quarters of a mile upstream to get into wild fish, including some Kern River rainbows and an occasional golden, it'll seem much farther.

THE TULE RIVER

This small western-slope river is not part of the big Kern River drainage area, but has its own canyon just to the north, flowing from the high country to Springville and Porterville. It drops sharply through a deep canyon until it flows into Lake Success, near Porterville, but by that time it is a warm water fishery more suited to bass than trout. However, there is some good fly fishing in the higher regions.

At Cedar Slope, just east of Camp Nelson, there is access to the Middle Fork of the Tule, and anglers can work their way downstream to Camp Nelson. On the North Fork, Wishon is the easiest spot to get to the river. From Coffee Camp downstream is pounded pretty heavily by all sorts of anglers, and as a result the fly fishing isn't that good.

SUMMING UP

Easy access and golden trout are the two main reasons to fish here. Anglers from the Los Angeles area can make it a day trip or an easy weekend trip and have plenty of time to fish. The angling may be better on the Owens River and Hot Creek, but they're another couple of hours up Highway 395.

But where else can you catch drive-up golden trout! These little beauties are noted for living in inaccessible hike-in areas so high they'll pop your lungs. Not so—there are a handful of drive-up creeks, namely, **Salmon, Taylor, Fish,** and **Trout Creeks,** where you can park or camp and catch dozens of these little fellows. Goldens also can be found on the **South Fork of the Kern River** in Monache Meadows at the end of a 6-mile jeep road that demands a 4x4 and good clearance. Just kick the cattle out of the way and go at it, and you can catch a half a hundred of them in a day. This area was declared a Wild Trout section in 1997, and perhaps some agreement will be reached so the cattle can be fenced away from the river and the broken-down banks allowed to regenerate. If you want to avoid the cattle at Monache Meadows, drive upstream as far as you can go and then start walking. It's pretty country and has lots of browns and rainbows, in addition to the goldens. Just remember that golden trout aren't big. Ten inches is one to be proud of, but they are fighting machines that don't ever give up.

For those with strong legs and a love of hiking, this is the part of the world that offers access to a tremendous variety of walk-in lakes and streams that have larger fish—the Golden Trout Wilderness. There isn't any vehicle access—you have to do it on your own.

The 4-mile Wild Trout section of the main stem of the Kern River upstream from Johnsondale Bridge has bigger fish, some up to seventeen inches, and should get even better as time goes on. There's a good trail from the bridge upstream that allows plenty of access. For the most part, this is a fall fishery, when the water flow drops below 500 cubic feet per second, usually in late August or early September.

✦✦✦✦✦

ADDITIONAL INFORMATION

FLY SHOPS

High Sierra Flyfisher, 337 W. Ridgecrest Boulevard, Ridgecrest, CA 93555; (760) 375-5810. Ridgecrest, off Highway 395 in the desert a few miles before it intersects with Highway 14, is an unlikely place for a full-service fly shop, but this area of about 30,000 people has a very active fly-fishing club that does much to support it. The shop also is a blessing for Southern Californians headed north who have left something behind and need fly-fishing gear.

Martin's Rod and Reel, 13220 Sierra Way, Kernville, CA 93238; (760) 376-3835. This shop has all types of fishing gear, including some flies and fly-fishing equipment.

HOSPITALS

Kern Valley Hospital, 6412 Laurel Avenue, Mountain Mesa, CA; (760) 379-2681.

PUBLIC CAMPING

There are numerous U.S. Forest Service campgrounds throughout the area, but they fall under different jurisdictions. Most of them are in the Sequoia National Forest, which is also helpful in routing requests that aren't in their jurisdiction. They are at 900 West Grand Avenue, Porterville, CA 93257; (559) 784-1500.

Information on campgrounds in Sequoia National Park can be obtained from the park headquarters, Sequoia–Kings Canyon National Park, Ash Mountain Headquarters, Three Rivers, CA 93271; (559) 565-3341.

Part of the Kern River drainage is in the Inyo National Forest. The best source for campground information is the Mount Whitney Ranger Station, 640 South Main Street, Lone Pine, CA 93545; (760) 876-6200.

Other U.S. Forest Service stations that are useful for information are:

Kernville Ranger Station, 105 Whitney Road, Kernville, CA 93238; (760) 376-3781.

Hot Springs Ranger District, 43474 Parker Pass Drive, California Hot Springs, CA 93207; (805) 548-6503.

WILDERNESS PERMITS

Visitors to the Golden Trout Wilderness must obtain a wilderness permit and a campfire permit if they plan on staying overnight. Wilderness permits are not necessary for hikers or campers in the South Sierra Wilderness or the Dome Land Wilderness, but fire permits are necessary for overnight campers. Permits are free and can be obtained from the Blackrock Visitor Station on the Kern Plateau, on Forest Service Road 21S03, near the intersection with Sherman Pass Road (22S05), or from any of the following locations:

Sequoia National Forest, 900 West Grand Avenue, Porterville, CA 93257; (559) 784-1500.

Tule River Ranger District, 32588 Highway 190, Porterville, CA 93257; (559) 539-2607.

Carnell Meadow Ranger District, 105 Whitney Road, Kernville, CA 93238; (760) 376-3781.

Mount Whitney Ranger Station, 640 South Main Street, Lone Pine, CA 93545; (760) 876-6200.

Sequoia–Kings Canyon National Park, Ash Mountain Headquarters, Three Rivers, CA 93271; (559) 565-3341.

MORE SOURCES

The Kernville Chamber of Commerce, P.O. Box 397, Kernville, CA 93238; (760) 376-2629.

The Lake Isabella Chamber of Commerce, P.O. Box 567, Lake Isabella, CA 93240; (670) 379-5236.

The Lake Isabella Visitors Center, 4875 Ponderosa Drive, Lake Isabella, CA 93240; (760) 379-5646.

CHAPTER 14: THE CARSON RIVER AREA

From Wild Trout to Planted Rainbows.

Paolo Marchesi

THE Carson River drainage is the northern end of the justly famous Sierra Nevada eastern slope—home to some of the best fishing water in the state and some of the biggest trout California can boast. The really prime water (dare I mention Hot Creek and the Owens River yet again?) is a couple of hundred miles south, but that doesn't detract from the fishing here. First, there is just about every type of water you can enjoy, from small creeks to rivers to alpine lakes. Second, there are a lot of fish, many of them big enough to offer sport to the most serious of anglers. Third, compared with much of the rest of the Sierra Nevada, there are fewer anglers.

Chalk up a bonus point for the little town of Markleeville, a throwback to the mining days that hasn't quite turned into one of the ubiquitous "Get your gold pan here!" wide spots in the tourist road that dot the northern Sierra Nevada. In Markleeville's case, it was silver, rather than gold, and despite a "rush" in the early 1860s, silver was so expensive to mine that the area quickly went broke.

As you may have guessed, I love the Carson and its tributaries. I've fished and camped here as much as any place in the Sierra, and I've spent way too many evenings enjoying the pleasures of the politically incorrect, brassiere-bedecked

Scott Milener looks for rises at Heenan Lake after an autumn snowstorm. The Lahontan cutthroat trout here grow quite large.

Cutthroat Saloon, Markleeville's longtime watering hole.

But enough of such esoteric pleasures. Let's get down to the business of fishing.

The Carson River system is just south of the Truckee River basin, starting at South Lake Tahoe and covering almost 350 square miles. Made up mostly of snowmelt, the Carson flows from about 10,000 feet to 5,000 feet, where it enters Nevada's Carson Valley as the West and East Forks of the Carson River. The rivers are not dammed, so they flow high in the spring and early summer, then get low in the late summer and fall.

Much of the Carson River drainage is in Alpine County, which has the smallest population of any county in California—about 700 full-time residents at last count. There are several ways to get there. From South Lake Tahoe, Highway 89 splits off from Highway 50 and heads southeast over 8,573-foot-high Carson Pass, joining Highway 88 on the way. At Woodfords, Highway 88 forks east to Nevada, while Highway 89 winds south through Markleeville and then to Highway 395 near Topaz Lake. Another route, to my mind one of the prettiest drives in California, is Highway 4, which passes through Angels Camp, Arnold, and Dorrington before it crosses the spine of the Sierra Nevada at 8,731-foot-high Ebbetts Pass. Highway 4 ends at Highway 89, a few miles south of Markleeville. For Southern Californians, an alternative is to follow Highway 395 north and then take Highway 89 or 88 to wherever they want to fish.

There are two forks of the Carson River, the West Carson, which flows through Hope Valley north of Markleeville, and the East Carson, just south of Markleeville. For fishing purposes, they are separate rivers, since they flow deep into Nevada before converging.

THE WEST FORK OF THE CARSON RIVER

The West Fork of the Carson River originates near Carson Pass and flows north 26 miles through Faith Valley and Hope Valley into western Nevada. The West Carson is first accessible from Blue Lakes Road, where it is little more than a stream, then it joins Highways 88 and 89 where they converge at Hope Valley.

This 7 miles of river to the town of Woodfords is the most heavily fished—and heavily stocked—section of the West Carson, with riffles and runs, pocket water, and a few bigger pools. From Woodfords to the Nevada border, the river drops sharply through Woodfords Canyon and provides good pocket-water fishing, although there is little fishing access because of private land. Some of the river can be accessed via Carson River Road, which turns east off Highway 88, about a mile east of the Highway 88 and Highway 89 split, or Diamond Valley Road, off Highway 88, not far from the Nevada border.

THE EAST FORK OF THE CARSON RIVER

The East Fork of the Carson River is typical of many Sierra waters—it offers both easy-access, roadside fishing for stocked rainbows and more difficult fishing in areas where anglers need to work to get to the river, but are rewarded with wild fish. It even has a 12-mile Wild Trout section that should be, but somehow isn't, blue-ribbon water. More about that later.

The East Carson River comes out of the Carson-Iceberg Wilderness, dropping sharply through a deep canyon until it reaches Wolf Creek Meadows, the first spot where an angler can gain reasonably easy access. In the upper stretches of the Carson above the natural barrier made by Carson Falls, 14 miles upstream from Wolf Creek, there still are Lahontan cutthroat. Above Carson Falls, which is strictly hike-in territory, the river and its tributaries are closed to protect this fish, which once was the main trout of the area.

From Wolf Creek to the headwaters, about 28 miles, the East Carson is one of California's original Wild Trout streams singled out for special attention in 1971. The Wild Trout Program's objectives are to maintain the wild-trout populations and to preserve the natural character of the streams, and in the case of the East Carson, to "emphasize maintenance of the remote secluded quality of the angling experience."

To get to Wolf Creek Meadows, take the clearly marked turnoff to the south from Highway 4 just as the highway and

the river join, 7 miles southwest of Markleeville. For the first mile, Wolf Creek Road is paved and parallels the river, which is part of the put-and-take fishery, with stocked rainbows. Then Wolf Creek Road climbs and turns to gravel, while the river stays in its canyon.

At Wolf Creek Meadows, 6 miles from the Highway 4 turnoff, the road drops into the meadow. The left branch leads past several homes and ranch buildings and across Wolf Creek to a corral before cutting steeply uphill. A sign says "Dixon Mine, 2 miles" but the road dead-ends at the Carson River after about a mile. It's a bumpy, rough mile, but can be done without four-wheel drive unless the weather is bad. The road branches into several fingers just before it reaches the river, all of which end on a bluff a hundred feet above the East Carson. There are no facilities, but there is plenty of level space to camp. Numerous trails lead to the river, and access is no problem.

Anglers can work downstream, where Wolf Creek enters the Carson. A number of deep holes make great holding places for bigger trout. It is possible to rockhop downstream all the way to where Wolf Creek Road climbs and leaves the river, but it is several miles and a tough hike.

Upstream from the Dixon Mine area the terrain is more demanding, and there is more pocket water. The fishing can be better, however, since fewer anglers are willing to try it. This is typical rainbow country, with a fair number of fish, but few of them more than twelve inches.

Attractors are fine, along with caddis imitations and mayflies such as the Adams and Pale Morning Dun, while nymphs such as Pheasant Tails, Zug Bugs, and Hare's Ears—with bead heads or not—are effective. As always, carry some ant and grasshopper patterns and a few Woolly Buggers to probe those few deep pools. Sizes for both dries and nymphs usually range from 12 to 16, seldom smaller. I've always favored a Royal Wulff as an attractor, although most Sierra anglers prefer Red or Yellow Humpies.

Wolf Creek itself offers good fishing—fly fishers can go upstream from where it enters the Carson or park in Wolf Creek Meadows and fish downstream. There are mostly resident browns in this mile-long section of Wolf Creek. In the meadow area, Wolf Creek is stocked in the spring, but gets too low for planting in the late summer and early fall. Rather than fish in the meadow, where cattle graze and some private land is fenced off, stay right at the fork in Wolf Creek Road as it enters the valley and follow it to the upper end of the meadow, where it ends at a campground.

Working upstream from the campground—a well-used trail follows Wolf Creek for some miles—is fun fishing and gets the angler away from stocked trout. Some surprisingly large fish can be found in the pocket water where the creek tumbles down out of the mountains. For patterns, try the same as for the Carson River, but perhaps a size smaller.

At the Wolf Creek Road turnoff from Highway 4, Silver

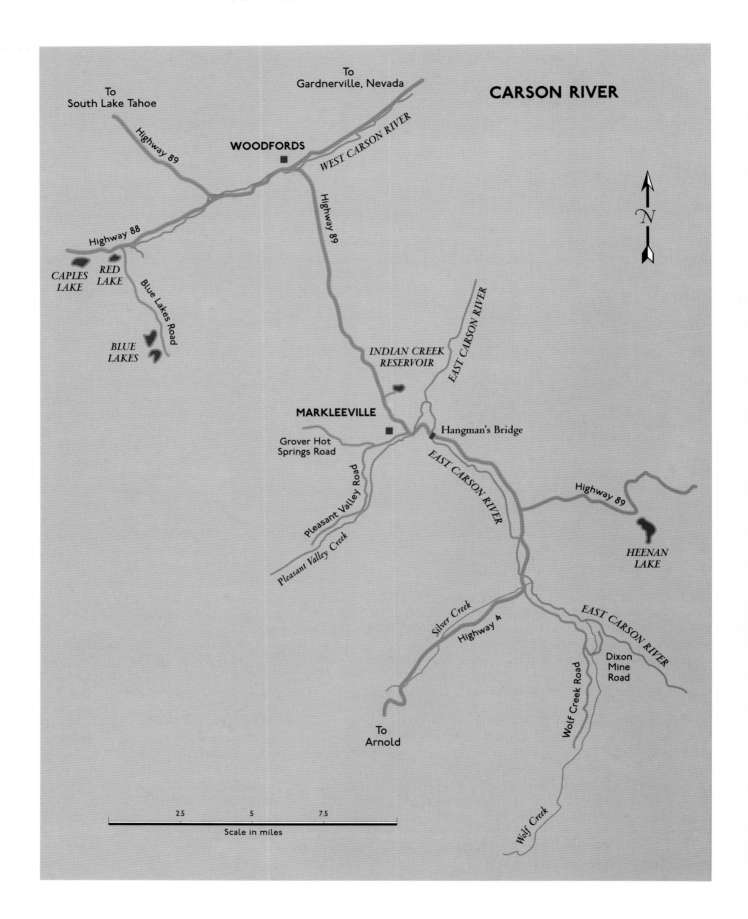

CARSON RIVER

To
South Lake Tahoe

To
Gardnerville, Nevada

WOODFORDS

WEST CARSON RIVER

Highway 89

Highway 89

Highway 88

CAPLES
LAKE

RED
LAKE

Blue Lakes Road

BLUE
LAKES

EAST CARSON RIVER

INDIAN CREEK
RESERVOIR

MARKLEEVILLE

Hangman's Bridge

Grover Hot
Springs Road

EAST CARSON RIVER

Highway 89

HEENAN
LAKE

Pleasant Valley Road

Pleasant Valley Creek

Silver Creek

Highway 4

EAST CARSON RIVER

Wolf Creek Road

Dixon
Mine
Road

To
Arnold

Wolf Creek

N

2.5   5   7.5

Scale in miles

Creek (see below) flows into the Carson. And from this area 6 miles downstream, to Hangmans Bridge near Markleeville, there are numerous access points along the road. The entire section is heavily stocked and heavily fished, not only by Californians, but by Nevada anglers from nearby Gardnerville and Carson City. In addition to hatchery rainbows, there are occasional big Lahontan cutthroats put into the river by the Department of Fish and Game after spawning at Heenan Lake.

Although this entire stretch is heavily pounded by Power Bait and lure anglers, there are areas where a wading fly-line type can find some decent fishing, since there is a solid population of native trout. You just have to pick your spots and get away from bankside pull-ups that get fished day after day, all season.

The Wild Trout section of the river that stretches 12 miles from Hangmans Bridge downstream to the Nevada border is a different matter. Fishing is restricted to barbless lures and flies, with a two-fish, fourteen-inch-minimum limit. There is no easy access—walking or floating the river is the only way to fish it. By the way, Hangmans Bridge got its name in 1874 when vigilantes stopped a group taking a man to Bridgeport to be tried for murder and executed him in the tradition of the Old West by looping a rope around his neck.

This section of the East Carson was designated a Wild Trout stream in 1986 with the hope it would become a blue-ribbon fishery. It hasn't, and nobody seems quite sure why. Some local anglers place the blame on white-water rafters, who they claim take as many big trout as they want while drifting the river in spring and early summer, decimating the natural brood stock. Note that this is what they claim, not what anybody actually knows is happening.

Anglers willing to work their way from the bridge downstream can expect reasonable, but not great fishing. The river is large enough so that bankside walking is possible and a day-long expedition can cover several miles of water. There are long stretches of almost barren water, so the fly fisher needs to hit likely spots, and if the fish don't respond, go on to the next riffle or hole. Don't bother pounding a piece of water that doesn't produce.

There is parking on either side of Hangmans Bridge and numerous signs stating current regulations. Access to the south side of the river is over a private gate (at this time the owner does not object), and the hiking here is easier than on the north bank.

Judy Warren, who guides in this area, says the favorite flies are Prince Nymphs, either with or without a bead head, a Hare's Ear Beadhead, and black Woolly Buggers. For dries, try any of the Adams flies—Parachute, Irresistible, or standard, in size 14, 16, or 18—along with a White Miller. In the fall, grasshopper patterns and Muddler Minnows work well.

ALPINE COUNTY LAKES

In addition to the forks of the Carson River, Wolf Creek, and Pleasant Valley Creek, there are more than sixty lakes in Alpine County, alone, most of them with fish. Here are just a few of them that are accessible from West Carson country.

Upper and **Lower Blue Lakes** actually are a series of lakes 12 miles off Highway 88 near Carson Pass. A bit farther west up Highway 88 there is access to **Red Lake,** which has good-sized brookies. **Red Lake Creek** emerges from Red Lake near Carson Pass and flows through shallow, forested canyons and high meadows to the West Fork of the Carson in Hope Valley. There are shallow riffles, some runs, and plenty of pocket water. This used to provide excellent fishing and may again be prime water, although it has gone through a low spell when its fishing could best be described as routine. What happens depends on what the Department of Fish and Game, which now owns the lake water, decides to do.

Caples Lake is a few miles west along Highway 88, near the Kirkwood Ski Resort, and provides its best fishing at ice-out. During the summer, float tube near the two dams at the eastern end of the lake early and late in the day. There are numerous campgrounds in this area, along with boat ramps, resorts, and stores. This lake is a favorite for a number of anglers and is home to some big Mackinaws, which generally are deep and can be reached only by trolling.

A lake worth mentioning that falls in between the two forks of the Carson is **Indian Creek Reservoir,** which is near the Markleeville airport, just north of town. It is only 4 miles from Highway 89 along a paved road and is a great area for an angler who wants to float tube or use a small pram or canoe, or a small boat with an electric motor. It also can be fished from the shore.

Chances of hooking large rainbows, Lahontan cutthroats, brook trout, and Kamloops are excellent. The most effective flies are black or olive Woolly Worms or Woolly Buggers, Matukas, and any dark nymphs. Sizes 10 to 12 do best. Dries can work in the evening, depending on the hatches. There is a first-come, first-served BLM campground at the lake, and the big Turtle Rock Park Campground is not far away on the west side of Highway 89.

If you really want to get into fishing the lakes in this region, buy a U.S. Forest Service map of the Toiyabe National Forest and do some backcountry exploring. You can't go wrong. For all the lakes, use the normal Sierra dries and nymphs, along with scud patterns, Woolly Buggers, and Muddlers.

HEENAN LAKE

Heenan Lake deserves special mention. It used to be the closest thing to a guaranteed public big-trout lake in California—Lahontan cutthroats to thirty inches and more! It still has them, and folks still are catching them, but sometimes it seems you can walk across its 129 surface acres on the tubes of avid anglers.

The lake is 8 miles east of Markleeville on Highway 89 as it heads over Monitor Pass. The lake is a few hundred yards off the highway on an unmarked dirt road 4.2 miles from the junction of Highways 89 and 4. You can't miss it because of the cars parked there.

Heenan sits at 7,200 feet, surrounded by sagebrush-dotted hills still used for cattle grazing. Since it was acquired in 1982 by the Wildlife Conservation Board, it has been used as the only breeding area in California for Lahontan cutthroat, which are listed as a threatened species.

Regulations are complicated. It is open on Fridays, Saturdays, and Sundays from Labor Day through the last Sunday in October. Its policy is strictly barbless hooks, no bait, and let 'em go. The entire lake is fenced, and a Department of Fish and Game warden checks it regularly. It used to be that a game warden was on hand during fishing hours collecting a $3.00 fee, but at the moment there is no permanent warden, and the fishing is free. This could change, so check the regulations.

Small portable boats with electric motors can be used (gas engines are not permitted) and can be taken by auto almost to the water down a short access road from the dirt parking lot. Float tubes are the favorite means of fishing the waters, although a number of anglers do well from the bank, since the cutthroat tend to hang out in water three to eight feet deep fairly close to shore.

A jam-packed parking lot and a couple of portable toilets are the main fixtures—visitors make the trek for the fishing, not the scenery. There are a few smaller fish, but twenty-inchers are hooked regularly and fish up to thirty inches aren't unheard of. DFG biologists who take spawners from the lake to breed them say there are some even larger, and I know of one thirty-three-incher caught on a fly.

The Heenan Lake breeders are a full-bodied fish native to the area, a strain that comes from the prehistoric Lake Lahontan that used to cover a good portion of what is now Nevada. The remnants of Lake Lahontan today are Pyramid and Walker Lakes. Due to commercial overfishing late in the last century, Lahontan cutthroat died out in Pyramid Lake and became hybridized in most of the remaining eastern-slope areas.

Eggs from Heenan are distributed to the Hot Creek and Mount Shasta hatcheries. In turn, the grown fish are put into a number of streams and lakes, including Pyramid Lake, Pleasant Valley Creek, and the East Carson River.

For the first few years, Heenan was an undiscovered hot spot, but since the early 1990s, when it became well known, it has been jammed on fall weekends—at least until the weather turns cold and windy. There have been some ecological scares, too, including a major drawdown of water by the Nevada

rancher who owns the water rights and then an algae bloom that drained the oxygen from the lake and caused a major die-off. Despite this, there still are plenty of large cutthroat in the lake, and the fishing remains good, although it is more difficult than in the early days, when a Woolly Bugger trolled by float tubers generally would garner a strike.

Woolly Buggers still catch fish, as do black, purple, or green Matukas, but make sure to keep them a solid color with no red. I wish I could tell you why. Several local anglers who fish Heenan regularly, including Judy Warren, told me this. I can't prove it from personal experience, however, since I find that dark nymphs—Pheasant Tails, Zug Bugs, and Bird's Nests, size 12 or 14—work better. There also is an Antron caterpillar pattern called the Heenan Special that is favored for the lake . Only occasionally is a Heenan Lahontan caught on a dry fly, and then usually in the evening. If you want to try, the usual mayfly or caddis imitations in size 14 or 16 are best.

SILVER CREEK

Silver Creek, which parallels Highway 4 for almost 4 miles before it runs into the East Carson, often is overlooked because it is so close to the road and is so brushy. This typical, tumbling Sierra stream is mostly pocket water. And brushy it is. The big problem for fly-line anglers is finding a place to fish because of the brush that chokes Silver Creek from both sides. About the only places that are easy to fish are where Highway 4 crosses the creek and it widens into riffles, allowing anglers to work up or down the stream.

On the other hand, the biggest fish are in those areas where it is hardest to cast to them. It can be frustrating work, and cost a lot of hung-up flies, to fish Silver Creek, but it also can be productive. It is fishable until late in the season, since unlike many other streams in the area, it does not become a thin trickle by early fall.

PLEASANT VALLEY CREEK

Alas, what used to be one of the better fishing spots in the Carson River area no longer is open to the public. Pleasant Valley, only three miles from Markleeville, is a privately-owned ranch that had been open to fly fishers for more than half a century. Beginning with the 1998 season, the owners, fed up with trash, campfires, bad manners and the general hassle, turned Pleasant Valley Creek into a pay-to-play fly-fishing stream. Permits can be purchased through Alpine Fly Fishing in nearby Markleeville. (See below for details.)

SUMMING UP

The Carson River drainage is what you want to make of it—fishing for stocked trout in easy-access areas or working harder to get to wild trout, some of them big. The two forks of the Carson River—the **West Carson** north of Markleeville and the **East Carson** to the south of town—are roadside fisheries that are popular with anglers of all types and are regularly filled with hatchery rainbows. The Wild Trout area of the East Carson, from Hangmans bridge 12 miles downstream to the Nevada border, never developed into a blue-ribbon fishery as hoped.

In the fall, from Labor Day Weekend until the end of October, **Heenan Lake** provides catch-and-release fishing for huge Lahontan cutthroats. This is the only breeding area for Lahontans in California and is run by the state Department of Fish and Game. Float tubing is best, but small boats without gas motors can be used. My personal favorite, however, is **Wolf Creek,** upstream from the campground at the end of Wolf Creek Meadows off Highway 4. It is not stocked, and although the trout aren't big, it is fun fishing into the canyon.

♦ ♦ ♦ ♦ ♦ ♦

ADDITIONAL INFORMATION

FLY SHOPS

Angler's Edge, 1420A Highway 395, Gardnerville, NV 89410: (702) 782-4734. This is a full-service fly shop.

Alpine Fly Fishing, inside Grover's Corner, 14841 Highway 89, Markleeville, CA 96120; (530) 542-0759 or (530) 694-2562. This fly shop is in what used to be Monty Wolf's in Markleeville and handles permits to fish Pleasant Valley Creek. Permits can be purchased by stopping at the shop or writing Alpine Fly Fishing well in advance of the desired date at P.O. Box 10465, South Lake Tahoe, CA 96158.

Tahoe Fly Fishing Outfitters, 3433 Lake Tahoe Boulevard, South lake Tahoe, CA 96150; (530) 541-8208. Web site: http://www.sierra.net/flyfishing. E-mail: flyshop1@sierra.net.

HOSPITALS

South Lake Tahoe: Barton Memorial Hospital, 2170 South Avenue, South Lake Tahoe, CA 96150; (530) 541-3420.

Carson City: Carson Tahoe Hospital, 775 Fleischmann Way, Carson City, NV 89703; (702) 882-1361.

Gardnerville: Carson Valley Medical Center, 1107 Highway 395, Gardnerville, NV 89410; (702) 782-1500. Carson Valley Health Center, Stratton Center, 1538 Highway 395, Gardnerville, NV 89410; (702) 782-8181.

PUBLIC CAMPING

There are numerous public and private campgrounds throughout the area. For information, contact the Alpine County Visitor's Information Bureau, 3 Webster Street, Markleeville, CA 96120; (530) 694-2475. Fax: (530) 694-2478. E-mail: alpcnty@telis.org.

Paolo Marchesi

Lahontan cutthroat trout were once found in many waters of the Lake Tahoe region. They're much rarer now; Heenan Lake is used by the Department of Fish and Game to raise broodstock for stocking other rivers.

MORE SOURCES

Contact the Alpine County Visitor's Information Bureau via one of the means listed above.

Sorenson's Resort, 14255 Highway 88, Hope Valley, CA 96120; (530) 694-2203.

Angling Alpine: A Field Guide for Fly Fishing Alpine County, by J. E. Warren. The book costs $12.95 and can be purchased at several local stores. It offers detailed suggestions on what flies to use on area rivers, lakes, and creeks.

CHAPTER 15: THE BRIDGEPORT AREA
Trophy Trout Country, Incredible Fishing.

Rick E. Martin

THE streams and lakes in the Bridgeport area of the Sierra Nevada eastern slope offer some of the best and most varied trout fishing in California. For big-trout anglers, there are Bridgeport Reservoir and the East Walker River, which is a premier stream for fly fishers. Then there's Green Creek, a small mountain stream holding trout so big they have no right to be there. Not far up the road is Kirman Lake, a walk-in pond with trophy-sized brook trout and a few Lahontan cutthroats.

Add a couple of dozen other lakes and myriad streams that hold both wild and stocked trout. The Bridgeport Chamber of Commerce is quick to point out that it has thirty-five lakes and 500 miles of streams within a 15-mile radius. That's a lot of water, folks, and they aren't just being local boosters when they claim most of it is worth fishing. Fishing is important to Bridgeport, even though its main industry is cattle ranching. Unlike Mammoth Lakes, 35 miles to the south, there is no winter ski trade here, and most businesses must make their living from summer tourists, many of whom come for the angling.

The downside is that since the influx is seasonal, tourist businesses such as motels and gas stations soak the cus-

tomers with prices higher than just about anyplace else in California. For the most part they are up front about it—"We've only got a few months in which to make a living"—but that doesn't help me when I'm forking out an extra thirty cents a gallon for gas or additional twenty dollars for a motel room.

Bridgeport is about the same distance, at least in driving time, from Southern California as from the San Francisco Bay area. Southern Californians can shoot north on Highway 395, while Northern Californians can cross the Sierra Nevada via Highway 120 or 108 if they don't mind narrow, twisty roads. An alternative is to take Interstate 80 to Reno and then head south on Highway 395, which is a longer drive, but easier motoring.

Once you're there, the Bridgeport area offers numerous campgrounds, many easily accessible and others higher in the mountains, but still reachable by gravel or dirt roads. For those willing to shoulder a pack and sleeping bag along with their fishing gear, the selection of high-country streams and lakes is limited only by stamina and time. The base elevation is about 7,000 feet, and many of the waters are much higher, so the season doesn't really get started for many areas until June or even July.

Although there is a lot of water around here, it is scattered. This chapter deals first with the East Walker River and

July, and there's still plenty of snow on the mountains above Lower Virginia Lake south of Bridgeport. The lake offers good fishing for planted rainbows.

Bridgeport Reservoir, since they are the best known of the areas. Other sections are the Highway 108 area north of Bridgeport, including Kirman Lake, the Little and West Walker Rivers, and Topaz Lake; the area near Bridgeport, including Twin Lakes, Robinson Creek, Buckeye Creek, Barney Lake, and the Highway 120 area south of Bridgeport, including Green Creek and the Virginia Lakes.

Bridgeport is the only town around, and Ken's Sporting Goods on Main Street is an excellent source of up-to-date fishing information. Owner Rick Rockel, an avid fly fisher, opens early, closes late, and keeps abreast of the situation on just about every piece of water in his territory. It also is worth stopping just to see the huge trout in a freezer in front of the shop—you may want to let yours go, but at least this gives you an idea of what waits to be hooked in some of the local waters.

THE EAST WALKER RIVER

The lower East Walker, which flows from Bridgeport Reservoir to the Nevada border, has a history of both fine fishing and major problems. But it has been resurrected and should remain blue-ribbon fishing for the foreseeable future. The last disaster came during the 1988–89 drought, when Bridgeport Reservoir was drained to fulfill the demand for water by the farmers and ranchers in Nevada who control the water rights. As the reservoir emptied, it carried tons of silt into the East Walker, killing many of the trophy-sized trout there. Local anglers did what they could to save the fish, but most of them died.

The uproar led to legal action and a court ruling that prevents this from happening again. It took years for the 7 miles of the East Walker between the reservoir and the Nevada border to come back as a trophy trout area, but it would appear that the bad old days are over, and excellent fishing will prevail in the future.

Like most popular big-trout waters, the East Walker isn't an easy river to fish. How you fly fish it depends on the time of year. From the opener in April until the end of May or early June, when the river runs high, large streamers, heavy leaders, and sink-tip lines are necessary. Light leaders leave almost no chance of landing these big fish, so use 1X or even 0X to handle streamers tied on size 2 or 4 hooks. Flies that imitate minnows are the ticket, including black or white Marabou streamers, Woolhead Sculpins, and Matukas. When the water drops, switch to large nymphs that imitate caddis—Bitch Creek Nymphs are one favorite. As summer comes on, the size of the nymphs gets smaller, down to 12 and 14. Caddis imitations and general patterns such as Zug Bugs are recommended. Hopper patterns fished on top also are effective, particularly in the late summer and fall, when weeds sometime make nymphing difficult. A favorite time of year for fishing the East Walker is in October (the season here closes October 31), when browns move up to the base of the

dam to spawn. The Big Hole pool just below the dam becomes jammed with anglers, and with good reason, since many of the biggest fish are there.

The East Walker flows through private land, but there are a number of access points available. Just remember that it is private land, so leave it cleaner than you found it.

The best fishing is in the 1.5-mile stretch from the dam downstream to the Highway 182 bridge. It is limited to barbless lures and flies only, with a one-fish limit, eighteen inches or longer. From the bridge to the Nevada border, two fish, fourteen inches or longer, can be kept, but tackle restrictions remain the same. The section to the bridge is flatter water, with more long runs. The water downstream of the bridge has more riffles, and although fishing is good, there aren't as many large trout.

The upper section of the East Walker is the major tributary to Bridgeport Reservoir, flowing into the lake from the south. Most of it is on private land, but it can be reached from the Highway 395 at the eastern end of Bridgeport. It is a meandering meadow stream noted for springtime fishing for spawning rainbows and fall fishing for spawning browns. There is little cover in the stream itself, but undercut banks furnish good protection for big fish. Use the same streamers in the spring as on the East Walker below Bridgeport Reservoir and hopper imitations in the summer. There aren't a lot of fish, but the ones you'll find there are large.

BRIDGEPORT RESERVOIR

Bridgeport Reservoir is noted for bait and lure fishing, but there are times when fly fishers will have a chance at hooking some of its huge rainbows and browns. The water is murky most of the time, which hampers fly fishing. But in the spring and fall, float tubing near the dam with large sculpin and leech patterns can bring some vicious strikes by big fish. There are two boat ramps on the lake.

The reservoir, fed by the East Walker and several creeks, is shallow, except near the dam at the northern end, and can be waded at the southern tip, where the East Walker enters. This is a particularly nutrient-rich lake, with fantastic weed and insect growth that quickly turns trout into behemoths There also are scuds and a variety of minnows.

HIGHWAY 108

This twisty two-lane from Sonora Pass to Highway 395 16 miles north of Bridgeport offers access to a variety of lakes, including **Kirman Lake,** famed for football-shaped brook trout that weigh four or five pounds. Kirman (sometimes called Carmen Lake) also holds a few equally large Lahontan cutthroats raised from Heenan Lake stock. (See the Carson River chapter.)

The trail to Kirman Lake is a rancher's private dirt road that goes south off Highway 108 half a mile from where it

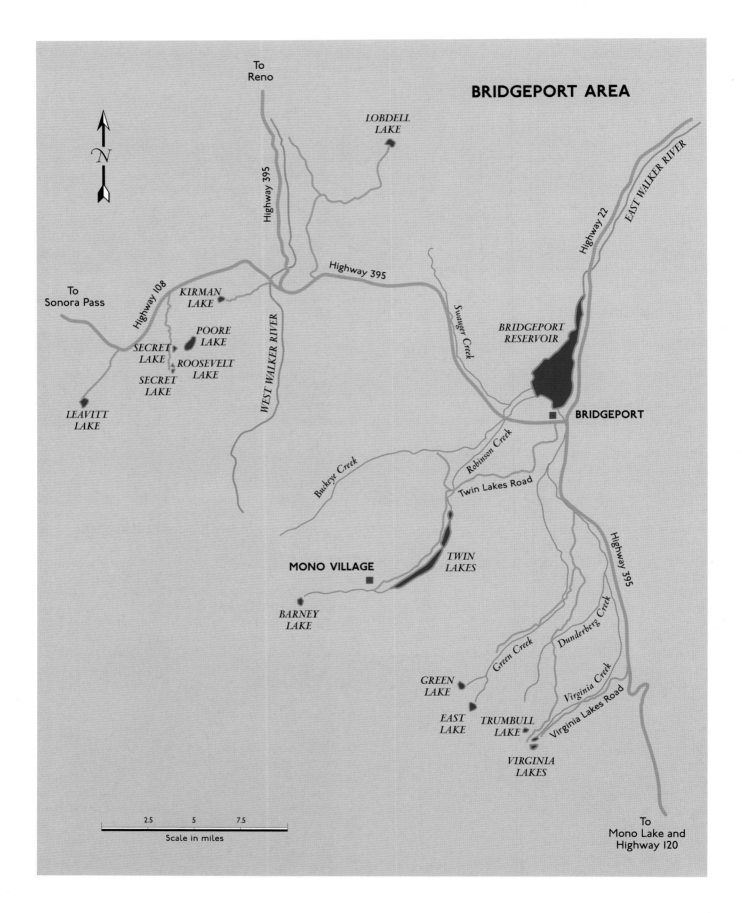

BRIDGEPORT AREA

N

To
Reno

LOBDELL
LAKE

Highway 395

EAST WALKER RIVER

Highway 22

BRIDGEPORT
RESERVOIR

To
Sonora Pass

Highway 108

KIRMAN
LAKE

Highway 395

Swauger Creek

POORE
LAKE

SECRET
LAKE

ROOSEVELT
LAKE

SECRET
LAKE

WEST WALKER RIVER

BRIDGEPORT

LEAVITT
LAKE

Robinson Creek

Buckeye Creek

Twin Lakes Road

Highway 395

TWIN
LAKES

MONO VILLAGE

BARNEY
LAKE

Dunderberg Creek

Green Creek

GREEN
LAKE

Virginia Creek

EAST
LAKE

TRUMBULL
LAKE

Virginia Lakes Road

VIRGINIA
LAKES

To
Mono Lake and
Highway 120

2.5   5   7.5

Scale in miles

intersects Highway 395. Near a cattle guard there is parking on both sides of Highway 108, and the dirt road can be reached by climbing a wooden stairway over a fence on the southern side. It is an easy walk to the lake—about an hour for a little less than 3 miles. However, anglers need to haul along a float tube, and carrying that gear can make the hike seem double the distance. The road is perfect for a mountain bike if you can set it up to carry a tube.

Shoreline fishing is limited, although there is some early and late in the season, when the fish are cruising the shallows or trying to spawn. Otherwise, a float tube is about the only way to pick up good-sized trout. For flies, try small Olive Matukas, Spruce Matukas, small leech patterns, Zug Bugs, and freshwater shrimp patterns. The main trout fodder in Kirman is shrimp, but tossing a shrimp pattern at them means you are competing with millions of naturals. Only artificial, barbless flies and lures can be used on Kirman Lake, but two trout that are sixteen inches or longer can be kept.

Kirman has a reputation for offering hot fishing one year, then being almost barren the next. The DFG has checked the lake, and the fish are always there—it's just catching them that seems to be the problem.

Continuing west on Highway 108, Leavitt Meadow, across from the U.S. Marine Corps training center, is an excellent jumping-off point for easy hikes to a series of lakes that offer trout fishing. There is a campground with convenient roadside parking for anglers who want to walk in to **Poore Lake, Lane Lake, Roosevelt Lake, Secret Lake,** and **Hidden Lake.** These lakes can be reached in a walk of an hour and a half to two hours, less, if you use a mountain bike. Poore Lake, like Kirman, has trophy brook trout in the four-pound to five-pound range and Kamloops rainbows that run nearly as big. The four smaller lakes—Hidden Lake is the longest hike—have brook and Lahontan cutthroat trout that run up to a couple of pounds in size.

The usual Sierra nymphs such as Zug Bugs or Gold-Ribbed Hare's Ears work well, along with leech patterns, including Woolly Buggers and Woolly Worms. In Poore Lake, the big brookies feed on Lahontan redside suckers, so take along streamer patterns such as a multicolored Marabou Muddler that contains some red and gold. These streamers are particularly effective early and late in the day, when trout are feeding on the suckers on the shallow shelves that surround the lake.

Near the Sierra crest on Sonora Pass, about 10 miles from the Highway 395 turnoff, a four-wheel-drive road leads to **Leavitt Lake.** The lake has great brook trout and Kamloops fishing, but at 9,500 feet it is cold and generally is iced over until late June or early July. Because it is deep, bait fishing is the best bet for anglers, although occasionally flies can be effective in the early morning or late evening. Two nearby lakes, **Latopie** and **Koenig,** also have fishing and can be reached by easy hiking.

For details on fishing the western side of Sonora Pass, see the Highway 108 chapter.

THE WEST WALKER AND LITTLE WALKER RIVERS

The West Walker and East Walker are separate bodies of water, not only in fact, but in character. The West Walker is a typical freestone stream, tumbling out of the Sierra alongside Highway 108. As it approaches Highway 395, it is joined by the Little Walker and then parallels 395 north. For about a dozen miles it offers drive-up fishing, then spills into Antelope Valley and becomes a meandering meadow stream until it ends at Topaz Lake, on the California-Nevada border.

The section of the West Walker that parallels Highway 395 north was devastated in the January 1997 flood. So much water smashed through the narrow canyon that it took out huge sections of the highway, rerouted the river channel, and stripped the banks of all vegetation. Although the highway was rebuilt within six months and the river rechanneled back into its preflood bed, there was not much that could be done with the banks that once had been lush with riparian growth. Huge sections along the river now are marked by little more than boulders and tree stumps left behind during cleanup efforts. This was mostly an area of stocked fish, although there were some wild browns, and it is being heavily planted with hatchery fish again. But how long it will be until enough growth returns to offer protection to whatever wild fish remain is an open question. Still, this section of the river offers fun dry-fly fishing in September and October.

A better bet for fly fishers, however, is to follow the West Walker downstream from the picnic area on Highway 108 about 2 miles west of the junction with 395. The river is planted at the picnic area and is fished heavily, but from that point on it moves away from the highway and cuts northeast through a canyon to intersect with Highway 395 some 2 miles away. It takes several hours to fish this section of the river, and it is a good way to spend a morning or afternoon. Dry-fly attractors, including Yellow Humpies, Royal Wulffs, and Hornberg Specials, work well through here.

Not much of the West Walker is fishable in Antelope Valley, where the towns of Walker and Coleville are located and the West Walker changes from a mountain freestone stream to a slow-flowing meadow river. This area is owned by ranchers and farmers, and access is difficult. Once on the river, anglers can work their way up or down the stream, but must stay within the high watermark and not step onto private property. Wading without leaving the water can be worth the trouble, since the Antelope Valley portion of the West Walker is home to large brown trout. But be careful—the water level goes up and down quickly as irrigation demands vary.

The West Walker feeds into **Topaz Lake,** which is split by the boundary between California and Nevada. Because of this, like Lake Tahoe, it can be fished with either a California or Nevada fishing license. There are plenty of rainbows in the range of twelve to eighteen inches in Topaz, and fishing is permitted from January 1 to September 30, but it isn't noted as a fly-fishing lake. Topaz also is home to the so-called tiger trout, a cross between a brookie and a brown trout that is stocked by the Fish and Game Departments in California and Nevada.

A quick word about **Lobdell Lake,** which can be reached via a dirt road that turns east off Highway 395 14 miles north of Bridgeport. A sign saying "Burcham Flats / Lobdell Lake" indicates the road. About 4 miles along the road, a branch to the right eventually leads to Lobdell Lake, a man-made reservoir that turns into little more than a large mud puddle late in the season. Until the mid-1990s, Lobdell contained a thriving population of Montana graylings, the only place you could catch them in California. They were all killed in an unexplained winter die-off, and since then, kokanees have been planted in Lobdell.

A creek worth mentioning is **Swauger Creek,** which parallels Highway 395 from the Bridgeport Ranger Station north for several miles. Although close to the road, it is choked with brush and willows, and few people fish it, not realizing it has a good population of wild brown trout. It isn't easy fishing, but for anglers willing to work, it is productive. An added bonus is that probably nobody else will be fishing it.

TWIN LAKES AND OTHER BRIDGEPORT AREA WATERS

Upper and **Lower Twin Lakes** can be fly fished, particularly in the early morning or late evening along the banks, but they are much better for bait and lure angling, particularly trolling. Only 15 miles from Bridgeport, Twin Lakes has campgrounds, stores, rental boats, and other facilities aimed at attracting the vacation trade.

Both lakes are much clearer and deeper than Bridgeport Lake—Lower Twin goes to 160 feet and Upper Twin to 120 feet. They are heavily stocked with rainbows and kokanees, but they also have some big brown trout. The state record for a brown—twenty-six pounds, eight ounces, caught in 1987—was from Upper Twin. The kokanees generally are small. They are easy to catch, particularly in the evening, when they come near the surface, on Black Gnats, attractors like Royal Wulffs, or streamers such as size 8 and 10 Olive Matukas or Hornberg Specials. Catching trophy browns on flies is unlikely, since most of them are hooked by deep trolling.

Another popular water in this area is **Robinson Creek,** the outlet for Twin Lakes. This feeder stream for Bridgeport Reservoir follows the road north toward Bridgeport and is perhaps the most popular of the family fishing areas. It has five Forest Service campgrounds, including the big Robinson Creek Campground just a mile from Lower Twin Lake, and a steady supply of stocked rainbows. There also are some wild browns in the stream. Fly fishers can do well with Royal Wulffs, various caddis patterns, Yellow Humpies, and small

Scott Milener checks his knots before fishing the East Walker River. No one wants to lose a large fish through carelessness.

Hornberg Specials.

The upper section of Robinson Creek is a major feeder stream for Upper Twin Lake. Anglers can follow a well-marked Forest Service trail from Mono Village at the end of

Paolo Marchesi

Upper Twin and hike to **Barney Lake,** about an hour and a quarter walk upstream. It is ideal for a day hike. Barney Lake, not to be confused with the lake of the same name near Mammoth Lakes, offers easy-to-catch brook trout in the eight-to-twelve-inch range.

Buckeye Creek, another Bridgeport Reservoir feeder stream, is in the drainage to the north of lower Robinson Creek

and can be reached either by a dirt road that cuts north at Bogards Camp, about 2.5 miles north of Twin Lakes on the road to Bridgeport, or by an unimproved dirt road that heads south from the Bridgeport Ranger Station on Highway 395 west of Bridgeport. Several campgrounds on Buckeye Creek offer easy access to fishing. The lower stretches of Buckeye are planted during the summer, but by working upstream and away from the road, an angler can find wild brook trout. There also are some brookies and browns in the lower stretches, along with the planted rainbows.

HIGHWAY 395 SOUTH OF BRIDGEPORT

Green Creek is to my mind one of the most enjoyable fly fishing areas on the eastern slope of the Sierra Nevada. It also is very demanding—anglers have little chance of catching bigger fish (we're talking in the fourteen-to fifteen-inch class) unless they have reasonable technical skills. The waters are clear, the fish are spooky, and along much of the creek, heavy brush makes casting difficult and affords excellent protection for the fish.

The turnoff to Green Creek is an unmarked dirt road west off Highway 395 just as it begins to drop into Bridgeport Valley. The road forks after a mile, with a sign showing Green Creek to the left. After another 1.5 miles, the road forks again with a hard, uphill turn to the right leading to Green Creek. Going straight on the road leads to Virginia Lakes Road and can be used as an alternate way of getting to Green Creek

The road joins Green Creek at a pond known as the Gauging Station and then parallels the creek, which is shaded by aspen and other trees and brush, for about 3 miles. There also is a meadow where the creek has been slowed by beaver ponds. The ponds are tough fishing because every step creates movement that scares the fish, but making the effort can be rewarding.

Green Creek trout will take the usual Sierra patterns, but you'll need long, light leaders to avoid scaring your quarry. Some favorites for the area are black Flying Ants in size 16, attractor patterns like the Royal Wulff or Yellow Humpy, size 16, or caddis or mayfly patterns in size 14 and 16. Caddis patterns should have an olive thorax and the mayflies should be light-colored, such as the Light Cahill or Pale Morning Dun.

The road ends at a campground, which also is the trailhead for three popular lakes—Green Lake, East Lake, and West Lake. They all contain rainbows, browns, and brookies, some of them quite large. East Lake and Green Lake are the most popular for summer fishing with bait and lures. West Lake has sixteen-inch to twenty-inch brown trout that can be caught on flies in October when they are spawning. If you want to do a bit more hiking, the trail to Green Lake and East Lake goes on to Gilman Lake, Hoover Lakes, and Summit Lake, all of which hold rainbows and brook trout.

Little Virginia, Big Virginia, and Trumbull Lakes are popular fishing areas and are easily accessed by way of an 8-mile paved road that turns southwest off Highway 395 at Conway Summit. They are stocked with both rainbow and brook trout, and there are some wild browns. There are campgrounds both on the lakes and on Virginia Creek, which follows the road to Highway 395. Easy access means the entire area is heavily

fished. The lakes are at about 9,500 feet, and snow usually cuts them off until early or mid-June. They are popular with bait and lure anglers, but also can be fly fished from a small pram or with a float tube. A trail that begins near the Virginia Lakes goes to Cooney Lakes, Frog Lakes, and Blue Lake, and then to the series of lakes that also can be reached from Green Creek. There are fish in the lakes, but most are small.

Virginia Creek, which flows out of Little Virginia Lake, drops into a gorge as it parallels Highway 395 toward Bridgeport, but it still is accessible and can provide good fishing for anybody willing to do a little hiking. As it nears Bridgeport, Green Creek flows into Virginia Creek, and Virginia Creek becomes more accessible. It is stocked, but most anglers pass it by, so dropping an attractor fly into its fast-moving water can be productive.

Dog Creek and Dunderberg Creek also converge and flow into Virginia Creek about 8 miles from Bridgeport. The down timber and beaver ponds can make it tough going in spots, but the reward is larger browns, along with big rainbows and brookies.

HIGHWAY 120

Highway 120 branches east from Highway 395 just south of Lee Vining, heading over the Sierra crest at Tioga Pass and into Yosemite National Park. There are a number of creeks and lakes in the area, all of which are planted wherever they are accessible. (See the Yosemite Park Area chapter for details on Yosemite National Park .)

The main fishing creek is Lee Vining Creek, which flows into and out of Ellery Lake, then down to Highway 395 and into Mono Lake. Upper Lee Vining Creek above the lake can be reached where it crosses Highway 120, 9 miles west of the turnoff from Highway 395. To get to the creek below Ellery Lake, take Azusa Camp Road, which turns off Highway 120 3 miles from the Highway 395 intersection, and follow it 5 miles until it crosses the creek. Working upstream or downstream gets away from planters and can lead to productive dry-fly fishing.

Ellery Lake and Tioga Lake are alongside Highway 120 near Yosemite and are heavily stocked, although there also are some wild browns and brookies. An alternative is Saddlebag Lake, reached by a turnoff from Highway 120 about 10 miles from the Highway 395 junction. Saddlebag Creek also can be reached via this road. Both the lake and creek are planted, but also have some wild fish. These all provide the typical fishing of the high Sierra, with attractor dries being the first choice. The fish aren't sophisticated, and they are more used to seeing Power Bait and worms than Royal Wulffs or Humpies.

SUMMING UP

To put it simply, this area has some of the best fishing in California, and plenty of it. The centerpiece is the **East Walker River** below Bridgeport Reservoir, home to big browns and rainbows and an excellent fly-fishing stream. After a series of ups and downs, it has regained its status as a blue-ribbon stream and by itself is worth the trek to Bridgeport, particularly in the fall, when the browns are spawning. **Bridgeport Reservoir,** just outside town, also is home to lunker fish, but fly fishing really is good only in the spring or fall. During the summer, algae bloom and weeds makes it tough going. **Kirman Lake,** a three-mile walk from Highway 108, has huge brookies, along with equal-sized Lahontan cutthroats, but you need to pack along a float tube to do this area justice because there is little fishing from the bank. Last but not least is **Green Creek,** south of Bridgeport. With clear water and ultraspooky trout, it is challenging, but an experienced fly fisher can hook some surprisingly big fish for such a little stream.

The Bridgeport Chamber of Commerce advertises 500 miles of streams and thirty-five lakes that can be fished within a 15-mile radius of town. Because of the abundance of fishable water, this also is an area where a little exploring and a minimum of hiking can put you on water without any company and with plenty of trout waiting to grab your fly.

In most areas, anglers can get by with simple attractor patterns such as a Royal Wulff or Yellow Humpy, although it helps to have a few caddisfly and mayfly patterns, along with the always-useful grasshopper and ant imitations.

◆ ◆ ◆ ◆ ◆ ◆

ADDITIONAL INFORMATION

FLY SHOPS

Ken's Sporting Goods, Main Street, Bridgeport, CA 93517; (760) 932-7707.

This is a general sporting-goods store, but has a good selection of flies and fly-fishing gear. Owner Rick Rockel and his staff are an excellent source of information on what is happening on area waters.

HOSPITALS

Mono County Medical Group, 1000 Twin Lakes Road, Bridgeport, CA 93517; (760) 932-7011.

PUBLIC CAMPING

The U.S. Forest Service Bridgeport Ranger Station, P.O. Box 595, Bridgeport, CA 93517; (760) 932-7070. For reservations at specific campgrounds, call (800) 280-2267.

MORE SOURCES

The Mono County Tourism Commission, P.O. Box 603, Mammoth Lakes, CA 93546; (800) 845-7922.

The Bridgeport Chamber of Commerce, P.O. Box 541, Bridgeport, CA 93517; (760) 932-7500.

The Lee Vining Chamber of Commerce and Mono Lake Visitor Center, Highway 395 and 3rd Street, Lee Vining, CA 93541; (760) 647-6629 or 6595.

CHAPTER 16: THE OWENS RIVER AREA

Where The Big Ones Are

Paolo Marchesi

THIS southeastern slope of the Sierra Nevada, really a high-plains desert, offers some of the best fishing in California. There's everything—spring creeks with unbelievable numbers of trout, rushing mountain waters tumbling through beautiful forestlands, lakes for float tubing, a smorgasbord of campgrounds, first-rate restaurants and lodging, and even several well-stocked fly shops. What more could the fly-line angler ask for? Well...maybe fewer people on some of the better-known streams, but you can't have everything.

This area stretches all the way from June Lakes in the north to Bishop in the south. It includes two of the biggest names in California fly fishing—the Owens River and Hot Creek. Toss in Lake Crowley, Rush Creek, and a handful of high Sierra streams and you have an anglers' heaven. It is equidistant from Southern California and the San Francisco Bay area, and even has a prime winter fishery in the form of the lower Owens River.

Its center is Mammoth Lakes, a major winter ski resort for Southern California that exists only because of the tourist industry. That tourist industry revolves around such outdoor activities as camping, hiking, sightseeing, and fishing in the summer, so the entire area is geared to take care of whatever needs the visitor might have. That means a variety of lodg-

The Owens River, really a large spring creek, meanders through the eastern slope's Owens River Valley and offers some of the best fishing in the Sierra.

ing, from cheap motels to first-class condos, and food from fast to gourmet.

From the Los Angeles area it is a quick shot up Highway 395, about 300 miles and five or six hours. It takes a bit longer from the San Francisco area, since the most direct ways to get there are on the curvy two-lane roads that climb over the spine of the Sierra, Highways 120 and 108. It's slow going, particularly in midsummer, when traffic creeps along behind trailers and motor homes that grind slowly up the steep grades. It's also Yosemite country—Highway 120 goes right through the national park—so there are myriad sightseers who aren't in a hurry to get to prime fishing. An alternative for Bay Area anglers is to take Interstate 80 to Reno, then shoot south on Highway 395.

Since the Owens River Valley, as this east-slope area is called, is about 7,000 feet high, the best fishing for the most part tends to be as the summer wears on. Early-season snowmelt, and sometimes early-season snowstorms, can make fly fishing difficult. And many high-country streams or lakes are generally impossible to reach until June or July, depending on the snow level.

The two best-known fishing areas here are the upper Owens River and Hot Creek. And with good reason. A California Department of Fish and Game electroshock survey of both streams found more than 11,000 fish per mile in each of them. At Hot Creek, they turned up 10,018 browns and

1,396 rainbows per mile, for a total of 11,414 fish. For the Owens River, it was 2,262 browns and 8,785 rainbows, for a total of 11,047. The fish came in all sizes, but with plenty of big ones.

That's the good news. The bad news is that there isn't much of either stream open to public access. What is fishable for free on the Owens is mostly limited to barbless fly or lure fishing with size and limit restrictions. Hot Creek is fly-fishing only, catch-and-release. Most of the length of both streams is in private hands, including "fishing ranches" on both Hot Creek and the Owens River. You have to stay there to fish their section of the water. They are heavily booked in advance and have restrictions on their fishing. The Alpers Owens River Ranch on the Owens River allows fly fishing only and is limited to barbless hooks, catch-and-release. Hot Creek Ranch on Hot Creek is the same, with an added restriction: dry flies only.

Hot Creek runs into the Owens River, which in turn feeds Lake Crowley, a large reservoir that sends its water downstream to Los Angeles. There also is good fishing on the Owens below Crowley, and much of it doesn't carry the restrictions that exist above the reservoir. For fishing purposes, the Owens is three rivers: the upper Owens above Lake Crowley, the Owens River Gorge, which extends from Crowley downstream to Pleasant Valley Reservoir, and the Wild Trout section of the Owens below Pleasant Valley. Regulations on the Owens River are varied and complicated. Always make certain you know which stretch of the river you are on and check the regulations, since they can change.

THE UPPER OWENS RIVER

The headwaters of the Owens are at Big Springs, just 2 miles off Highway 395 along Owens River Road. The water comes from two creeks trickling in from the Sierra, along with a major influx from springs that run year-round and give the upper Owens its spring-creek character. Owens River Road is a clearly marked turnoff to the east, 7 miles north of Mammoth Lakes. Big Springs is a public campground, and fishing is open to the public for about a mile downstream until the river hits the Alpers Owens River Ranch. Regulations are two fish, sixteen inches or larger, barbless lures or flies.

It is only about 13 air miles from Big Springs to Crowley, but the Owens is a meandering meadow stream that, with all its loops and twists, covers close to twice that distance. Throughout the fishing season, it is clear and clean, even though there is some snowmelt in the spring. Its water level varies little, and the smorgasbord of caddisflies, stoneflies, mayflies, and midges allows trout to grow quickly to trophy size.

It is a typical example of an excellent spring creek, and the same abundance of food and the clear water that allow trout growth also make it demanding fishing. Owens River trout see plenty of artificials and have the time to inspect an angler's offerings before taking—or refusing—them. As a result, long leaders, pinpoint casts with drag-free drifts, and match-the-hatch flies are a must.

Another difficulty is the wind. Although it may drop in late afternoon and evening, there are days when there is no letup, and tangled leaders and wind knots are the norm for everybody but the expert caster.

Finally, most of the surrounding countryside is open, with no bankside trees or brush to screen the angler, so creeping on hands and knees to get into position to cast to spooky trout can pay off. Remember, if you can see them, then they can see you, so the less of yourself that shows above the bank, the better chance you have of catching a lunker, rather than simply saying good-bye as it torpedoes downstream.

There's less than a mile of public access from Big Springs to the Alpers Owens River Ranch. The ranch has about 2 miles of stream, along with a man-made float-tube pond stocked with huge trout. This also is where the Alpers rainbows are bred, big, tough-fighting trout that are prime fish for the areas that buy them to stock streams or lakes.

The Alpers Ranch borders on Arcularius Ranch, which from 1919 until it was sold in 1998 was a fishing ranch that had fewer than twenty cabins and about 5 miles of the river for its customers. Now the fishing is available only to the owners. Another ranch downstream from Arcularius also is closed to the public. But below that, the Owens River is open to fishing down to where it feeds into Crowley. It is about 5 miles as the crow flies, but double that walking the streambank. In 1996, the Los Angeles Department of Water and Power and local ranchers installed a strong, barbed-wire fence on both sides of the river, preventing cattle from getting to the Owens. This stretch of the river already offered prime fishing, and if anything, should get even better.

There are two ways to get to the public section of the Owens. The first is to follow Owens River Road for more than 5 miles, past the various ranches. Just past a cattle guard and fence is a dirt road to the left (east) that goes to the river in what is known as the Long Ears section. (Long Ears was the name of the ranch that used to own the land.) A short hike across a couple of ditches puts you on the riverbank. Anglers also can open a wire gate (don't forget to close it behind you) and drive upstream a ways.

A more popular access is Benton Crossing Road, a two-lane blacktop reached from Highway 395 just south of the turnoff to Mammoth Lakes. It crosses the Owens about a mile upstream from where it enters Crowley, and dirt roads either north or south allow excellent access all along this stretch of river. The entire area offers prime fishing, and there is enough of it so anglers generally can have a stretch of river to themselves.

Caddis are a major food on the Owens, and the flies should match them. Just about any caddis pattern works, but the ubiquitous Elk Hair Caddis, size 12 to 16, is a perennial favorite. A CDC Caddis Emerger also is very effective, while for nymphs, try Gold-Ribbed Hare's Ears, size 12 or 14,

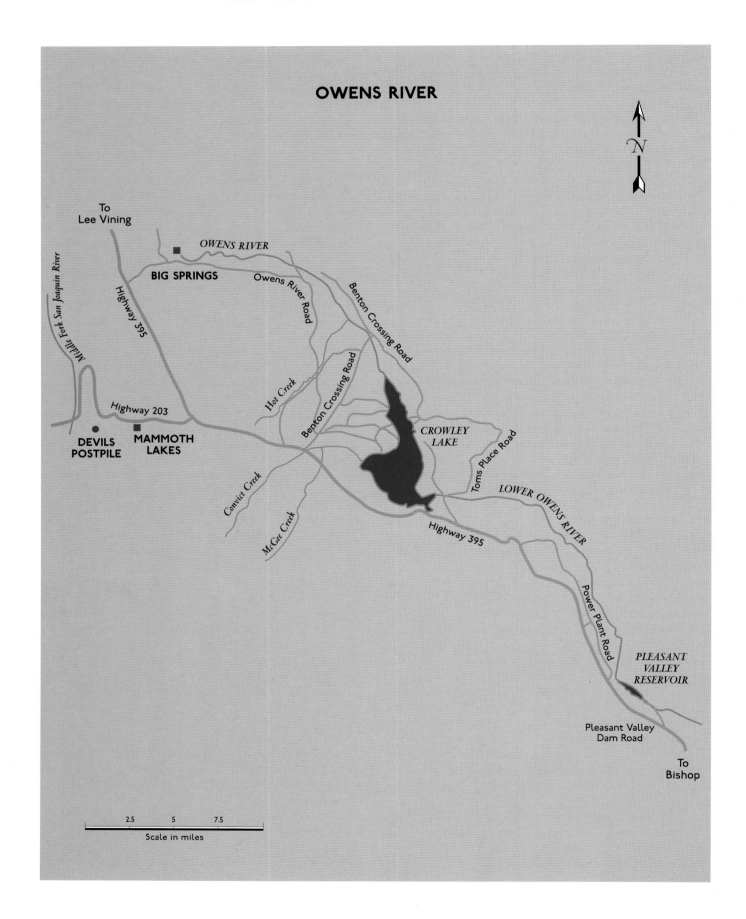

OWENS RIVER

N

To
Lee Vining

OWENS RIVER

■ **BIG SPRINGS**

Middle Fork San Joaquin River

Highway 395

Owens River Road

Benton Crossing Road

Hot Creek

Benton Crossing Road

Highway 203

● **DEVILS POSTPILE** ■ **MAMMOTH LAKES**

Conviet Creek

McGee Creek

CROWLEY LAKE

Toms Place Road

LOWER OWENS RIVER

Highway 395

Power Plant Road

PLEASANT VALLEY RESERVOIR

Pleasant Valley
Dam Road

To
Bishop

2.5   5   7.5
Scale in miles

Beadhead Pheasant Tails and Bird's Nests, size 12 or 14, and olive or orange scuds. Streamers attract big trout, so don't forget to bring along a selection of Woolly Buggers, Matukas, and Clouser Minnows, size 6 and 8.

The Owens River from Big Springs to Crowley, whether on public or private land, is fished the same way. The stream, the fish, and the insects are the same, and trout are everywhere. It is productive, but not easy fishing. Clear water, undercut banks, prolific hatches, and big, smart fish can intimidate novice anglers. Cautious approaches, accurate casts, and drag-free floats are crucial. For the fly fisher seeking to become an expert, this is one of the best training grounds I know. Proper presentation will be rewarded with fish; sloppy angling will mean only a handful of smaller trout.

The upper Owens is a migratory hatchery, with rainbows coming upriver to spawn in the spring and the big browns moving up from Crowley in the fall. Although there are plenty of large resident fish in the river in between, those are the periods when the biggest fish are caught. When the season opens in late April, the Owens is basically a nymph fishery, but within weeks, anglers can switch to dries and score on the big fish by using the classic Fall River drift technique, with long leaders and absolutely no drag. This technique involves drifting a fly downstream in a lane where the angler sees a fish feeding. Cast upstream a bit beyond this lane, quickly draw the fly back into the proper position by stripping in line, then feed line rapidly, so the fly makes its way downstream to the fish without dragging. It takes a bit of practice, but is an effective technique on any spring creek or similar stream where big fish are feeding constantly in one spot.

After spawning, along about the middle or the end of May, the big fish start moving downstream again to return to Crowley. It's then that the fishing picks up on the private ranches, or in the public stretch from below the ranches to Lake Crowley.

Fred Rowe, who has fished the area for years, says, "There are two ways to fish during this period—you either have to get flies down deep and into the holes, or you can strip them in and out of the cut banks and get the fish to come out and take them. The problem with fishing this section of the river is that it is real hit-and-miss because you have to find the fish. They are not podded up, so the trick is to cover a lot of territory to find one or two big fish."

"You cast and you cover the water, get the flies down deep. If you don't get anything, keep going. Cast and move, cast and move."

By the Fourth of July, most big fish have returned to Crowley, and although the action on dries becomes fast and furious on the Owens, most of the fish are smaller. In October, when the browns and rainbows again are spawning, they come out of Crowley and begin to work their way upriver. Yes, rainbows—there is a fall-breeding strain in Crowley, along with the more normal spring spawners.

As the fish move onto the ranches, if an angler hasn't booked the year before, it is tough finding room during this period. The spawners eventually will hit Big Springs once again as the season draws to a close. But remember, it's at about 7,000 feet elevation and can get cold, with snow flurries.

The regulations on this section of the river, from the private ranches to Benton Crossing Bridge, are artificial flies and lures, barbless hooks, and a limit of two trout, sixteen inches or smaller. From Benton Crossing downstream to the fishing monument, which is about a quarter of a mile upstream from the maximum lake level, there are no special restrictions. From the monument to Lake Crowley there are no special restrictions until August 1. From then until the end of the season (October 31 in this area), it is artificial lures, barbless hooks, and an eighteen-inch minimum for the two trout anglers are allowed to keep.

HOT CREEK

There isn't much of Hot Creek to fish, but what there is can provide a tremendous experience. This isn't exactly a secret, so fishing there without company is a rarity. Just below the hatchery is a short stretch of Hot Creek that is open to the public, but that was not well known for years. Now it is popular, with what appears at times to be almost as many anglers as fish. To get to this few hundred yards of Hot Creek, take an unmarked dirt road that turns off Hot Creek Hatchery Road just beyond the turnoff to the hatchery. If you go to the turnoff to Hot Creek Ranch, you've gone too far.

Below this section, a bit more than 2 miles of the stream belongs to the Hot Creek Ranch, a private resort that offers dry-fly fishing for guests who book its nine cabins. The creek meanders through an open meadow, and in the clear water, the fish are easy to spot. Catching them is a different matter—long leaders, sneaky tactics, and accurate casting are necessary. As I said, the rules on the ranch are dry-fly fishing only—nymphing isn't allowed. That stipulation was included in the sale of the ranch many years ago and is maintained today, making it one of the few places in the United States with such a regulation, perhaps the only one.

Below the ranch, about a mile of fishable stream is open to the public. Then hot water pours into the creek from thermal springs, wiping out the fishing from there until Hot Creek enters the Owens River above Lake Crowley. The hot water also traps the big fish in Hot Creek, so they don't migrate to Crowley.

This public-access section of Hot Creek is one of the most heavily fly fished stretches of water in California. It is limited to barbless flies and is catch-and-release. The walk down to the river from two small parking areas on the dirt road that parallels Hot Creek is fairly steep, but it is only a hundred yards long. The stream itself has the same meadow character as on the ranch upstream.

The public-access section does not have the same dry-fly

Paolo Marchesi

restriction as on the ranch, and early in the season, nymphs are particularly effective. Both mayflies and caddisflies are plentiful and flies that imitate them, such as Hare's Ear Nymphs, Pheasant Tails, or the A.P. series in olive, cream, or black in about a size 12, are popular. Beadhead versions can help get the flies down faster. There are even a few patterns developed in the area, such as the Burlap Caddis and Chamois Nymph. For dries, use any of the classic Baetis mayfly imitations, such as Blue or Olive Duns. For caddises, try both dark and light imitations up to size 16. Hot Creek's big fish call for big action, so an excellent technique is to cast good-sized streamers, say size 6 or 8, into openings in the weed beds and strip them back. Favorites are Clouser Minnows, Woolly Buggers, and Matukas in dark colors.

Speaking of weed beds, anybody who has fished Hot Creek from about the middle of July on knows all about them. They build up to such an extent that the lanes between them are only inches wide, and working those lanes is extremely difficult. It also is extremely productive because the trout use the weeds for protection and dart out to take bugs drifting through the water.

THE OWENS RIVER FROM LAKE CROWLEY TO PLEASANT VALLEY RESERVOIR

This is a river that is coming back to life, already offering good fishing that promises to get even better. But it is rugged country, with the river flowing deep in the Owens River Gorge.

A prime fishery many decades ago, the upper section of the 19-mile Owens River Gorge was reduced to a trickle of water when the Los Angeles Department of Water and Power dammed Lake Crowley and used its water to produce power for the Southland. The Owens from the dam down to what is known as the Upper Gorge Power Plant, a distance of about 9 miles, remained a viable small-trout stream, fed with water from springs and seepage from Lake Crowley. The lower 10 miles of the river disappeared—there was no water at all, and what once had provided fine fishing became a dusty ditch.

In 1991, a penstock that carried water from the Upper Gorge Power Plant to the turbines broke, spilling water into the desert. The county threatened legal action to get the spilling water diverted into what had been the river, bringing the Los Angeles Department of Water and Power to the negotiating table. The result was an agreement to provide a steady flow of water into the old Owens River streambed, a flow that started at 16 cubic feet per second and is being increased yearly until it is 106 cfs.

With water flowing through the lower gorge again, fishing was restored from the Upper Gorge Plant to Pleasant Valley Reservoir. Vegetation again began to grow, and the cad-

There isn't much of Hot Creek open to the public, but where it can be fished has an incredible number of trout—more than 11,000 to the mile.

dises, mayflies, and other aquatic insects quickly took up residence. The state Department of Fish and Game planted wild browns, starting a self-sustaining population that is doing very well indeed.

There's no road that actually leads to the river at the bottom of the 700-foot-deep gorge except just before the river reaches Pleasant Valley Reservoir at the Control Gorge Power Plant. You can park and walk upstream from there.

Adventurous anglers can take the Gorge Road from Highway 395 and then follow one of the many dirt roads that lead to the rim of the gorge. A number of them have steep, rude paths that lead to the river far below. It is a matter of probing the area until you find a path you are comfortable using. This also is an area favored by rock climbers, so parked cars don't necessarily mean anglers. Be smart about this: fish someplace else unless you're in reasonable physical shape, prepared to do some tough scrambling, and be on a first-name basis with rattlesnakes.

The only way to avoid major rock scrambling to get into the gorge section is to walk in along the two paved roads that branch off Gorge Road and lead to the Upper Gorge Power Plant and the Middle Gorge Power Plant. They are closed to vehicular traffic, but an angler can walk in and then work his or her way down to the water. It is about a 3-mile walk to the Upper Gorge Power Plant and about a mile to the Middle Gorge Power Plant. The upper gorge is reached via the road to Toms Place that turns off from Highway 395. There are a few spots to park near the river, but better fishing can be found by walking downstream along a dirt road. The trout here are much more wary than in the lower gorge—they've been fished over for years.

The Owens River Gorge is open to fishing all year, and there are no special regulations. Water levels remain constant, since the outflow from Lake Crowley is channeled through the penstocks, rather than down the river.

THE OWENS RIVER BELOW PLEASANT VALLEY RESERVOIR

The stretch of the river below Pleasant Valley Reservoir from the Pleasant Valley Dam downstream to the footbridge at the campground just below the dam is open from January 1 to September 30. Anglers must use artificial lures and flies and can keep two trout. From the bridge downstream is a 3.3-mile Wild Trout section that is catch-and-release.

This Wild Trout area is popular with Southern Californians and offers excellent fishing in the fall and winter, when the water flow from the reservoir is low. In the summer it is hot, and the river runs high. The only way to fish it in the summer is with nymphs and ton of lead to get them deep. Most anglers don't bother because there is better fishing on the upper Owens.

February and March are the best months to fish the Wild Trout section, and on weekends, a steady stream of vehicles pulls into the small campground. Still, with 3.3 miles of stream open to fishing, there is enough room to keep it from becoming shoulder-to-shoulder chaos.

Pleasant Valley Dam Road from Highway 395 north of Bishop leads to the campground. At the upper end of the campground, Chalk Bluffs Road turns south along the river and has good drive-up access to the entire Wild Trout section, although no camping is allowed there.

The population of trout is almost entirely browns, with a few rainbows in the lower stretches of the Wild Trout section. The favored flies are a variety of caddis, which is the primary aquatic insect in the area, along with Blue-Winged Olives, Light Cahills, leech patterns, Woolly Buggers, and streamers. For nymphs, the Beadhead Pheasant Tail is the most popular.

LAKE CROWLEY

Fishing Crowley is a must for every California angling enthusiast. Although it is a planted lake, the rate of growth is so fast that seven-inchers dumped in May will be fifteen inches long in October. And it is so big that many of the trout live for years to become five or more pounds.

Although Crowley boasts mayflies and caddises as part of its food chain, midges and perch minnows play the major role. At certain times of the year, fishing the weed growth along the banks, where big trout are feeding on perch minnows, can be exhilarating. Although Crowley is best fished from a float tube, anglers also can work from the bank.

Crowley has two distinct seasons—until the end of July, when regulations are open, and from August 1 until October 31, which is the trophy season and regulations limit anglers to barbless lures and flies, with a two-trout limit of eighteen inches or bigger.

Although many fly-line anglers don't fish Crowley until the trophy season, locals say this is a mistake. Float tubers need to be careful with so many boats on the water, but working the area where the Owens River enters Crowley at its northern end can yield excellent fishing. It helps that this area is shallow enough so that most boaters stay away.

For many lure and bait anglers, opening day on Lake Crowley is a tradition, and it is so jammed that you sometimes feel you could walk across it by stepping from boat to boat. By the time the weather heats up, most of the boaters have gone to cooler climes.

But Steve Kennedy, who owns The Trout Fitter in Mammoth Lakes, says fishing still is good. "You need to fish the first two hours of day and the last two—these are the times when the fish are feeding in the weed beds." Kennedy adds that although the special-restriction season begins August 1, the best fishing is from about mid-September on.

If you want a break from trout fishing, in May and June, the Sacramento perch come into the shallows to spawn. Fishing for them can be fun, and they are a fine-eating fish.

By August, the perch fry are big enough to imitate with lures and flies, and that's when fishing for the big trout that chase them into the bankside weed beds becomes exciting. But since they are in shallow water, the trout are spooky, so long casts are necessary to avoid putting them down. Float tubes are the favored way to fish. Get out beyond the weed beds and cast in to them. Often anglers can spot working fish, which sometimes seem to be in small schools. The trout smash these perch-fry imitations, so heavy leaders are called for—sometimes up to 1X.

The best road to both the western and eastern banks of Crowley is Benton Crossing Road, which turns east off Highway 395 just south of the Mammoth / June Lake Airport. Both the second and third roads turning off to the right lead to the lake. (The first turnoff at the Green Church does not go to Crowley). The second turnoff, at Whitmore Hot Springs, forks after a little more than half a mile. If you stay left from there on, you'll end up at the Green Banks section of Lake Crowley, which has good fishing all year around. Other turnoffs along that road all lead to the lake, but if you keep to the right forks, you'll find yourself at Sandy Point. The third turnoff is just beyond a cattle guard a bit over 3 miles from Highway 395. It leads to a honeycomb of roads as you approach Crowley, with the southernmost ending at Green Banks and the northernmost at the West Flats.

To reach the eastern side of the lake, continue along Benton Crossing Road until it crosses the Owens River, then turn right .7 miles from the bridge. This dirt road goes to the Owens and then splits. The road to the right leads to the upper Owens, the left one follows the lake shore to East Flats, Weed Point, and Leighton Springs. Alligator Point, one of the best fishing areas on Crowley, is about a mile south of where the road ends.

The western side of the southern end of Crowley can be reached by following Highway 395 south until a clearly marked turnoff leads to several bays. This is a boat-launch area and has camping facilities.

To get to the eastern side of southern Crowley, continue a bit farther south on Highway 395 and then take the road to Toms Place, which crosses Crowley at the dam. A dirt road on which four-wheel drive is advisable turns off to the left and offers a number of access points. The Toms Place road also allows access to the Owens River Gorge below the dam.

OTHER STREAMS WORTH TRYING
THE MIDDLE FORK OF THE SAN JOAQUIN

This lovely river flows through the Devil's Postpile National Monument area northeast of Mammoth Lakes and is typical of the high Sierra . There is one major drawback—in the summer, when the fishing is best, only shuttle buses are allowed into the area during the daytime. Private vehicles can make the 17-mile trek before 7:30 A.M. and after 5:30 P.M., but during the day, no private vehicles can go in along this road, although they can come out. This restriction usually ends after

Awesome fishing? How about awesome scenery.

Paolo Marchesi

Labor Day, but by then the water is so low that fishing is tough. For those who want to go during the day, the adult bus fare is $8.00 for a round trip, and there is no restriction on bringing along fishing gear.

The best fishing is in the Red's Meadow area up to Rainbow Falls. Access is easily gained by following the riverside trail. Waders are not necessary, but lightweight hip boots help, or just wear shorts and be prepared to get your sneakers wet.

The most negative part of the experience is that there are too many people around, including campers, hikers, sightseers, and picnickers, as well as those intent on catching the smallish rainbows and browns that are the mainstay of the San Joaquin.

A tip: work your way along the river, hitting only the best spots. It is a waste of time to fish one area hard because if it isn't productive right away, chances of coaxing a fish up by repeated casts are low.

The usual Sierra selection of flies works: Hare's Ears, Pheasant Tails, Zug Bugs, and so on for nymphs, the Adams, various caddis, ant, and hopper imitations for dries, along with Royal Wulffs and Red or Yellow Humpies for faster water.

RUSH CREEK

Rush Creek flows into and out of Lake Grant on the northern end of the June Lake Loop, north of Mammoth Lakes, crosses Highway 395, and empties into Mono Lake. There are no special restrictions on this stream above Grant Lake, but from the lake downstream, regulations call for barbless lures and flies and a zero limit.

There's not too much of it, but what exists offers good fishing, a secret well kept by locals. Rush Creek upstream from Highway 395 is accessed via the June Lake Loop. Downstream of Highway 395 it can be reached by a dirt road that turns east just north of where the creek flows under the highway. There are lots of riffles and runs, and there is plenty of water well into the fall, so some big rainbows and browns occasionally can be coaxed to a fly.

The joke that isn't a joke is that where Rush Creek flows into Mono Lake, which has a salinity level ten times higher than the ocean, anglers actually can fish in this desolate body of water. The heavy flow from Rush Creek pushes fresh water deep into the lake, and big browns will lie in the fresh water, but dash briefly into the salt water to feed on the tasty brine flies and brine shrimp that abound in the lake. I don't know of any specific brine fly or brine shrimp imitations, but a small black fly or light-colored scud should work.

MCGEE CREEK AND CONVICT CREEK

McGee Creek and its tributary, Convict Creek, flow from the mountains east across Highway 395 and into the upper end of Lake Crowley. On the eastern side of Highway 395,

they are under special regulations for part of the year. From the opening day in April through the Friday preceding Memorial Day and from October 1 to October 31, only barbless, artificial lures are allowed, and the limit is two fish a day, eighteen inches or larger. This is to protect the spawners that come up from Crowley.

These creeks can provide excellent early-season angling—fly fishers can find big browns that have come up from the lake. The downside is that it usually is cold and windy in this part of the world during late April and May. If you get a sunny day that brings off a heavy hatch, fishing these little creeks can be magnificent.

To the west of Highway 395 there are no special restrictions, and McGee Creek is a typical Sierra stream of pools and falls, along with plenty of brush to offer protection for trout. It holds mostly small rainbows and browns.

AREA LAKES

Despite the name of the town, there aren't any Mammoth Lakes. But there are a series of lakes near the town that can be fished—**Twin Lakes, Lake Mary, Lake George, Lake Mamie,** and **Horseshoe Lake.** They all are stocked and are pretty much in the put-and-take fishing category, more fun for families than for serious wild-trout anglers. Still, if you want to haul out the float tube, all of the lakes can be not only fun, but very productive. As with most eastern-slope waters, they have prolific plant growth that gives life to the aquatic insects that keep trout fat and happy.

Probably the most productive of the lakes is Mary, reached by paved Lake Mary Road from Mammoth Lakes. Lake Mary Road passes Twin Lakes on the way and then goes all the way around Lake Mary.

As for the other waters, Lake George is the highest (more than 9,000 feet) and the deepest, so fly fishing is possible only along the banks. Lake Mamie is shallow, but offers occasional good-sized browns in the area where water flows in from Lake Mary. Horseshoe Lake, which has a population of brookies, is at the end of a spur road from Lake Mary Road. Its water level fluctuates during the year because of the volcanic nature of its bed and often requires fishing in the middle of the lake.

A brief walk above Horseshoe Lake is **McCloud Lake,** which for a fly-line angler who wants a bit of solitary room is worth the stroll, even carrying a float tube and waders. It hosts some Lahontan cutthroat and is restricted to barbless flies and lures only, catch-and-release. Day hike lakes via a trail that leaves the Coldwater Campground at Lake Mary are **Heart, Arrowhead, Woods, Skeleton, Red,** and **Barney Lakes.** All have rainbows and brookies.

An additional stillwater fishery is **Sotcher Lake,** which is in Red's Meadow, near the San Joaquin River. Bankside fishing is limited, so a float tube is necessary, but you can drive right up to it using the road that goes from the Devil's Post pile to Red's Meadow. **Starkweather Lake** is another road-side water that can be reached in Red's Meadow, but it gets more pressure and doesn't offer as good fishing.

A bit farther south along Highway 395, the turnoff to the west on Rock Creek Road at Toms Place leads to a series of popular lakes that can provide decent fly fishing. The easiest access is at **Rock Creek Lake,** where float tubing can be productive, but day hikes can take you to a plethora of other stillwater fisheries, including **Serene Lake, Eastern Brook Lakes,** and **Patricia Lake,** just to name a few of the dozens and dozens of lakes in the area.

While the usual selection of flies work on all the lakes, both damselfly nymphs and dries also are important, particularly on Twin Lakes. Be sure to have some—they can be the key to a multifish day when the trout key on them.

SUMMING UP

The Mammoth Lakes area boasts two of California's most prolific trout streams—the **upper Owens River** and **Hot Creek.** As if that's not enough, the **lower Owens River** below Pleasant Valley Reservoir is a haven for first-rate winter trout fishing, a rarity in California. But the upper Owens and Hot Creek aren't easy fishing. Both are crystal-clear spring creeks that have educated trout. Anglers need to know what they are doing, with cautious approaches to the streams, accurate casts, and match-the-hatch abilities. There are all sorts of aquatic insects, and knowing what trout are feeding on becomes crucial. So anglers fishing this area for the first time would do well to hire a local guide for at least the first day. What you learn will be invaluable for the rest of the time you fish there. A novice fly fisher trying to learn on the spot without guidance is pretty much wasting time.

Lake Crowley early in the season is noted for its bait and lure fishing, although locals say fly-line anglers also can do well then. But most fly fishers wait until the restricted season begins on August 1 before venturing onto the lake in small prams and float tubes to fish the weed beds at the northern end of Crowley.

◆ ◆ ◆ ◆ ◆ ◆

ADDITIONAL INFORMATION

FLY SHOPS

The Trout Fitter, Shell Mart Center, Highway 203 and Old Mammoth Road, Mammoth Lakes, CA 93546; (619) 924-3676. A full-service fly shop.

The Trout Fly, Gateway Center, Mammoth Lakes, CA 93546; (619) 934-2517. A full-service fly shop.

Kittredge Sports, Highway 203 and Forest Trail, Mammoth Lakes, CA 93546; (619) 934-7566. A sporting-goods store with a large fly-fishing section.

Rick's Sports Center, Highway 203 and Center Street, Mammoth Lakes, CA 93546; (619) 934-3416. A sporting-goods store with a large fly-fishing section.

HOSPITALS

Mammoth Hospital, 85 Sierra Park Road, Mammoth Lakes, CA 93546; (619) 934-3311.

Northern Inyo Hospital, 150 Pioneer Lane, Bishop, CA 93514; (760) 873-5811.

PUBLIC CAMPING

The Mammoth Lakes Visitors Bureau, P.O. Box 48, Mammoth Lakes, CA 93546; (888) 466-2666. Web site: http://www.visitmammoth.com. E-mail: mmthvisit@qnet.com. The Visitor's Bureau is located in the same building as the U.S. Forest Service and has brochures with information on all campgrounds.

MORE SOURCES

In addition to the Mammoth Lakes Visitors Bureau listed above, write or call the Bishop Area Chamber of Commerce and Visitors Bureau, 690 N. Main Street, Bishop CA 93514; (760) 873-8405.

Fly Fishing Mammoth: A Fly Fisher's Guide to the Mammoth Lakes Area, by Mark J. Heskett, published by Frank Amato Publications, P.O. Box 82112, Portland, OR 97282, (503) 653-8108, is a helpful book on the subject. It costs $9.95.

INDEX